Creator, Writer & Art Director
ROYE OKUPE

Editor
AYODELE ELEGBA

Artist
SUNKANMI AKINBOYE

Colorist
RAPHAEL KAZEEM

Cover Art
GODWIN AKPAN

Special Thanks
MRS. SHERI WILLIAMS

Executive Producer
VOMOZ COMMUNICATIONS INC.

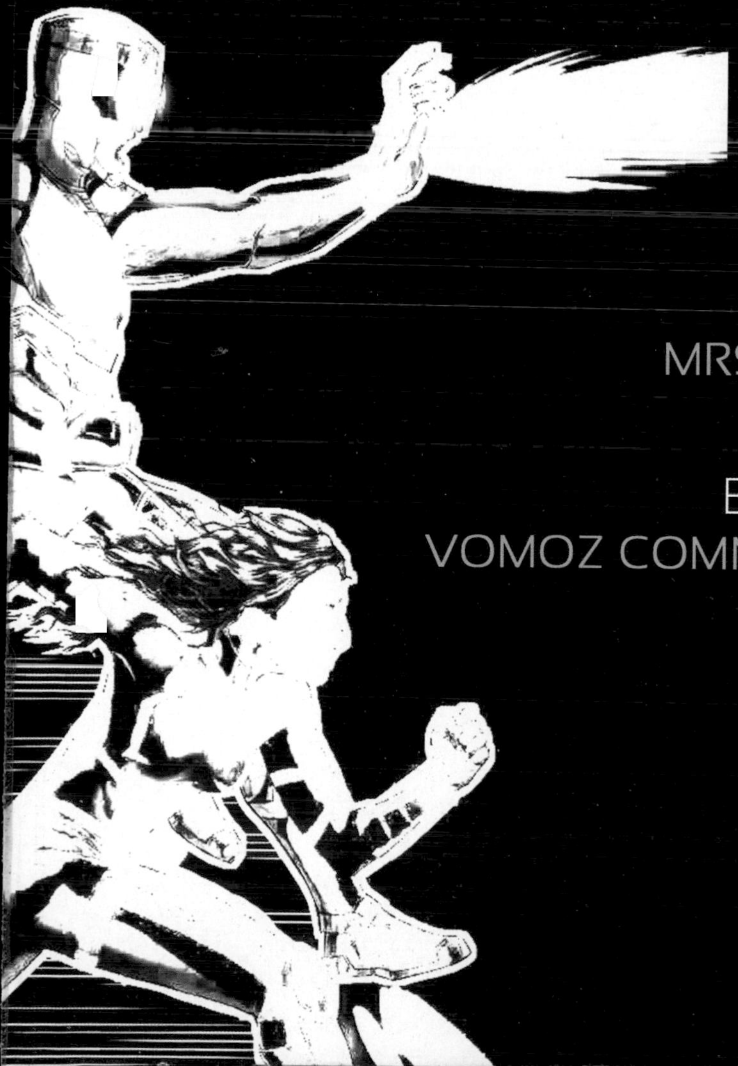

E.X.O.™

SAGA ONE | PART TWO

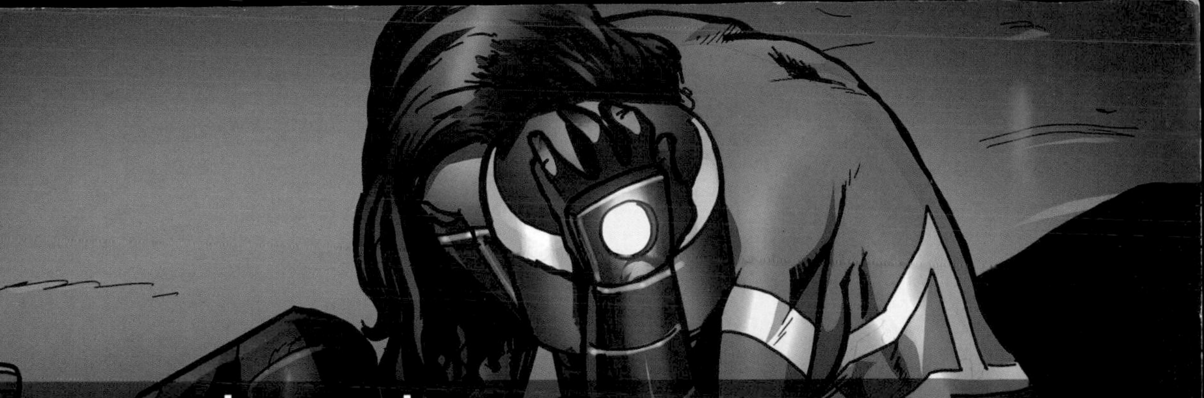

THE STORY SO FAR

Following the death of his mother in a lab accident caused by his father, Wale decides to abruptly depart from Lagoon City, leaving everything he knows and loves behind. But, after five years of concealing his movements as he wandered the globe, tragedy brings Wale back home when his father, Dr. Williams, mysteriously goes missing.

Upon returning home to protect his brother, Timi, and search for his father, Wale discovers a cryptic message left behind by Dr. Williams. The message leads him to a super-powered suit called E.X.O. (Endogenic Xoskeletal Ordnance), built by Dr. Williams.

Initially reluctant to investigate the purpose of E.X.O., Wale is forced to use the suit when a menacing group of robots, called the DREDs attack both his house and parts of the city. After Wale saves the day, he's branded a superhero by the general public, earning him the moniker, "EXO."

As Wale investigates the source of the attacks, he discovers that Prytek, a global leader in technology and innovation, and the terrorist organization The CREED, lead by the sociopathic Oniku, have been working in tandem. Before Wale can act, Timi is caught in the crossfire and ends up in a coma after being electrocuted by a DRED robot.

Thirsty for revenge, Wale, now suited up as EXO, sets out to put an end to The CREED, Oniku and Prytek, only to be urged to stand down by a mysterious female speedster. Little does Wale know that the mysterious speedster is in fact, Zahra, Wale's ex-girlfriend.

Refusing to heed her warnings, EXO (Wale) confronts Oniku at Prytek headquarters. After the battle with Oniku, he is left holding on for dear life but is saved by Zahra just as Oniku prepares to deliver the final blow. They both manage to escape from Oniku's grasp, but not before Oniku reveals himself to be Jide Williams. Dr. Williams brother and Wale's uncle!

CHAPTER EIGHT

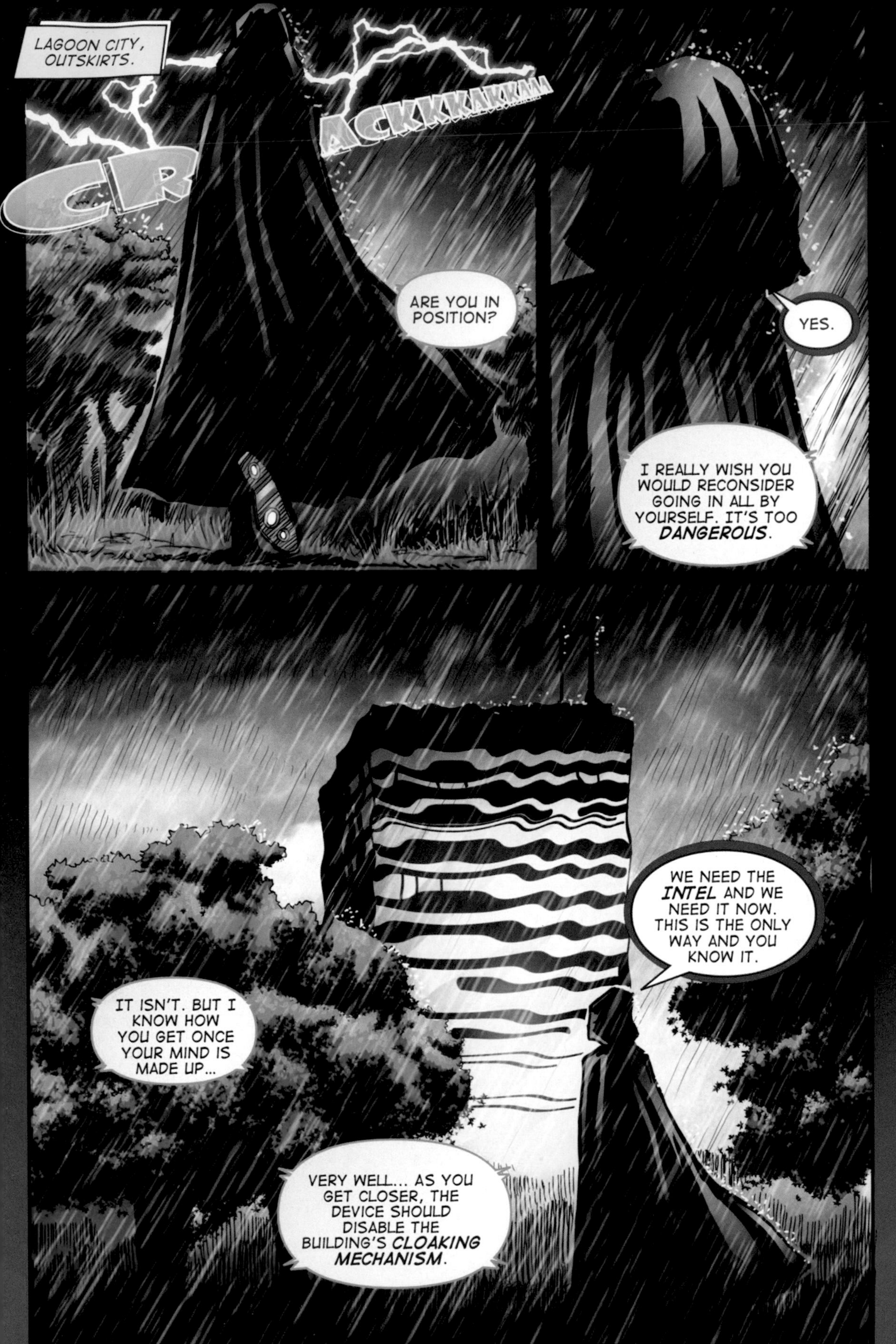
LAGOON CITY, OUTSKIRTS.
CRACKKKAKKKAM
ARE YOU IN POSITION?
YES.
I REALLY WISH YOU WOULD RECONSIDER GOING IN ALL BY YOURSELF. IT'S TOO DANGEROUS.
WE NEED THE INTEL AND WE NEED IT NOW. THIS IS THE ONLY WAY AND YOU KNOW IT.
IT ISN'T. BUT I KNOW HOW YOU GET ONCE YOUR MIND IS MADE UP...
VERY WELL... AS YOU GET CLOSER, THE DEVICE SHOULD DISABLE THE BUILDING'S CLOAKING MECHANISM.

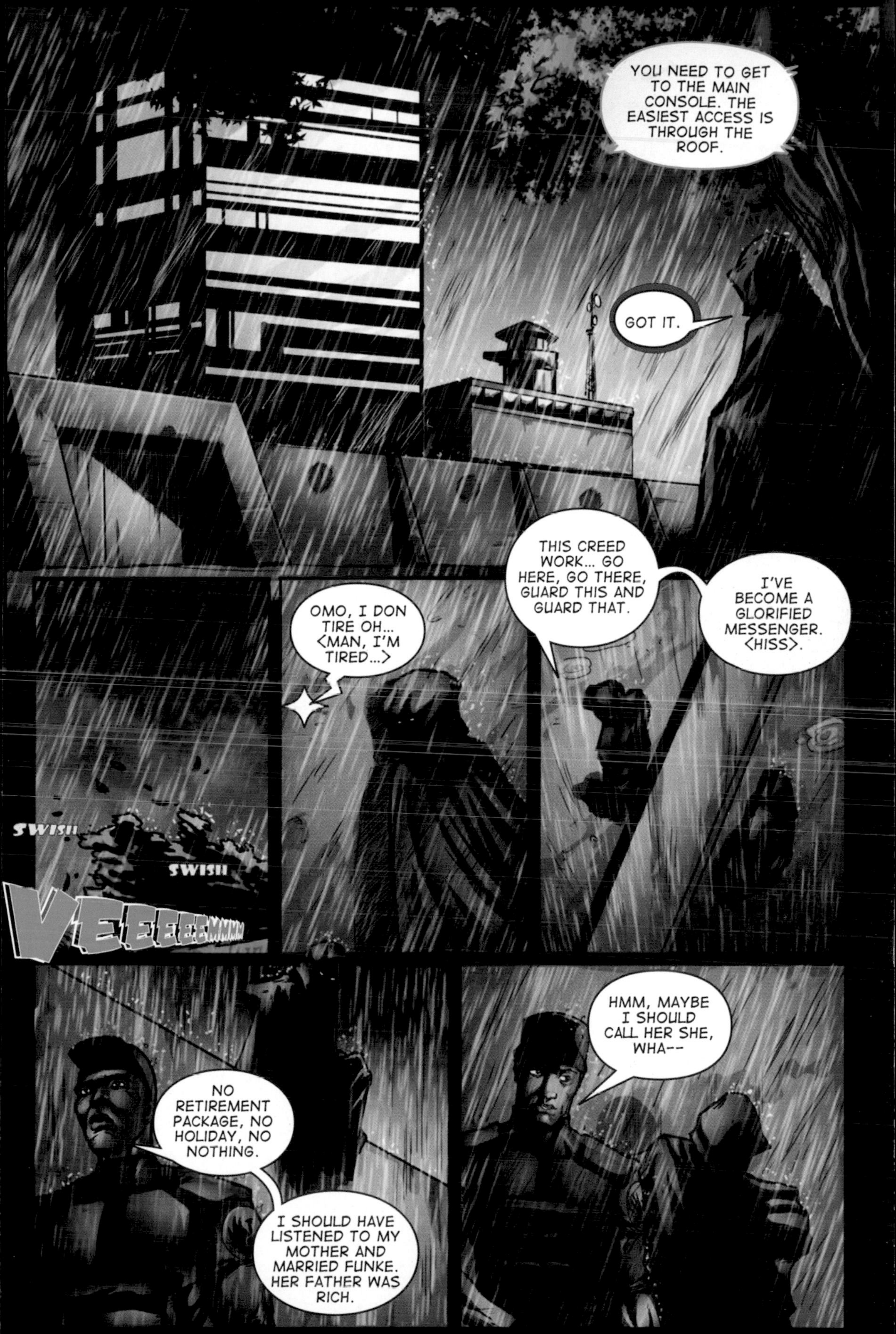
YOU NEED TO GET TO THE MAIN CONSOLE. THE EASIEST ACCESS IS THROUGH THE ROOF.
GOT IT.
SWISH
SWISH
VEEEEEMMMM
OMO, I DON TIRE OH... <MAN, I'M TIRED...>
THIS CREED WORK... GO HERE, GO THERE, GUARD THIS AND GUARD THAT.
I'VE BECOME A GLORIFIED MESSENGER. <HISS>.
NO RETIREMENT PACKAGE, NO HOLIDAY, NO NOTHING.
I SHOULD HAVE LISTENED TO MY MOTHER AND MARRIED FUNKE. HER FATHER WAS RICH.
HMM, MAYBE I SHOULD CALL HER SHE, WHA--

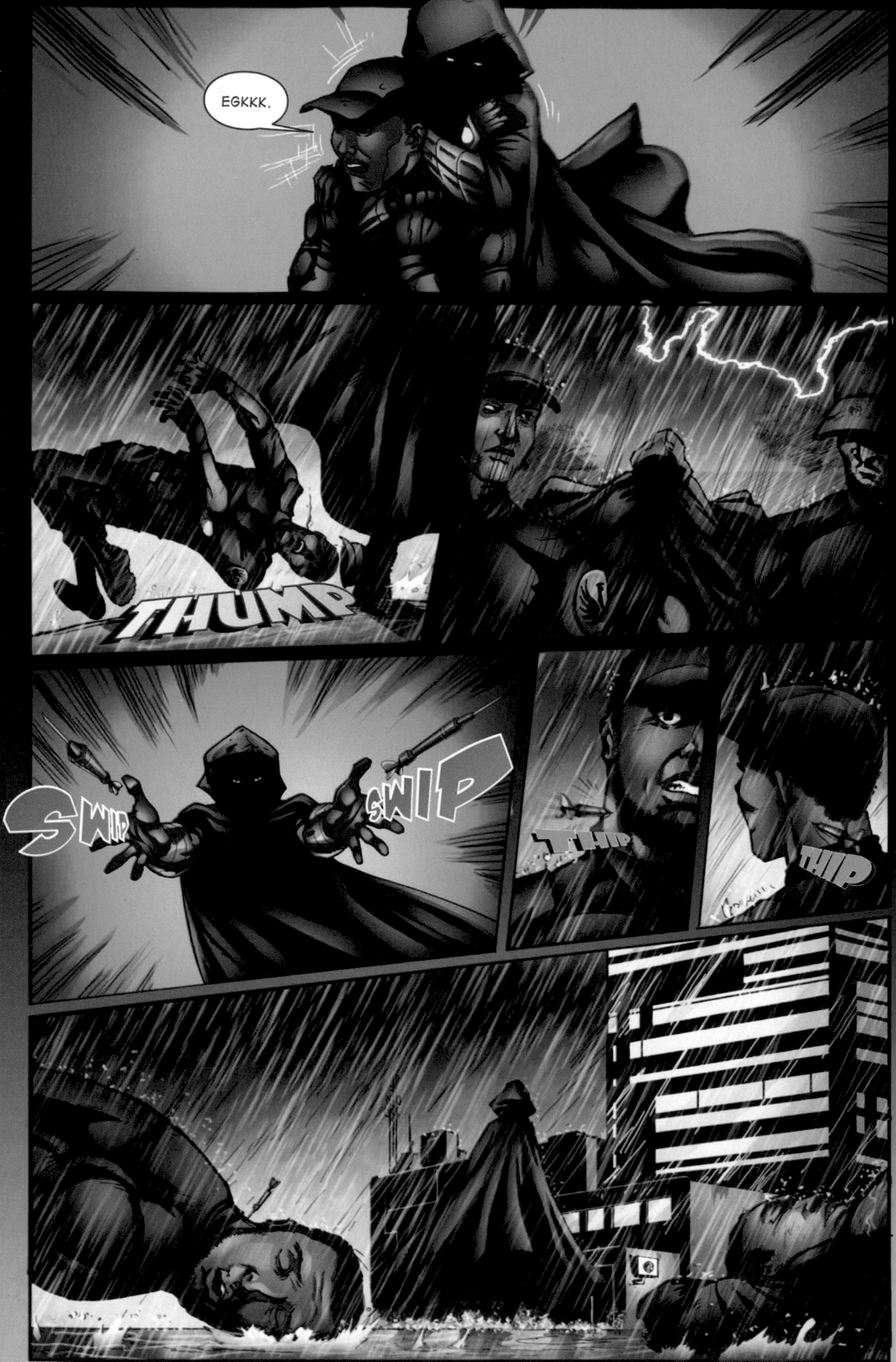
EGKKK.
THUMP
SWIP
SWIP
THIP
THIP

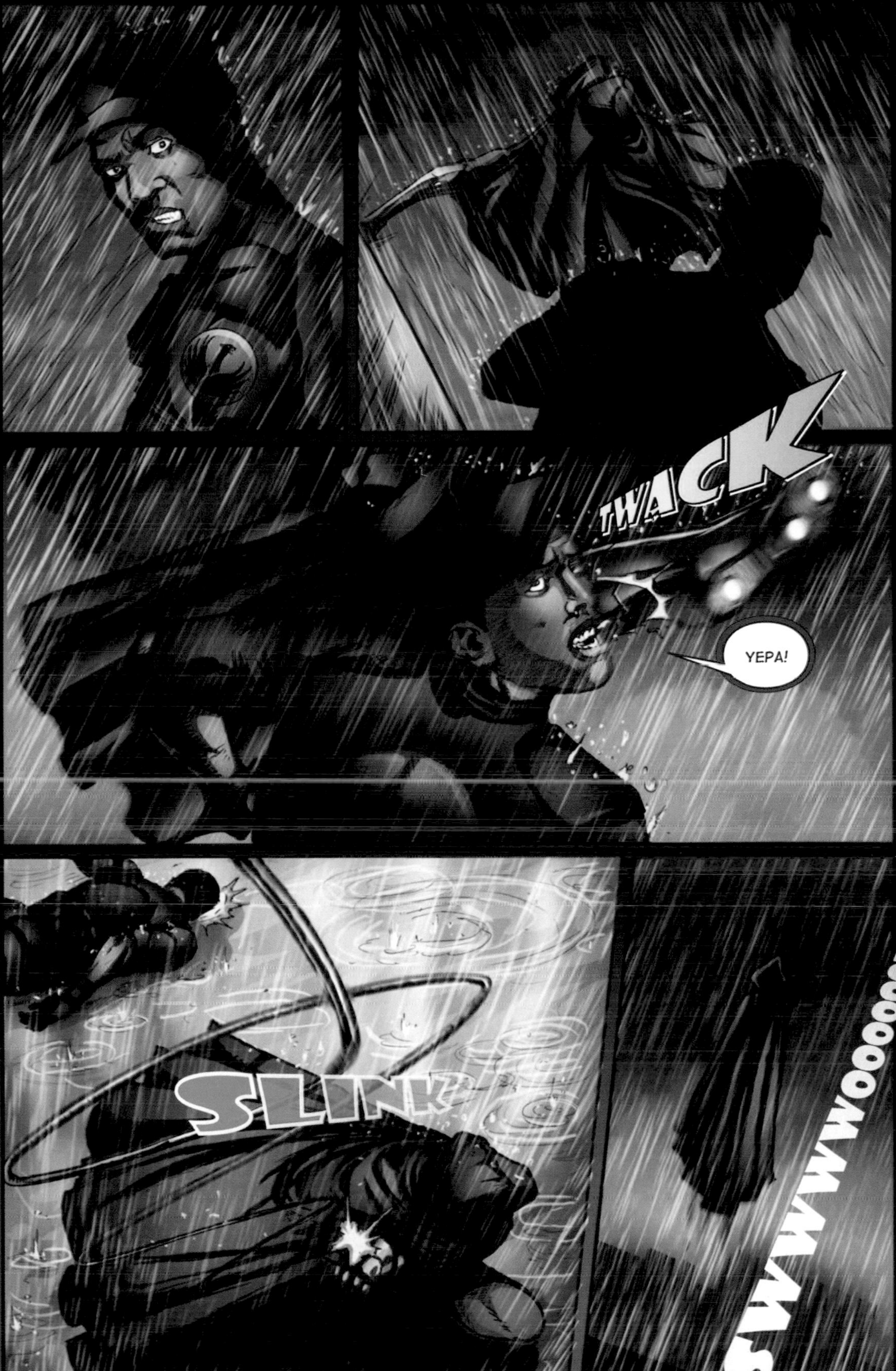

TWACK
YEPA!
SLINK
SWWWWOOOOOOP

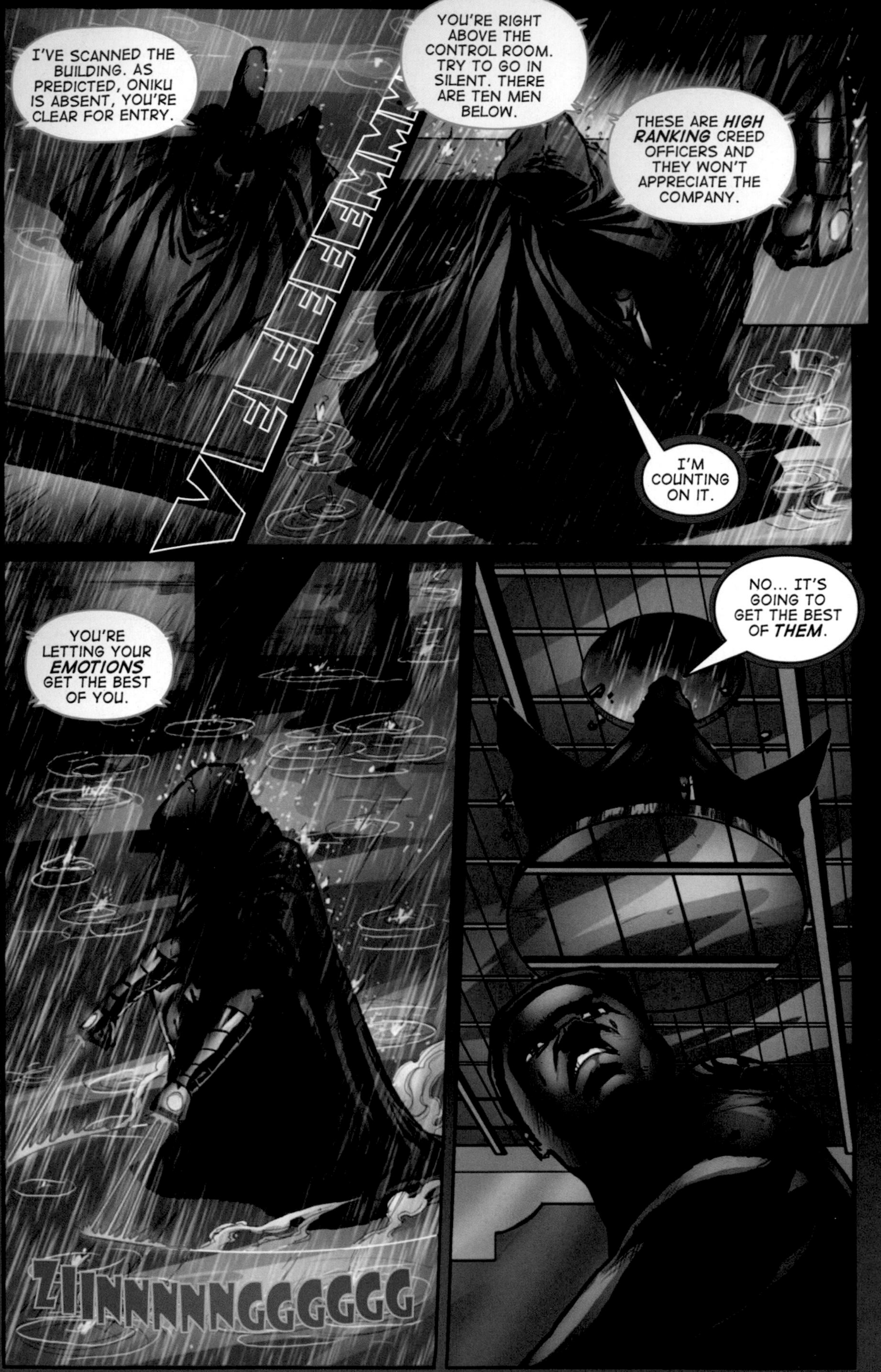
I'VE SCANNED THE BUILDING. AS PREDICTED, ONIKU IS ABSENT, YOU'RE CLEAR FOR ENTRY.
VWEEEEEEMMMMM
YOU'RE RIGHT ABOVE THE CONTROL ROOM. TRY TO GO IN SILENT. THERE ARE TEN MEN BELOW.
THESE ARE HIGH RANKING CREED OFFICERS AND THEY WON'T APPRECIATE THE COMPANY.
I'M COUNTING ON IT.
YOU'RE LETTING YOUR EMOTIONS GET THE BEST OF YOU.
ZIINNNNNGGGGGG
NO... IT'S GOING TO GET THE BEST OF THEM.

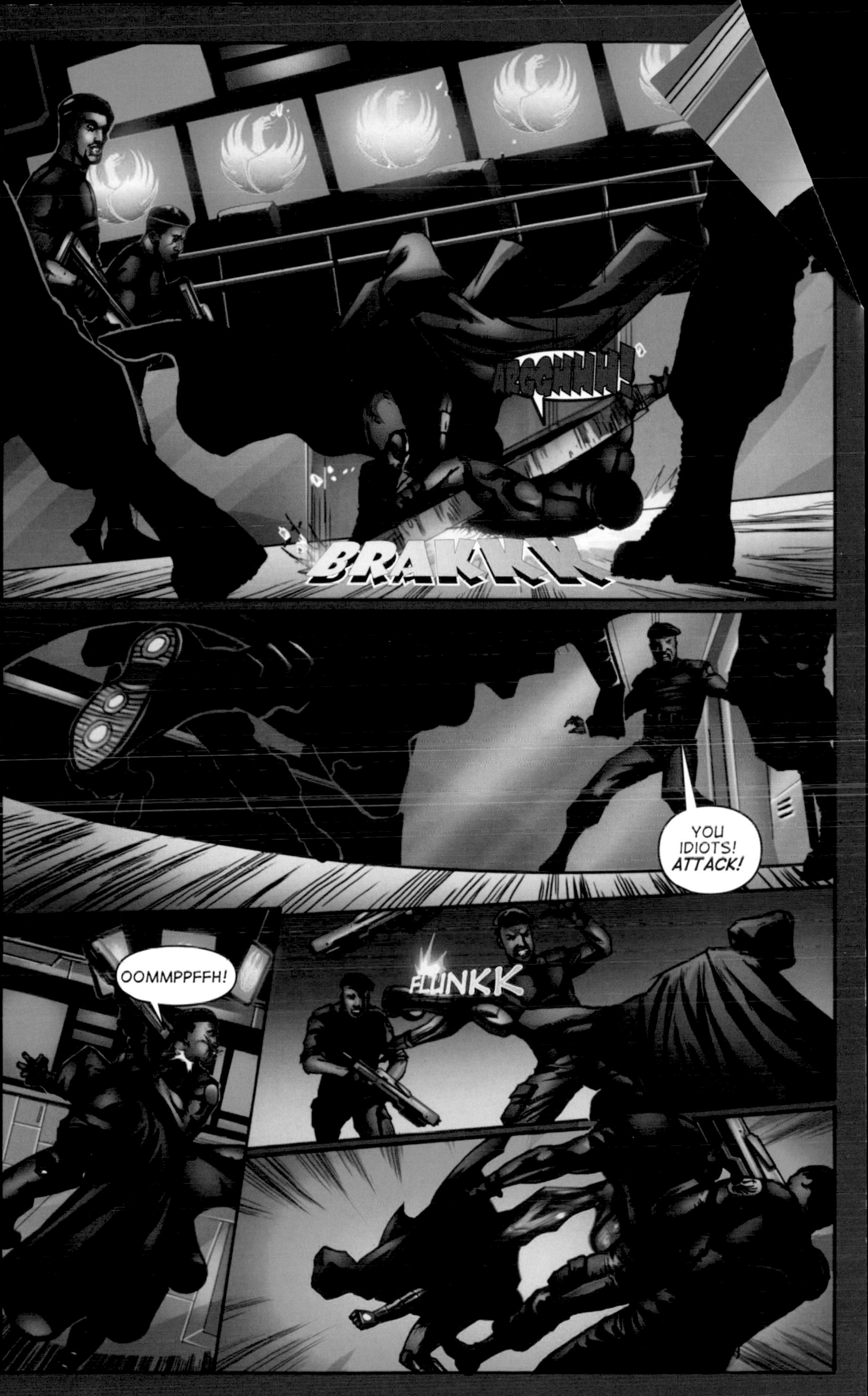
BRAKKK
YOU IDIOTS! ATTACK!
OOMMPPFFH!
FLUNKK

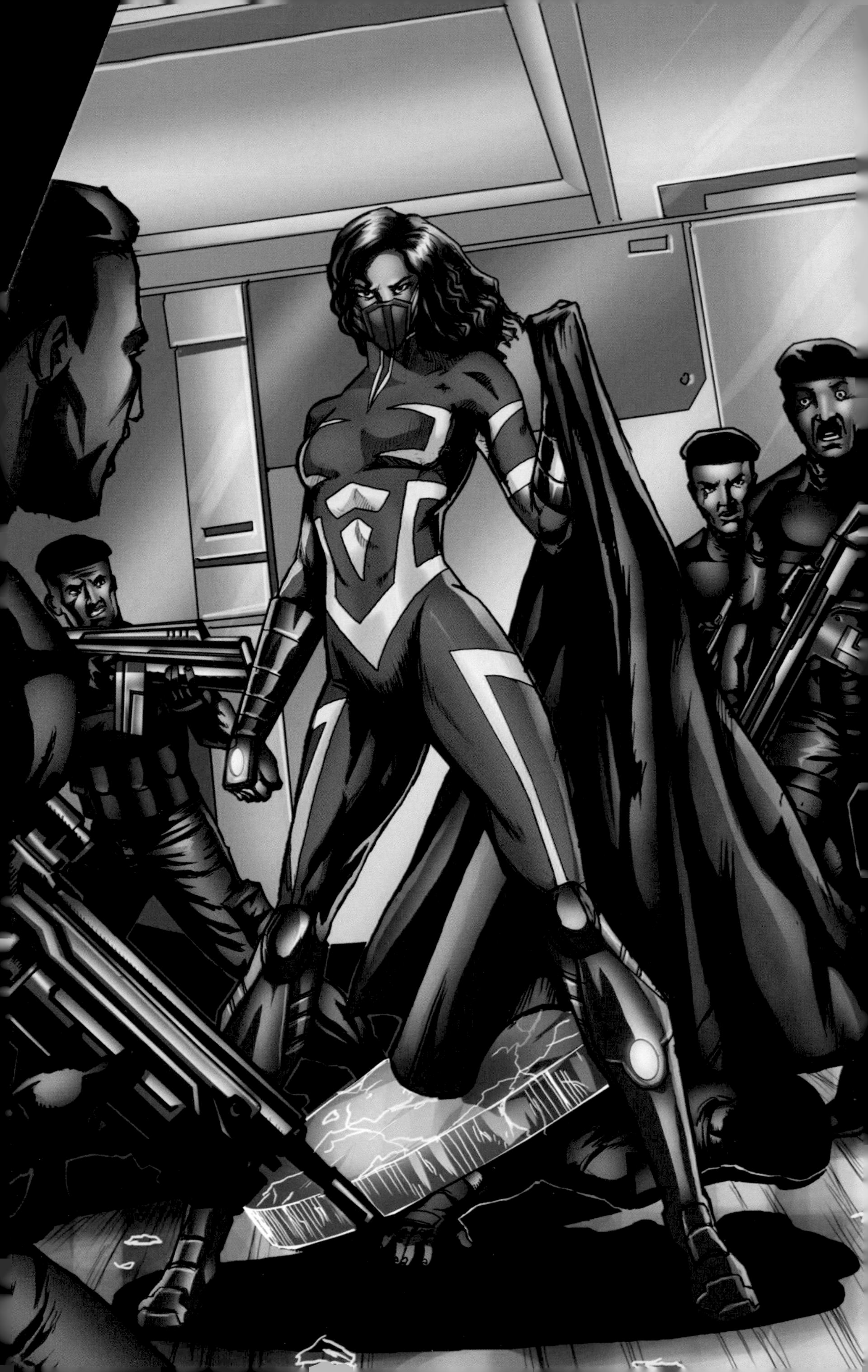

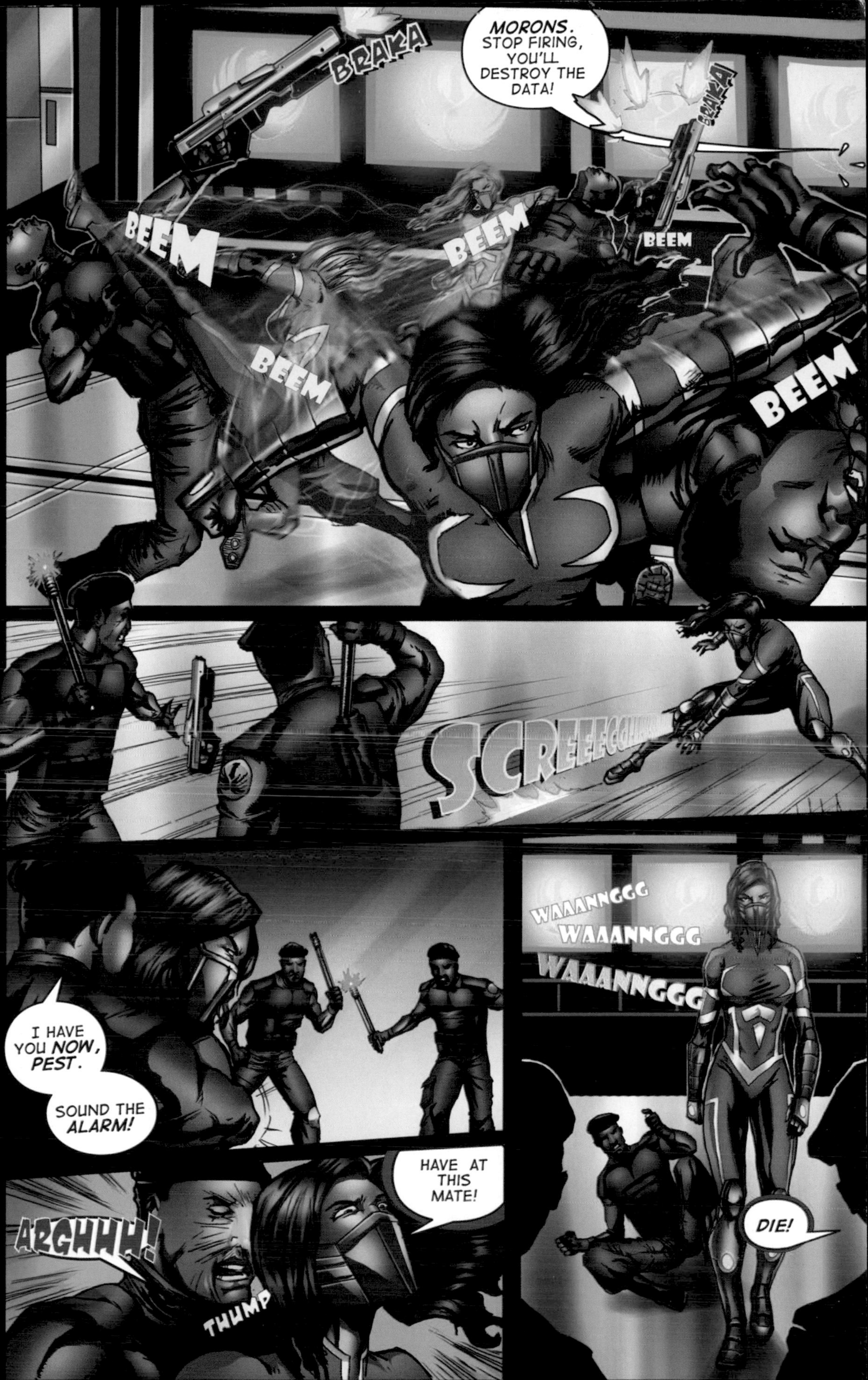
BRAKA
MORONS. STOP FIRING, YOU'LL DESTROY THE DATA!
BRAKA
BEEM
BEEM
BEEM
BEEM
BEEM
SCREEEGG
I HAVE YOU NOW, PEST.
SOUND THE ALARM!
HAVE AT THIS MATE!
ARGHHH!
THUMP
WAAANNGGG
WAAANNGGG
WAAANNGGG
DIE!

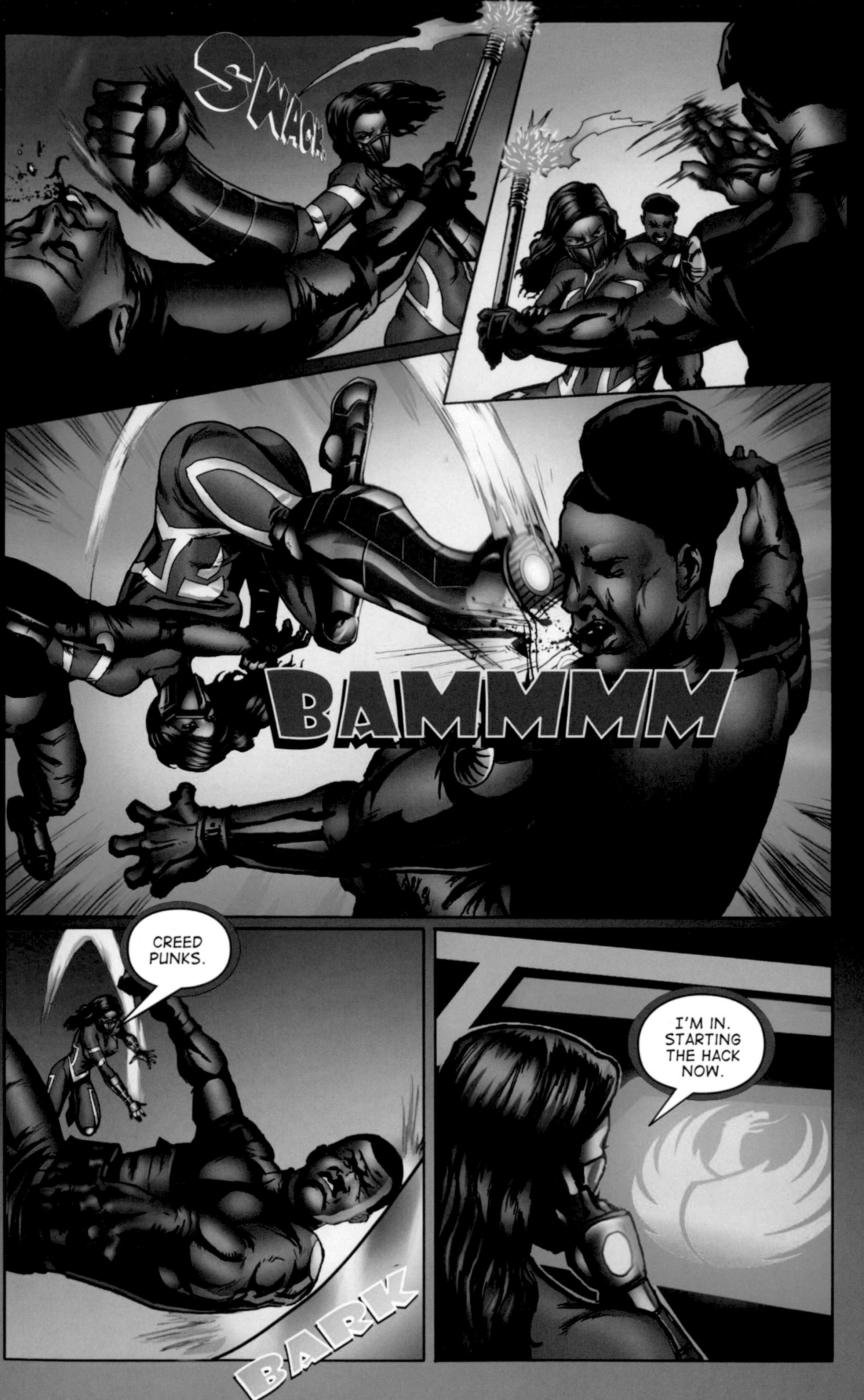
SWACK
BAMMMM
CREED PUNKS.
BARK
I'M IN. STARTING THE HACK NOW.

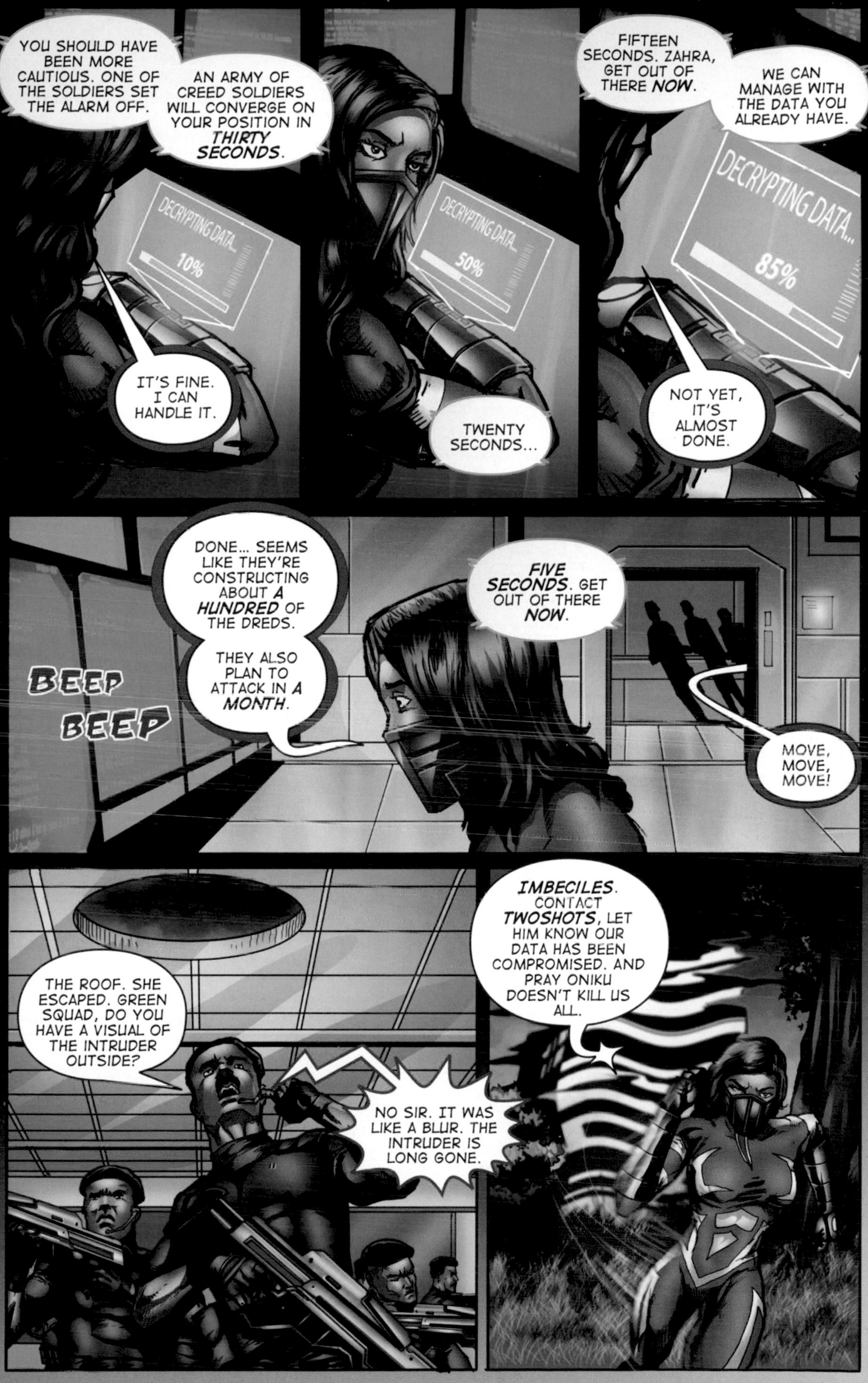
YOU SHOULD HAVE BEEN MORE CAUTIOUS. ONE OF THE SOLDIERS SET THE ALARM OFF.
AN ARMY OF CREED SOLDIERS WILL CONVERGE ON YOUR POSITION IN THIRTY SECONDS.
DECRYPTING DATA...
10%
IT'S FINE. I CAN HANDLE IT.
DECRYPTING DATA...
50%
TWENTY SECONDS...
FIFTEEN SECONDS. ZAHRA, GET OUT OF THERE NOW.
WE CAN MANAGE WITH THE DATA YOU ALREADY HAVE.
DECRYPTING DATA...
85%
NOT YET, IT'S ALMOST DONE.
BEEP
BEEP
DONE... SEEMS LIKE THEY'RE CONSTRUCTING ABOUT A HUNDRED OF THE DREDS.
THEY ALSO PLAN TO ATTACK IN A MONTH.
FIVE SECONDS. GET OUT OF THERE NOW.
MOVE, MOVE, MOVE!
THE ROOF. SHE ESCAPED. GREEN SQUAD, DO YOU HAVE A VISUAL OF THE INTRUDER OUTSIDE?
NO SIR. IT WAS LIKE A BLUR. THE INTRUDER IS LONG GONE.
IMBECILES. CONTACT TWOSHOTS, LET HIM KNOW OUR DATA HAS BEEN COMPROMISED. AND PRAY ONIKU DOESN'T KILL US ALL.

A SPECIAL THANK YOU TO OUR SPONSORS

mankindshoes.com

MANKIND is your exclusive luxury men's shoe boutique. Our customers value quality and style. From a day at the boardroom to a day at the country clubhouse, MANKIND is the store for men who want their footwear to not only be a statement of their personality, but also a reflection of their status. And because we perfectly understand this, our shoe selection is especially curated with this knowledge.

· EventKloud is an audience-driven marketing & advertising automation platform for events.

www.eventkloud.com

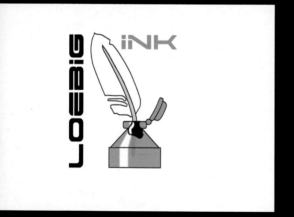

Loebig Ink, LLC is proud and privileged to support the creative, comic genius of Adewunmi (Roye) Okupe and E.X.O. The Legend of Wale Williams. From our first face to face meeting at Starbucks in downtown Silver Spring, MD, I knew that Roye and E.X.O were on a faith-inspired path to bring an amazing African Superhero story to life. Like E.X.O, Roye has answered a call to bring something special to a world that needs saving; a world that needs

www.vomozmedia.com

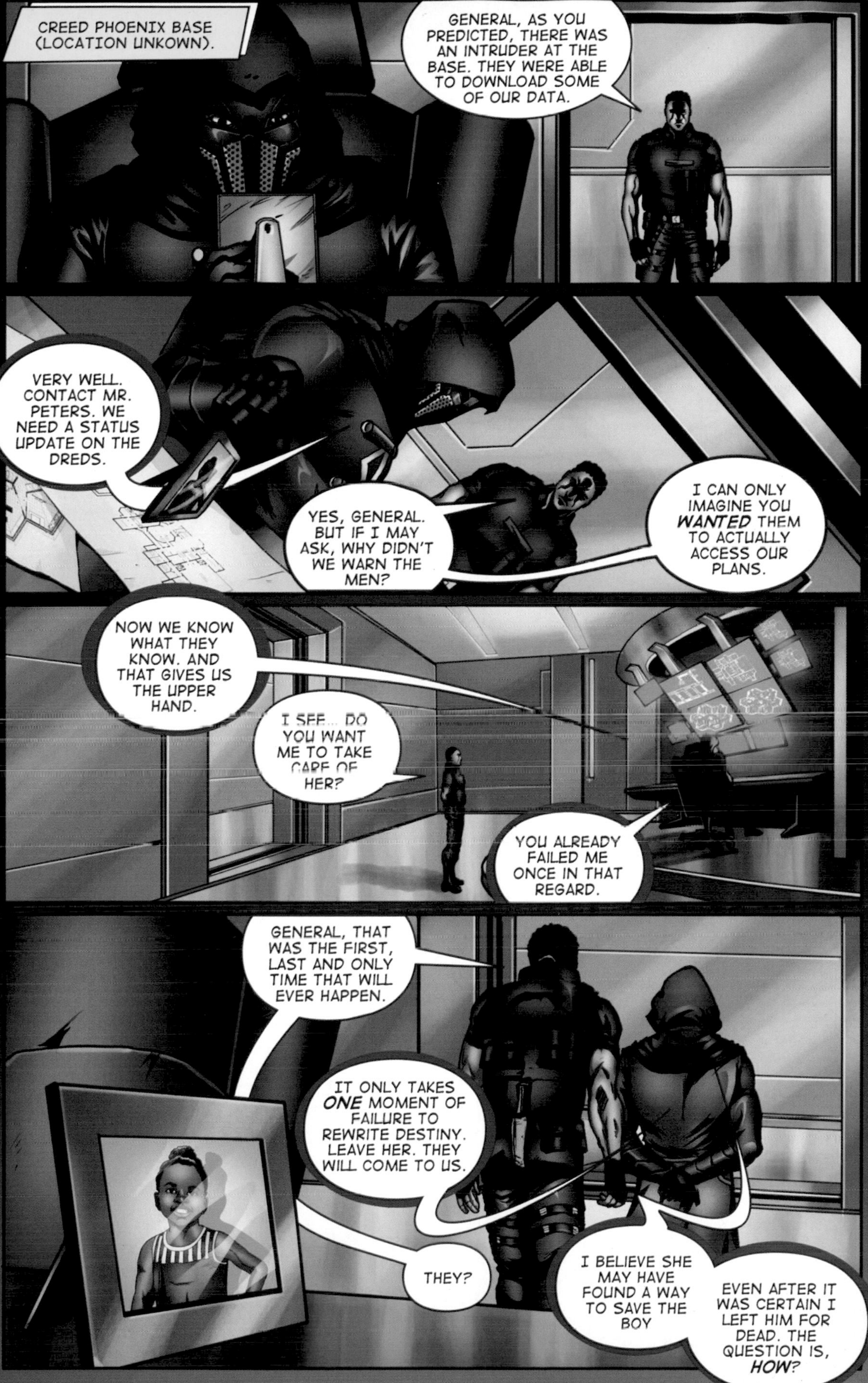
CREED PHOENIX BASE (LOCATION UNKOWN).
GENERAL, AS YOU PREDICTED, THERE WAS AN INTRUDER AT THE BASE. THEY WERE ABLE TO DOWNLOAD SOME OF OUR DATA.
VERY WELL. CONTACT MR. PETERS. WE NEED A STATUS UPDATE ON THE DREDS.
YES, GENERAL. BUT IF I MAY ASK, WHY DIDN'T WE WARN THE MEN?
I CAN ONLY IMAGINE YOU WANTED THEM TO ACTUALLY ACCESS OUR PLANS.
NOW WE KNOW WHAT THEY KNOW. AND THAT GIVES US THE UPPER HAND.
I SEE... DO YOU WANT ME TO TAKE CARE OF HER?
YOU ALREADY FAILED ME ONCE IN THAT REGARD.
GENERAL, THAT WAS THE FIRST, LAST AND ONLY TIME THAT WILL EVER HAPPEN.
IT ONLY TAKES ONE MOMENT OF FAILURE TO REWRITE DESTINY. LEAVE HER. THEY WILL COME TO US.
THEY?
I BELIEVE SHE MAY HAVE FOUND A WAY TO SAVE THE BOY
EVEN AFTER IT WAS CERTAIN I LEFT HIM FOR DEAD. THE QUESTION IS, HOW?

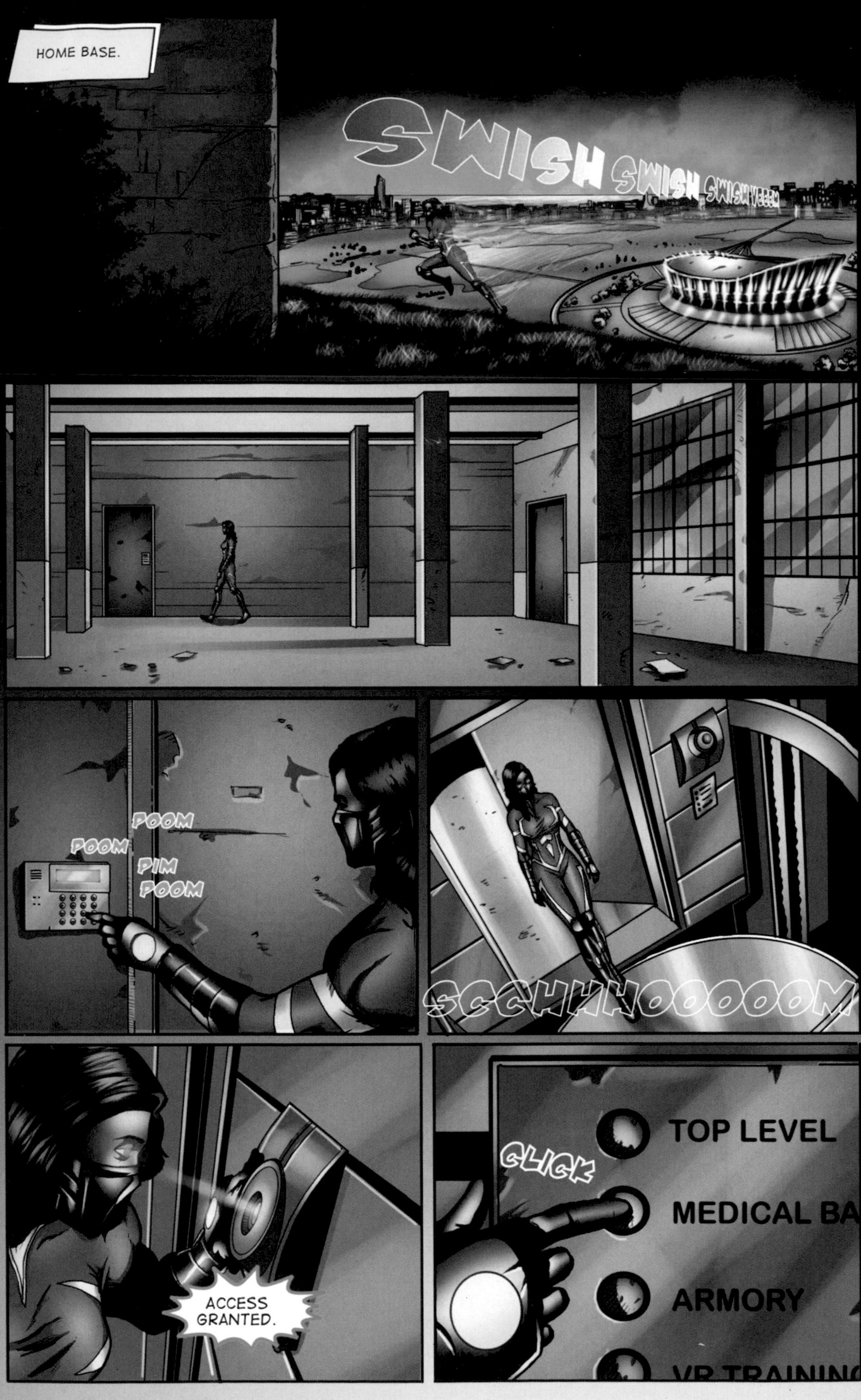
HOME BASE.
SWISH SWISH SWISH VEEEM
POOM
POOM
PIM
POOM
SCCHHHOOOOOOM
ACCESS GRANTED.
CLICK
TOP LEVEL
MEDICAL BA
ARMORY

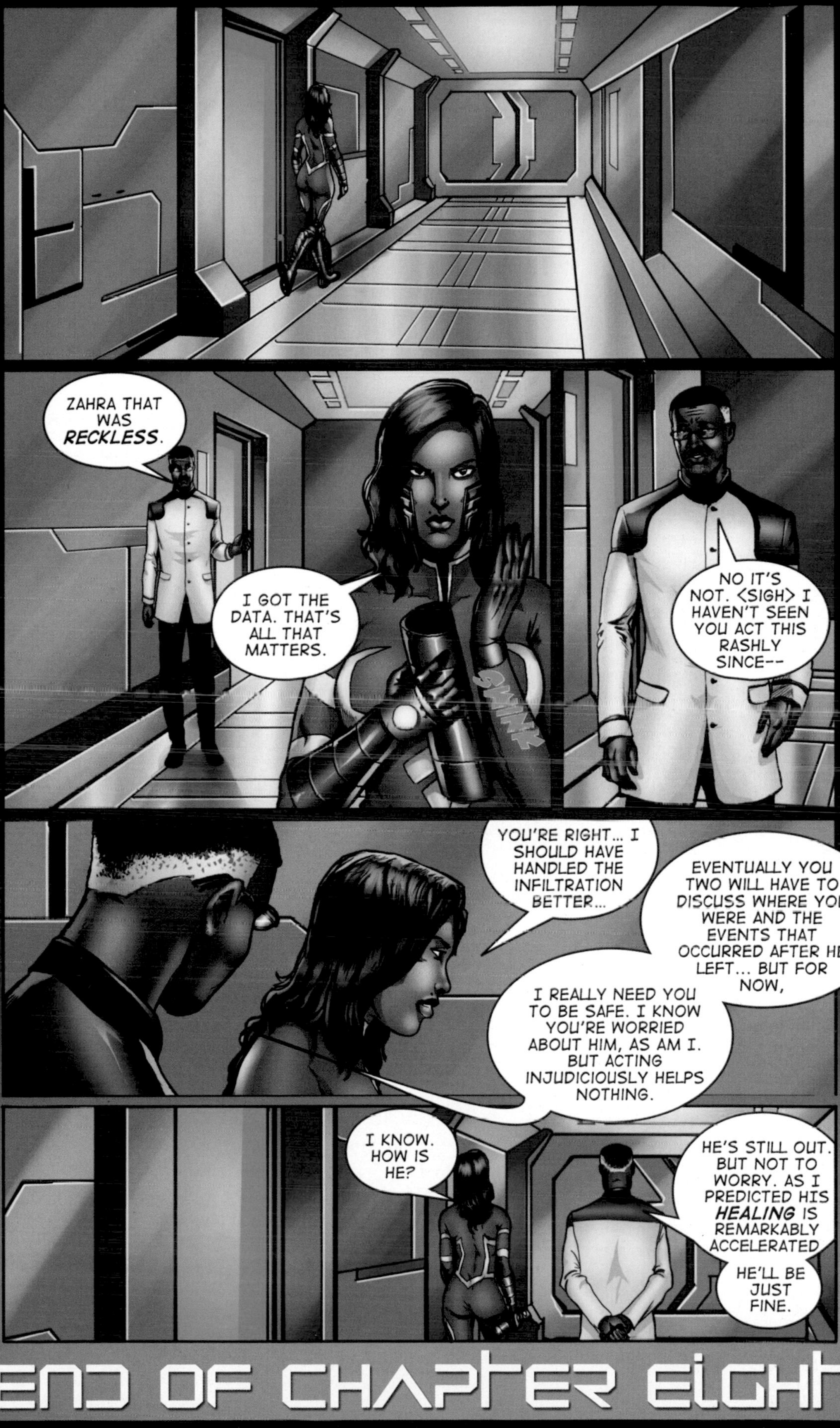
ZAHRA THAT WAS *RECKLESS*.
I GOT THE DATA. THAT'S ALL THAT MATTERS.
NO IT'S NOT. <SIGH> I HAVEN'T SEEN YOU ACT THIS RASHLY SINCE--
YOU'RE RIGHT... I SHOULD HAVE HANDLED THE INFILTRATION BETTER...
EVENTUALLY YOU TWO WILL HAVE TO DISCUSS WHERE YOU WERE AND THE EVENTS THAT OCCURRED AFTER HE LEFT... BUT FOR NOW,
I REALLY NEED YOU TO BE SAFE. I KNOW YOU'RE WORRIED ABOUT HIM, AS AM I. BUT ACTING INJUDICIOUSLY HELPS NOTHING.
I KNOW. HOW IS HE?
HE'S STILL OUT. BUT NOT TO WORRY. AS I PREDICTED HIS ***HEALING*** IS REMARKABLY ACCELERATED
HE'LL BE JUST FINE.
END OF CHAPTER EIGHT

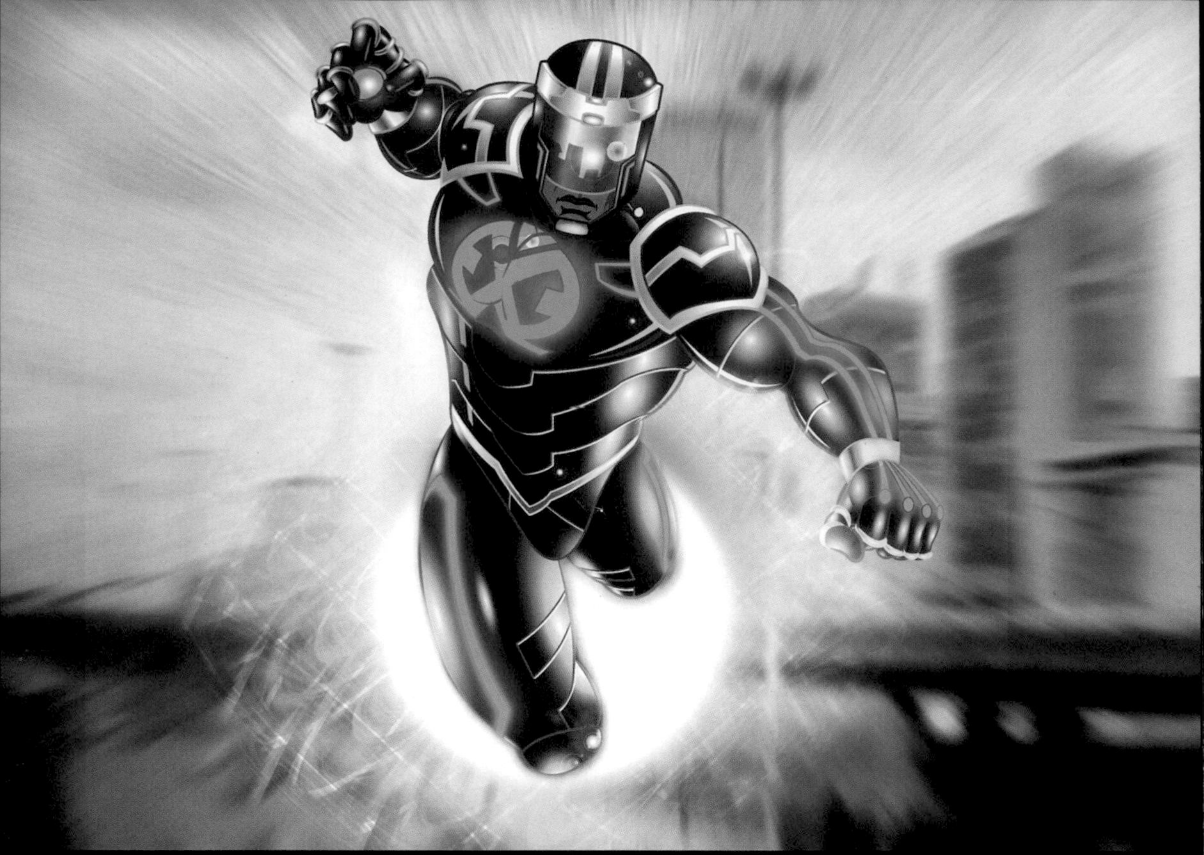

- Fan Art by Babajide Briggs Adebimpe

Fun Fact: E.X.O. stands for Endogenic Xoskeletal Ordnance and refers to the suit Wale wears. However, it is different from "EXO" (no periods), which is the moniker for Wale's superhero alter ego.

CHAPTER nine

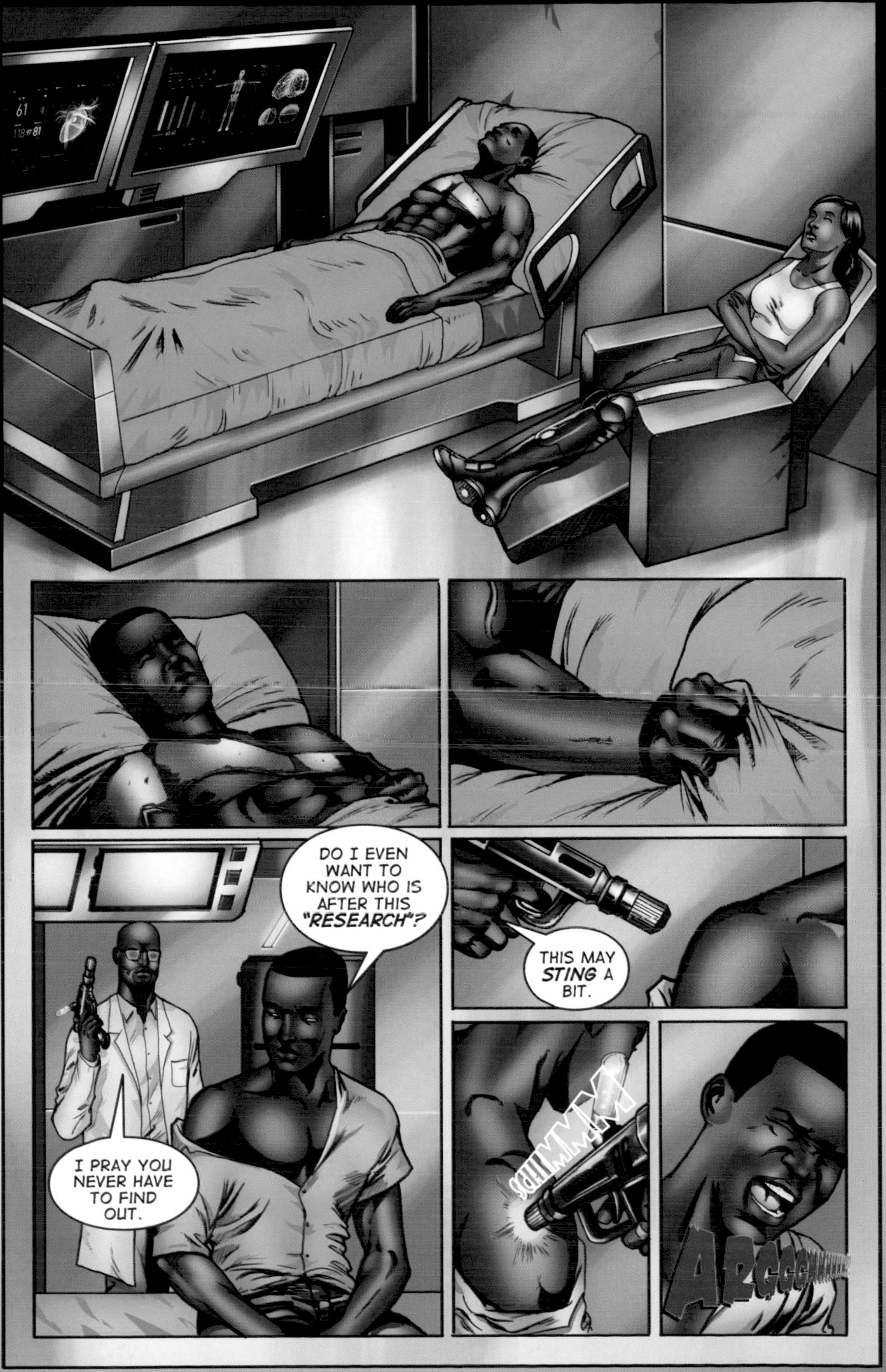
DO I EVEN WANT TO KNOW WHO IS AFTER THIS "RESEARCH"?
I PRAY YOU NEVER HAVE TO FIND OUT.
THIS MAY STING A BIT.

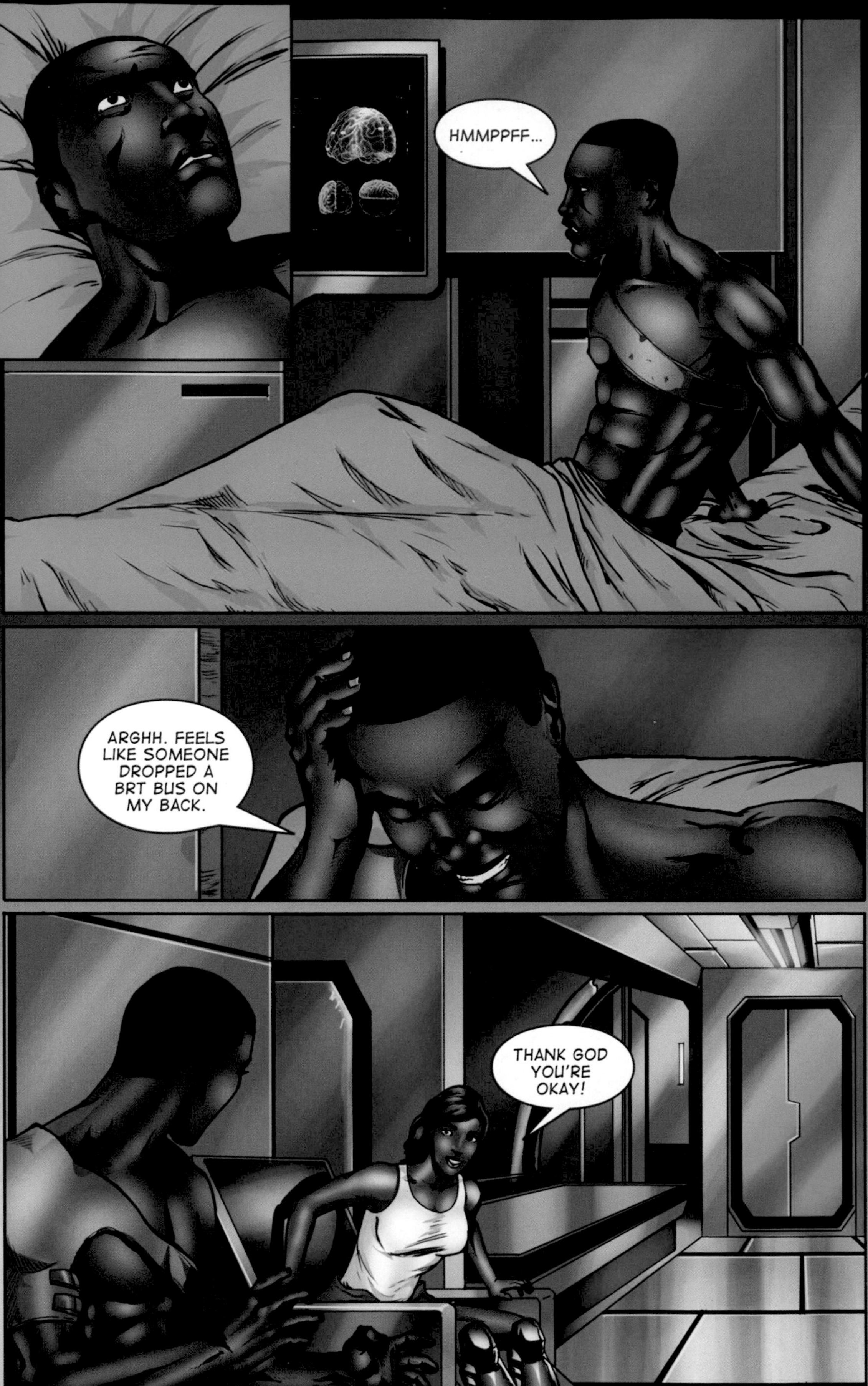
HMMPPFF...
ARGHH. FEELS LIKE SOMEONE DROPPED A BRT BUS ON MY BACK.
THANK GOD YOU'RE OKAY!

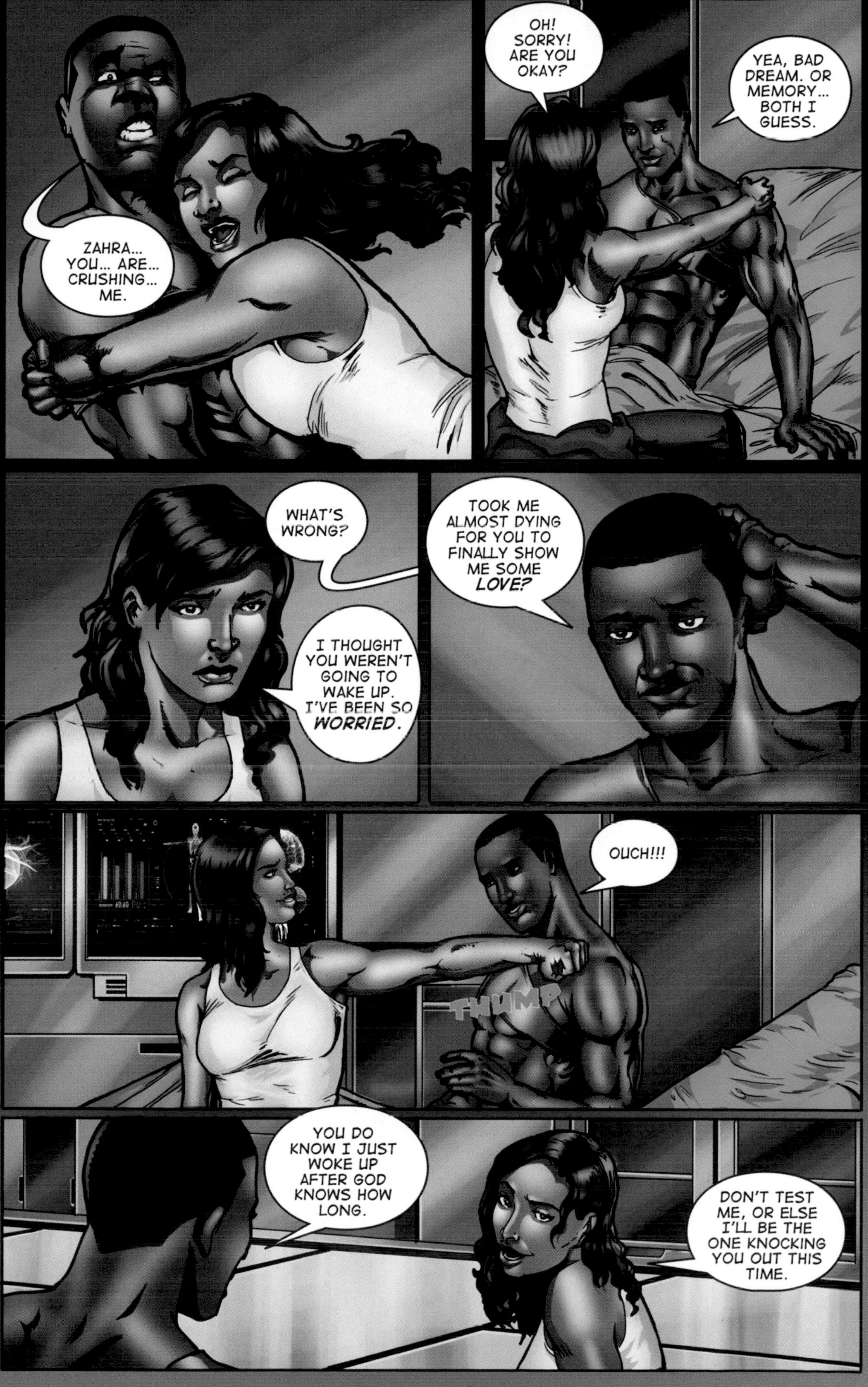
ZAHRA... YOU... ARE... CRUSHING... ME.
OH! SORRY! ARE YOU OKAY?
YEA, BAD DREAM. OR MEMORY... BOTH I GUESS.
WHAT'S WRONG?
I THOUGHT YOU WEREN'T GOING TO WAKE UP. I'VE BEEN SO WORRIED.
TOOK ME ALMOST DYING FOR YOU TO FINALLY SHOW ME SOME LOVE?
OUCH!!!
THUMP
YOU DO KNOW I JUST WOKE UP AFTER GOD KNOWS HOW LONG.
DON'T TEST ME, OR ELSE I'LL BE THE ONE KNOCKING YOU OUT THIS TIME.

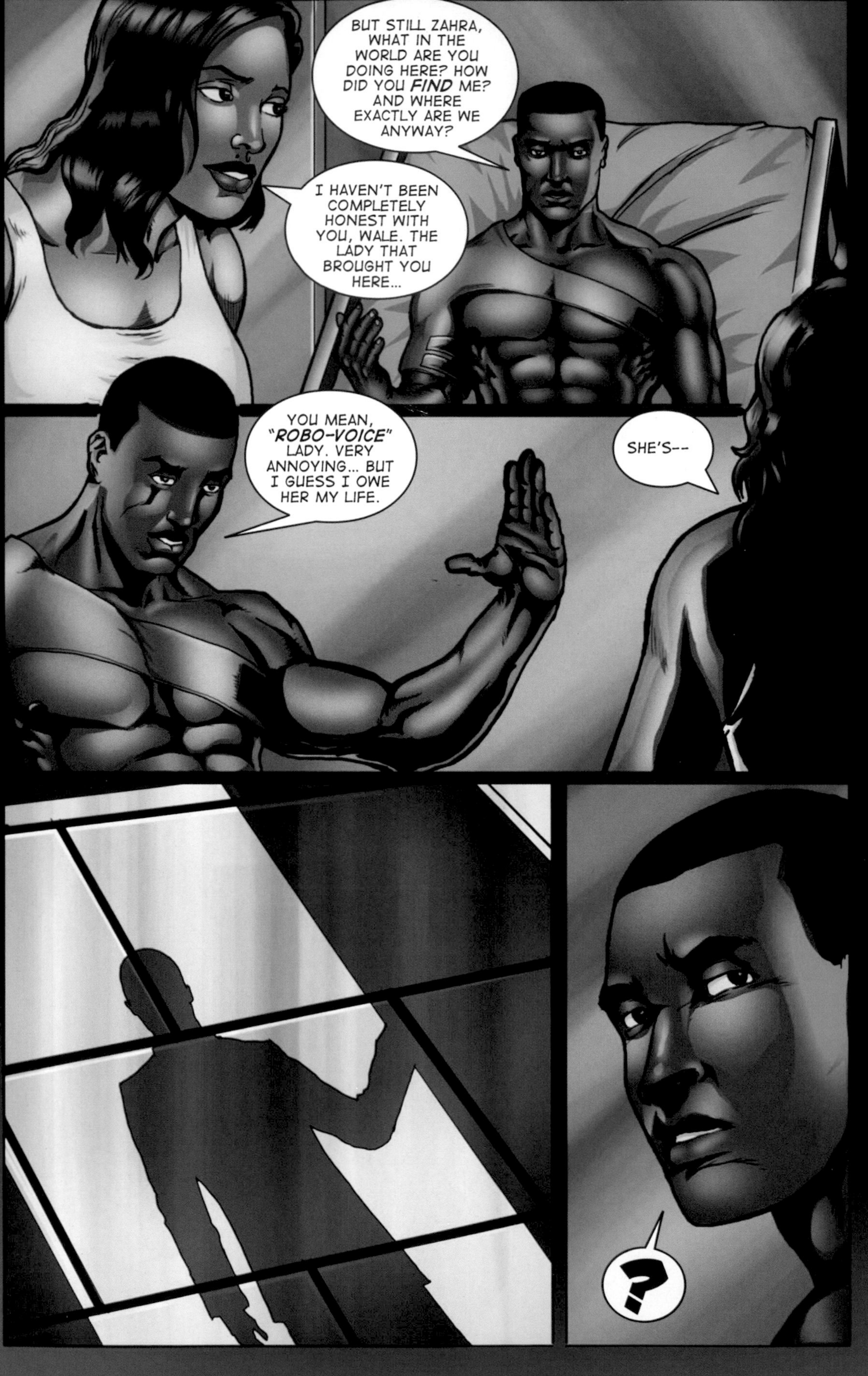
BUT STILL ZAHRA, WHAT IN THE WORLD ARE YOU DOING HERE? HOW DID YOU *FIND* ME? AND WHERE EXACTLY ARE WE ANYWAY?
I HAVEN'T BEEN COMPLETELY HONEST WITH YOU, WALE. THE LADY THAT BROUGHT YOU HERE...
YOU MEAN, "*ROBO-VOICE*" LADY. VERY ANNOYING... BUT I GUESS I OWE HER MY LIFE.
SHE'S--
?

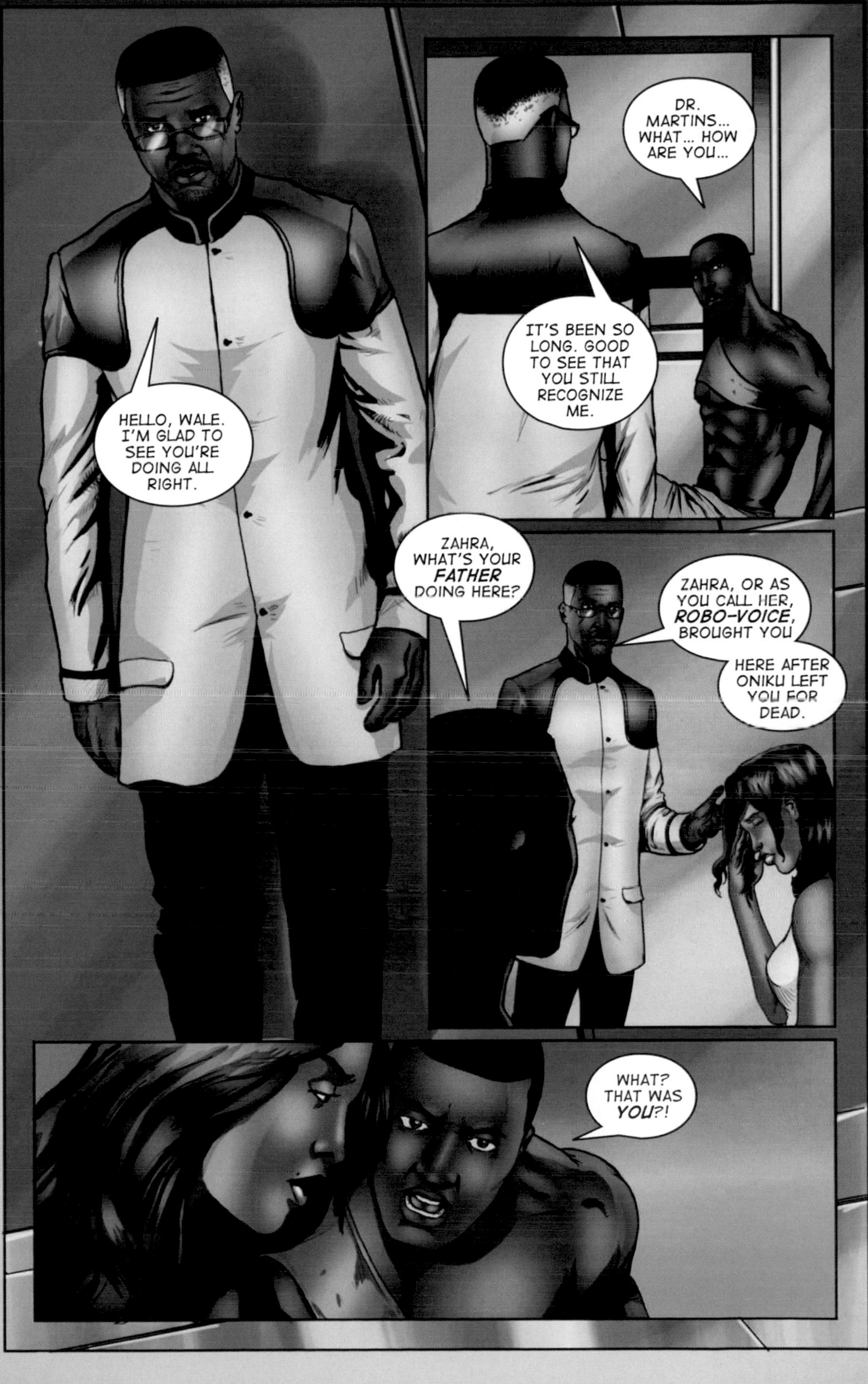
HELLO, WALE. I'M GLAD TO SEE YOU'RE DOING ALL RIGHT.
DR. MARTINS... WHAT... HOW ARE YOU...
IT'S BEEN SO LONG. GOOD TO SEE THAT YOU STILL RECOGNIZE ME.
ZAHRA, WHAT'S YOUR FATHER DOING HERE?
ZAHRA, OR AS YOU CALL HER, ROBO-VOICE, BROUGHT YOU
HERE AFTER ONIKU LEFT YOU FOR DEAD.
WHAT? THAT WAS YOU?!

YOUNEEK YOUNIVERSE
GENESYS

The beginning of a new era of heroes...

E.X.O.™

MALIKA™
Warrior Queen

WINDMAKER™

FIREFROST™

For more info visit
www.youneekstudios.com/genesys

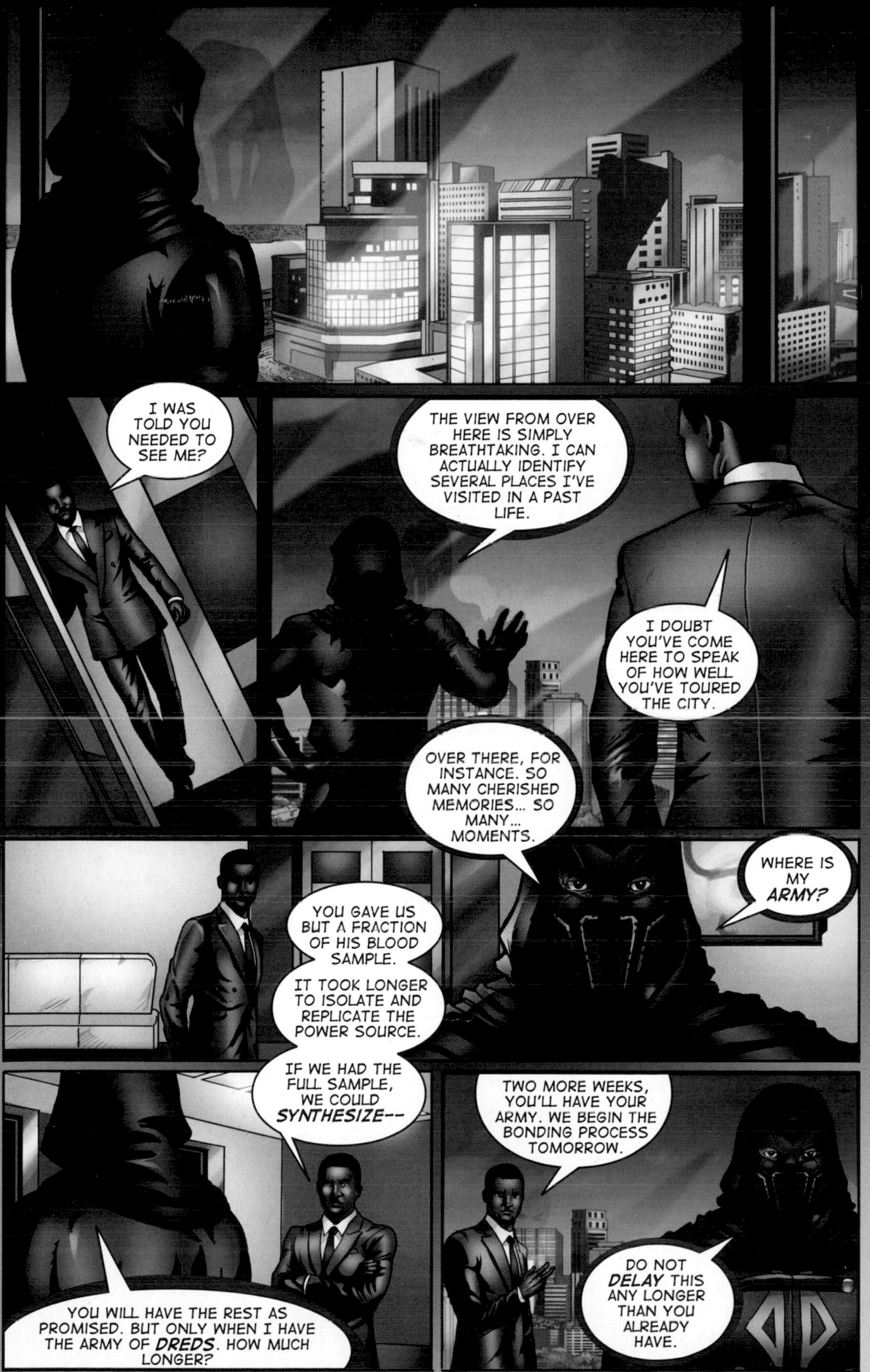
I WAS TOLD YOU NEEDED TO SEE ME?
THE VIEW FROM OVER HERE IS SIMPLY BREATHTAKING. I CAN ACTUALLY IDENTIFY SEVERAL PLACES I'VE VISITED IN A PAST LIFE.
I DOUBT YOU'VE COME HERE TO SPEAK OF HOW WELL YOU'VE TOURED THE CITY.
OVER THERE, FOR INSTANCE. SO MANY CHERISHED MEMORIES... SO MANY... MOMENTS.
WHERE IS MY ARMY?
YOU GAVE US BUT A FRACTION OF HIS BLOOD SAMPLE.
IT TOOK LONGER TO ISOLATE AND REPLICATE THE POWER SOURCE.
IF WE HAD THE FULL SAMPLE, WE COULD SYNTHESIZE--
YOU WILL HAVE THE REST AS PROMISED. BUT ONLY WHEN I HAVE THE ARMY OF DREDS. HOW MUCH LONGER?
TWO MORE WEEKS, YOU'LL HAVE YOUR ARMY. WE BEGIN THE BONDING PROCESS TOMORROW.
DO NOT DELAY THIS ANY LONGER THAN YOU ALREADY HAVE.

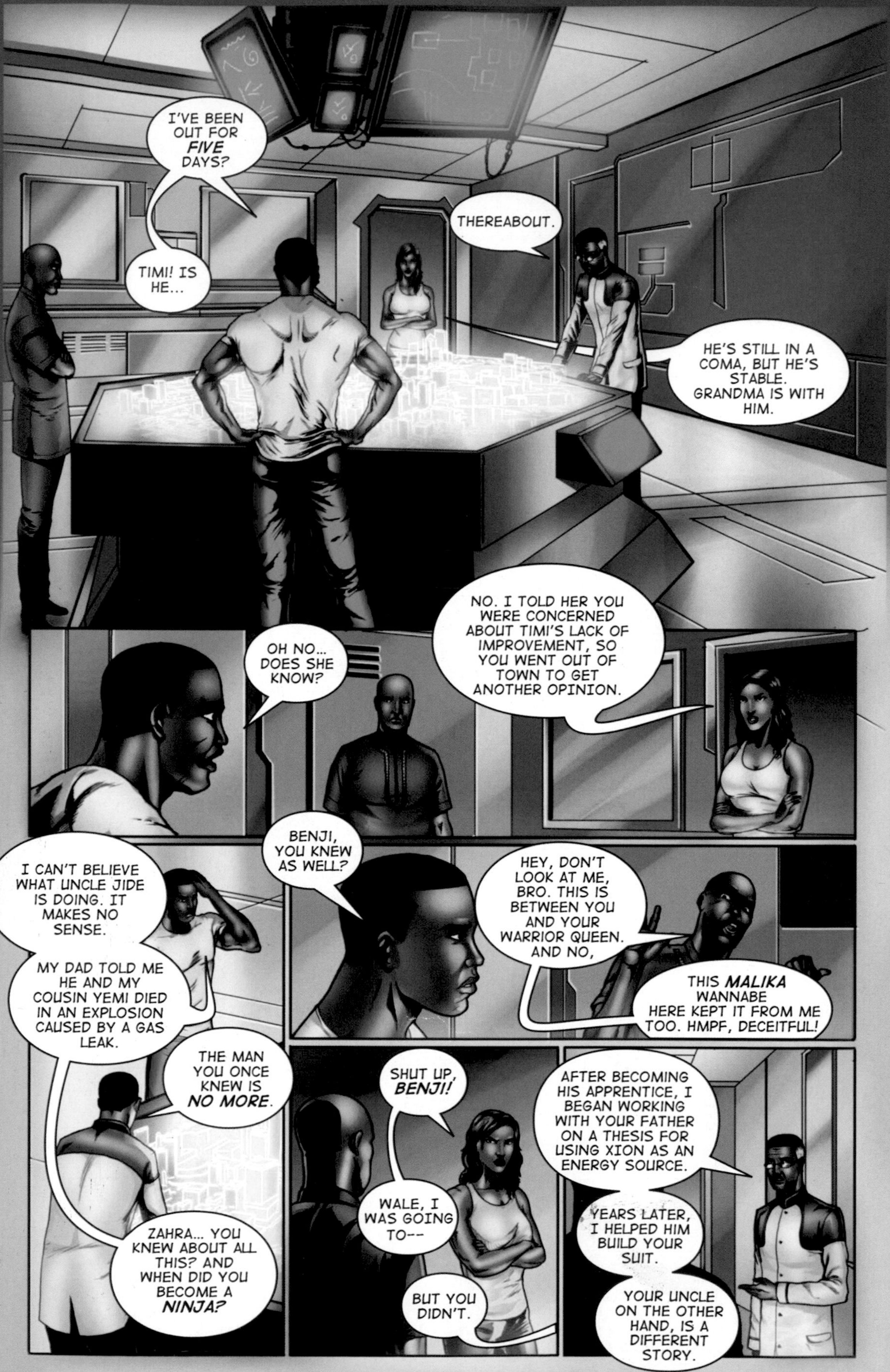

I'VE BEEN OUT FOR *FIVE* DAYS?
TIMI! IS HE...
THEREABOUT.
HE'S STILL IN A COMA, BUT HE'S STABLE. GRANDMA IS WITH HIM.
OH NO... DOES SHE KNOW?
NO. I TOLD HER YOU WERE CONCERNED ABOUT TIMI'S LACK OF IMPROVEMENT, SO YOU WENT OUT OF TOWN TO GET ANOTHER OPINION.
I CAN'T BELIEVE WHAT UNCLE JIDE IS DOING. IT MAKES NO SENSE.
MY DAD TOLD ME HE AND MY COUSIN YEMI DIED IN AN EXPLOSION CAUSED BY A GAS LEAK.
BENJI, YOU KNEW AS WELL?
HEY, DON'T LOOK AT ME, BRO. THIS IS BETWEEN YOU AND YOUR WARRIOR QUEEN. AND NO,
THIS *MALIKA* WANNABE HERE KEPT IT FROM ME TOO. HMPF, DECEITFUL!
THE MAN YOU ONCE KNEW IS *NO MORE*.
ZAHRA... YOU KNEW ABOUT ALL THIS? AND WHEN DID YOU BECOME A *NINJA?*
SHUT UP, *BENJI!*
WALE, I WAS GOING TO--
BUT YOU DIDN'T.
AFTER BECOMING HIS APPRENTICE, I BEGAN WORKING WITH YOUR FATHER ON A THESIS FOR USING XION AS AN ENERGY SOURCE.
YEARS LATER, I HELPED HIM BUILD YOUR SUIT.
YOUR UNCLE ON THE OTHER HAND, IS A DIFFERENT STORY.

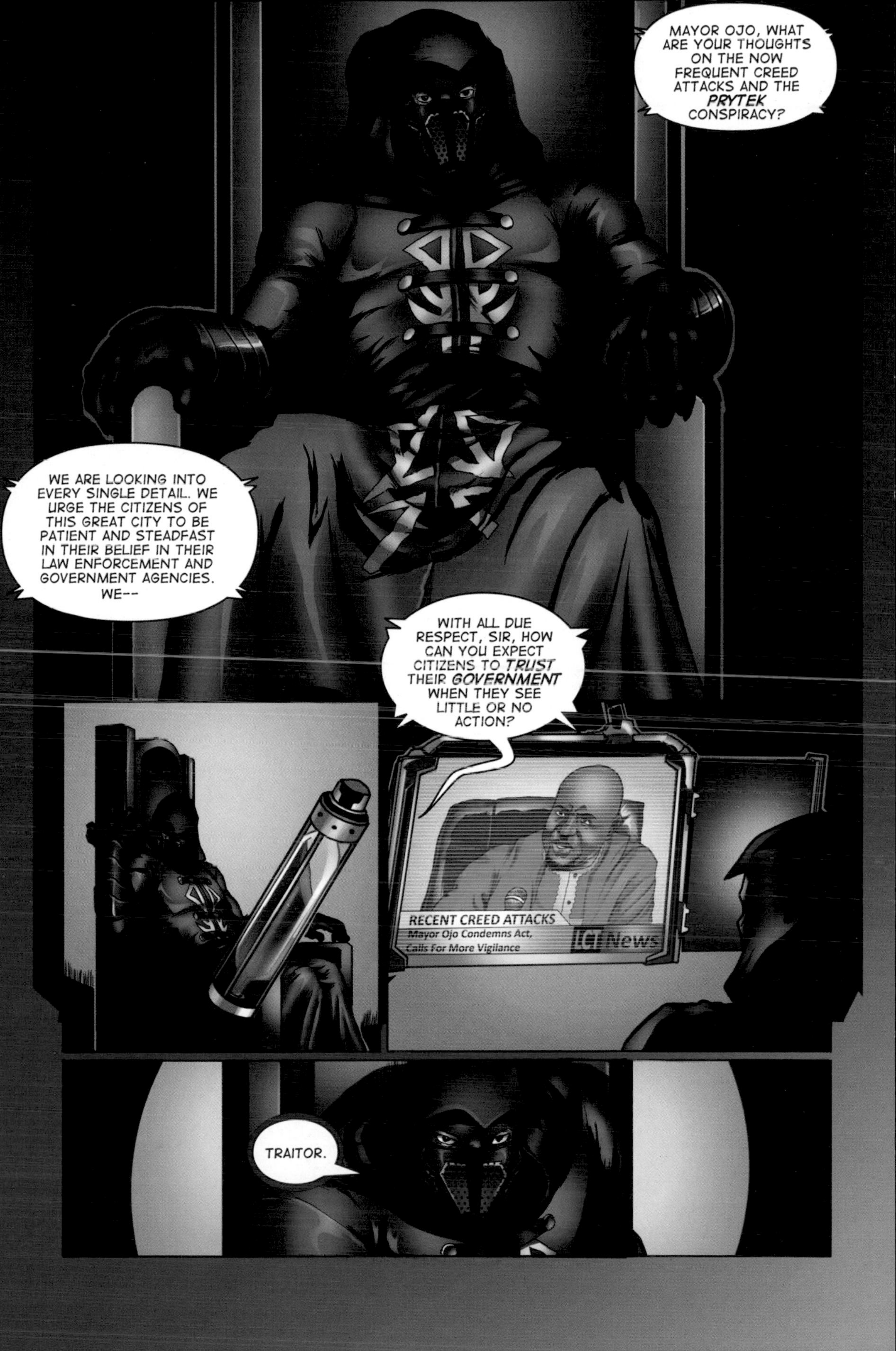
MAYOR OJO, WHAT ARE YOUR THOUGHTS ON THE NOW FREQUENT CREED ATTACKS AND THE PRYTEK CONSPIRACY?
WE ARE LOOKING INTO EVERY SINGLE DETAIL. WE URGE THE CITIZENS OF THIS GREAT CITY TO BE PATIENT AND STEADFAST IN THEIR BELIEF IN THEIR LAW ENFORCEMENT AND GOVERNMENT AGENCIES. WE--
WITH ALL DUE RESPECT, SIR, HOW CAN YOU EXPECT CITIZENS TO TRUST THEIR GOVERNMENT WHEN THEY SEE LITTLE OR NO ACTION?
RECENT CREED ATTACKS
Mayor Ojo Condemns Act, Calls For More Vigilance
ICT News
TRAITOR.

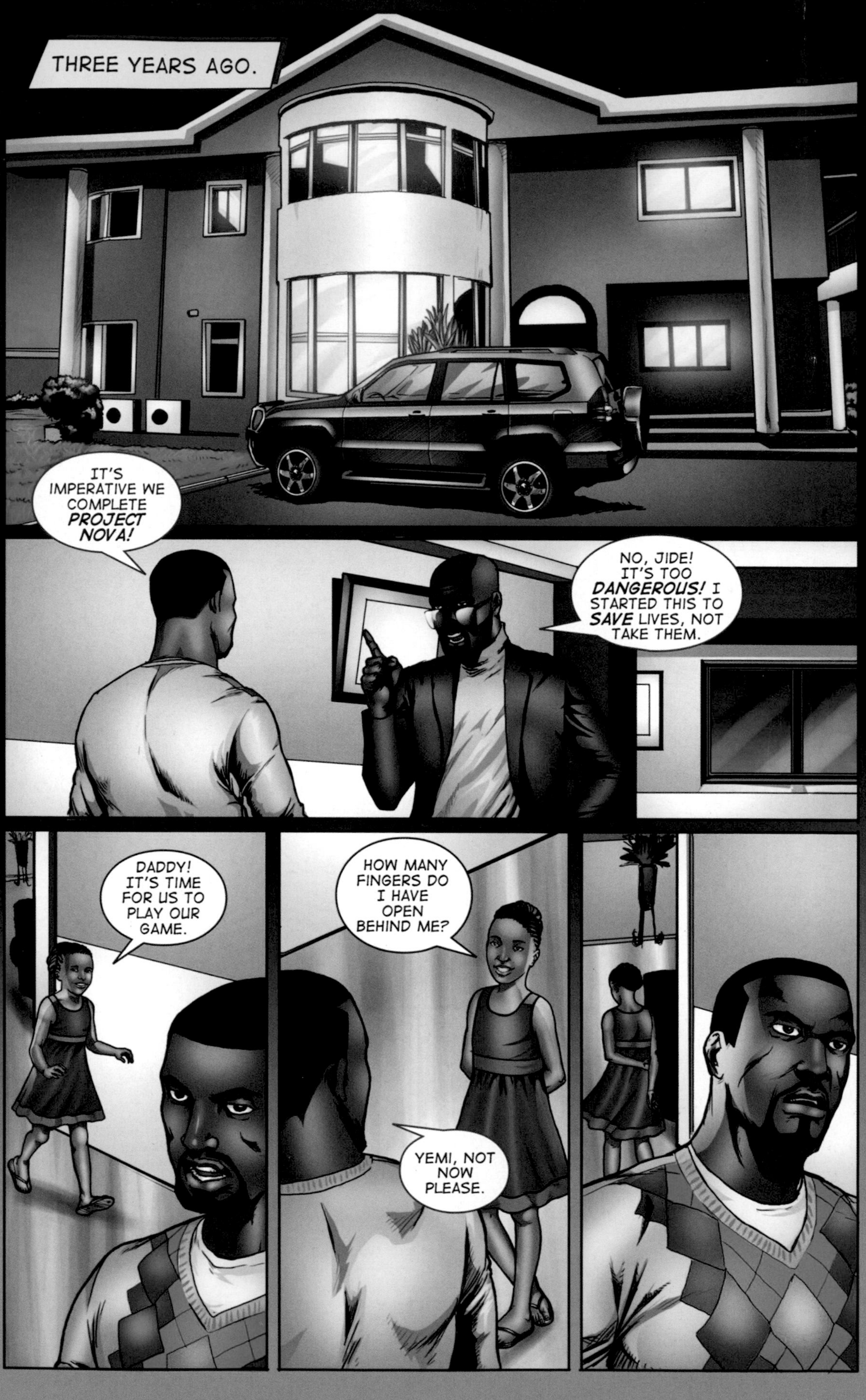
THREE YEARS AGO.
IT'S IMPERATIVE WE COMPLETE PROJECT NOVA!
NO, JIDE! IT'S TOO DANGEROUS! I STARTED THIS TO SAVE LIVES, NOT TAKE THEM.
DADDY! IT'S TIME FOR US TO PLAY OUR GAME.
HOW MANY FINGERS DO I HAVE OPEN BEHIND ME?
YEMI, NOT NOW PLEASE.

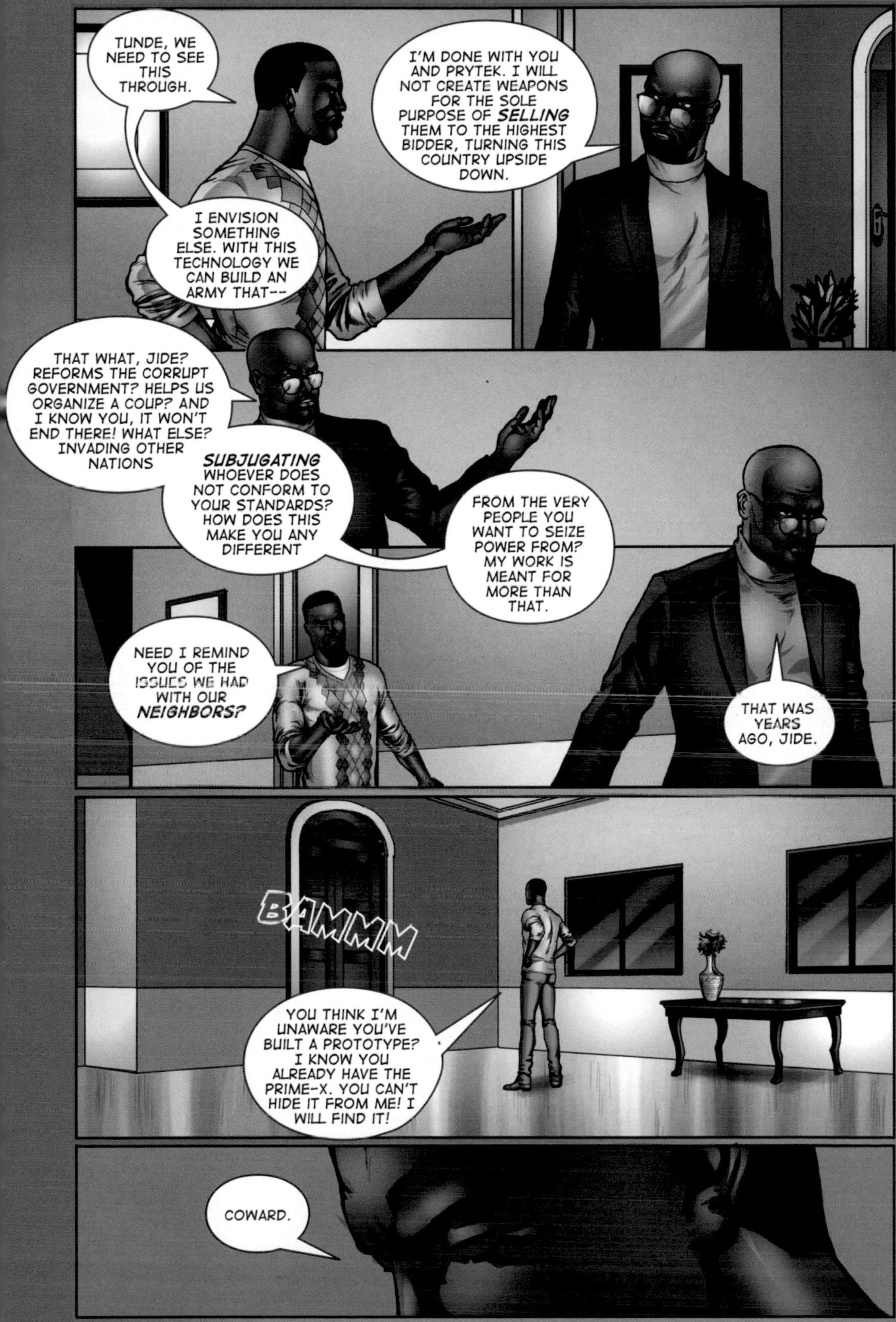
TUNDE, WE NEED TO SEE THIS THROUGH.
I'M DONE WITH YOU AND PRYTEK. I WILL NOT CREATE WEAPONS FOR THE SOLE PURPOSE OF SELLING THEM TO THE HIGHEST BIDDER, TURNING THIS COUNTRY UPSIDE DOWN.
I ENVISION SOMETHING ELSE. WITH THIS TECHNOLOGY WE CAN BUILD AN ARMY THAT--
THAT WHAT, JIDE? REFORMS THE CORRUPT GOVERNMENT? HELPS US ORGANIZE A COUP? AND I KNOW YOU, IT WON'T END THERE! WHAT ELSE? INVADING OTHER NATIONS
SUBJUGATING WHOEVER DOES NOT CONFORM TO YOUR STANDARDS? HOW DOES THIS MAKE YOU ANY DIFFERENT
FROM THE VERY PEOPLE YOU WANT TO SEIZE POWER FROM? MY WORK IS MEANT FOR MORE THAN THAT.
NEED I REMIND YOU OF THE ISSUES WE HAD WITH OUR NEIGHBORS?
THAT WAS YEARS AGO, JIDE.
BAMMM
YOU THINK I'M UNAWARE YOU'VE BUILT A PROTOTYPE? I KNOW YOU ALREADY HAVE THE PRIME-X. YOU CAN'T HIDE IT FROM ME! I WILL FIND IT!
COWARD.

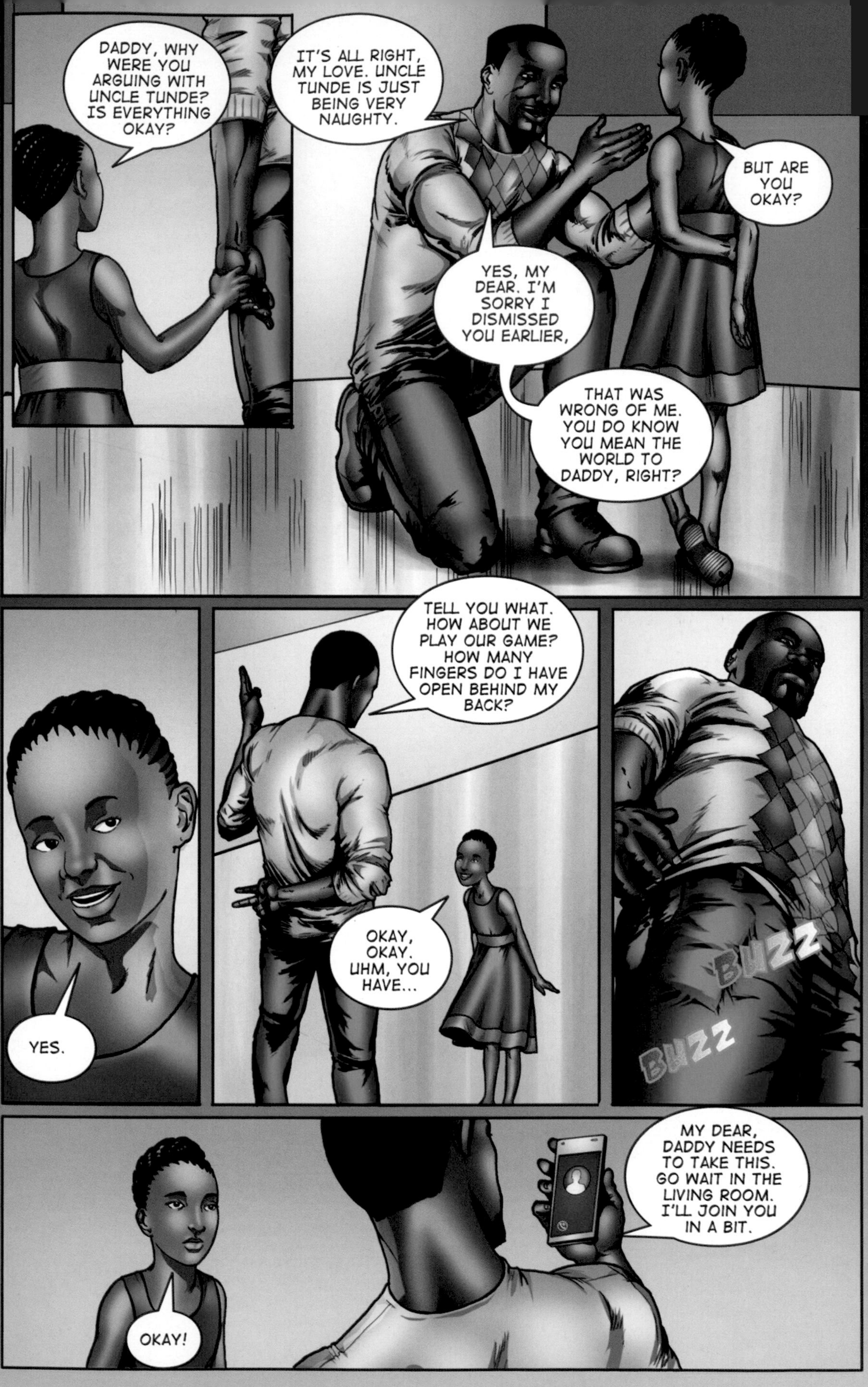
DADDY, WHY WERE YOU ARGUING WITH UNCLE TUNDE? IS EVERYTHING OKAY?
IT'S ALL RIGHT, MY LOVE. UNCLE TUNDE IS JUST BEING VERY NAUGHTY.
BUT ARE YOU OKAY?
YES, MY DEAR. I'M SORRY I DISMISSED YOU EARLIER,
THAT WAS WRONG OF ME. YOU DO KNOW YOU MEAN THE WORLD TO DADDY, RIGHT?
YES.
TELL YOU WHAT. HOW ABOUT WE PLAY OUR GAME? HOW MANY FINGERS DO I HAVE OPEN BEHIND MY BACK?
OKAY, OKAY. UHM, YOU HAVE...
BUZZ
BUZZ
MY DEAR, DADDY NEEDS TO TAKE THIS. GO WAIT IN THE LIVING ROOM. I'LL JOIN YOU IN A BIT.
OKAY!

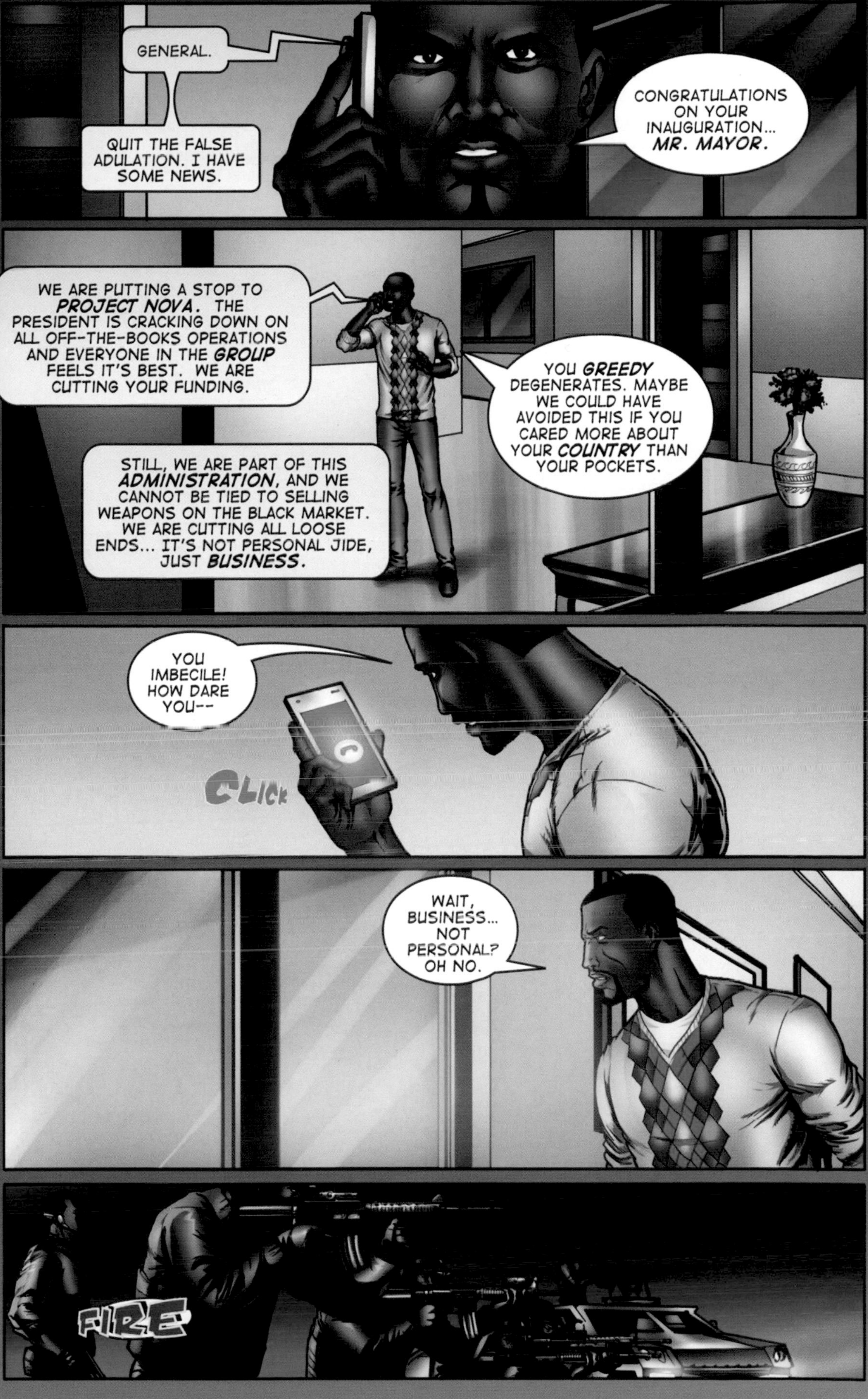
GENERAL.
CONGRATULATIONS ON YOUR INAUGURATION... MR. MAYOR.
QUIT THE FALSE ADULATION. I HAVE SOME NEWS.
WE ARE PUTTING A STOP TO PROJECT NOVA. THE PRESIDENT IS CRACKING DOWN ON ALL OFF-THE-BOOKS OPERATIONS AND EVERYONE IN THE GROUP FEELS IT'S BEST. WE ARE CUTTING YOUR FUNDING.
YOU GREEDY DEGENERATES. MAYBE WE COULD HAVE AVOIDED THIS IF YOU CARED MORE ABOUT YOUR COUNTRY THAN YOUR POCKETS.
STILL, WE ARE PART OF THIS ADMINISTRATION, AND WE CANNOT BE TIED TO SELLING WEAPONS ON THE BLACK MARKET. WE ARE CUTTING ALL LOOSE ENDS... IT'S NOT PERSONAL JIDE, JUST BUSINESS.
YOU IMBECILE! HOW DARE YOU--
CLICK
WAIT, BUSINESS... NOT PERSONAL? OH NO.
FIRE

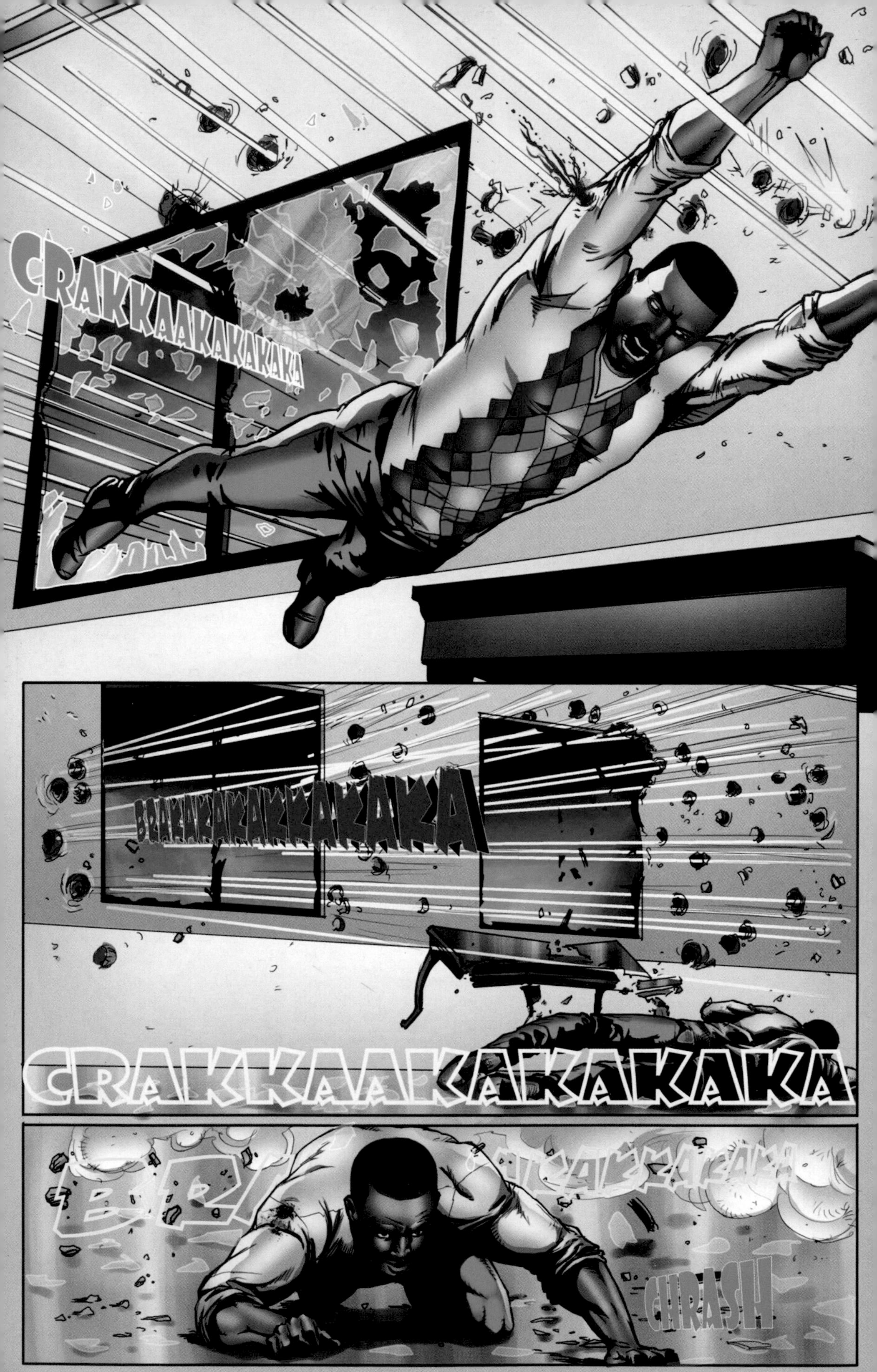
CRAKKAAKAKAKAKA
CRAKKAAKAKAKAKA
CHRASH

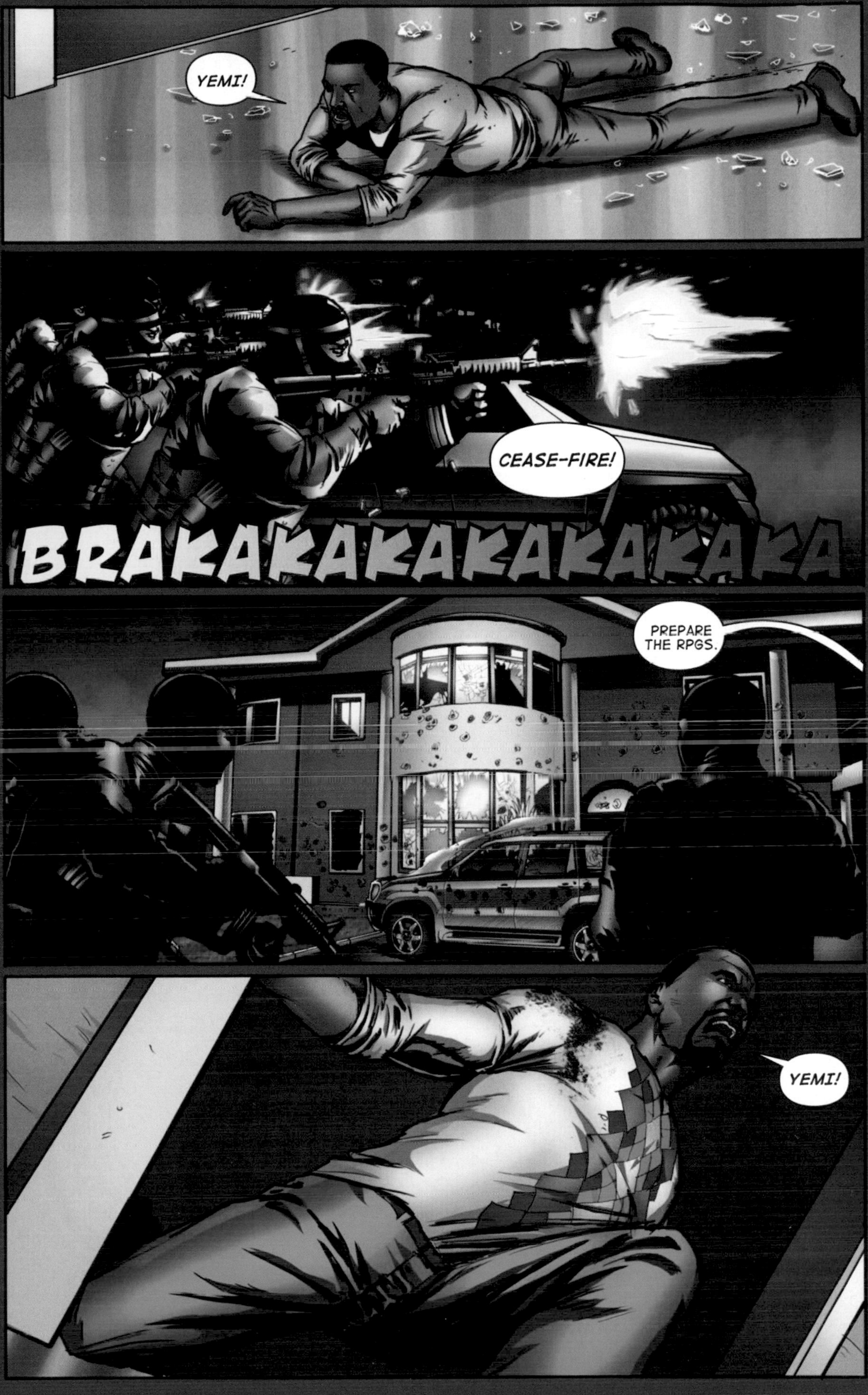
YEMI!
CEASE-FIRE!
BRAKAKAKAKAKAKAKA
PREPARE THE RPGS.
YEMI!

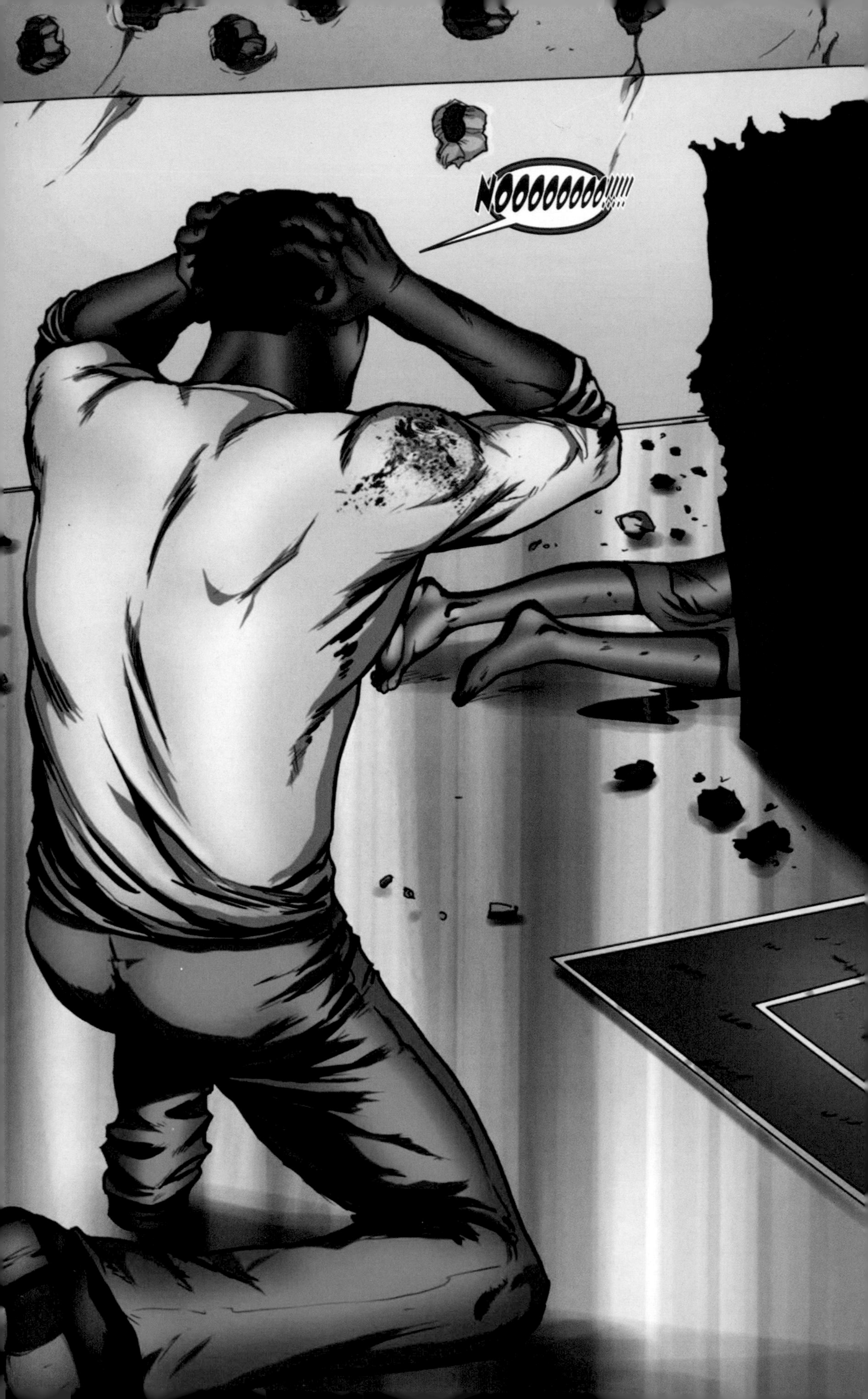
NOOOOOOOO!!!!!

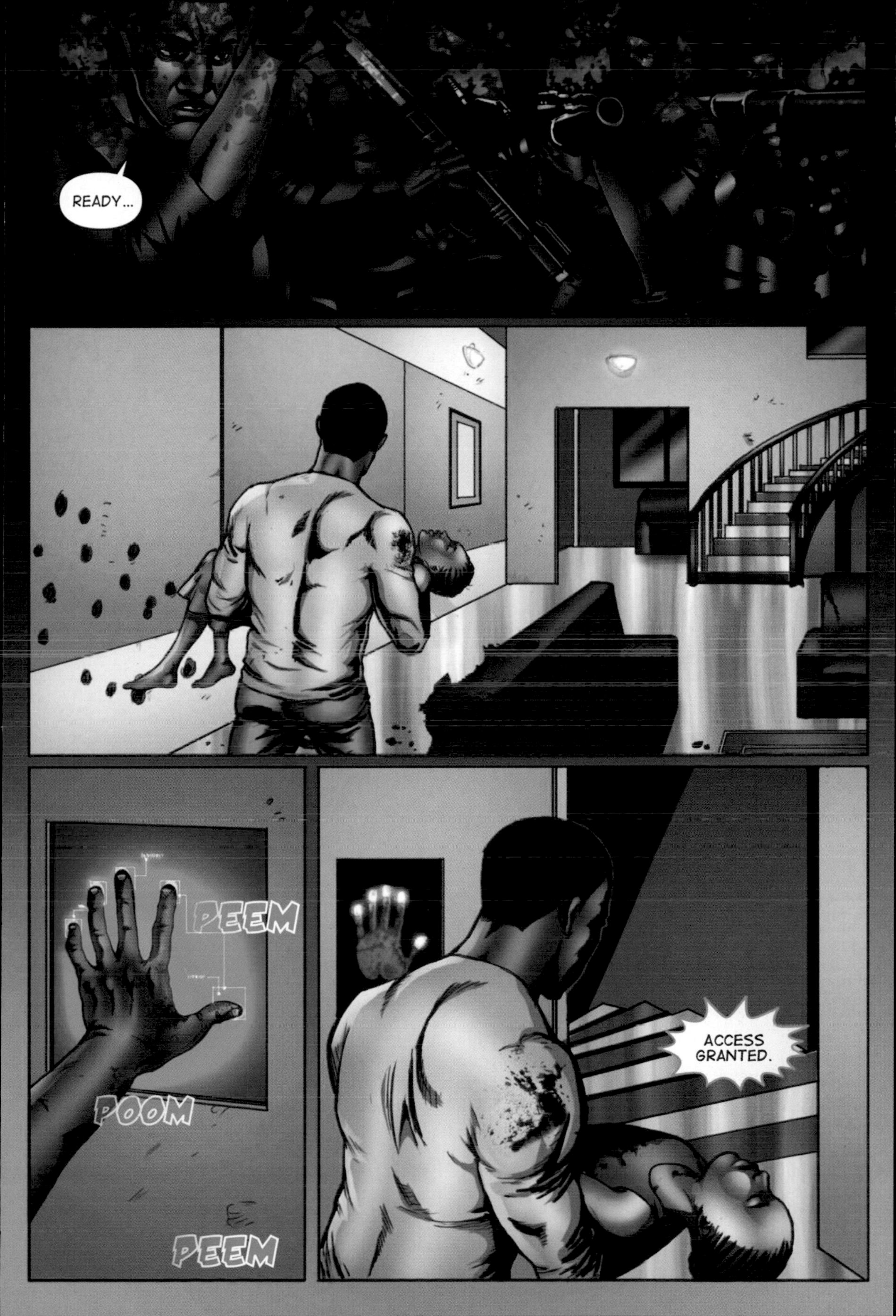
READY...
PEEM
POOM
PEEM
ACCESS GRANTED.

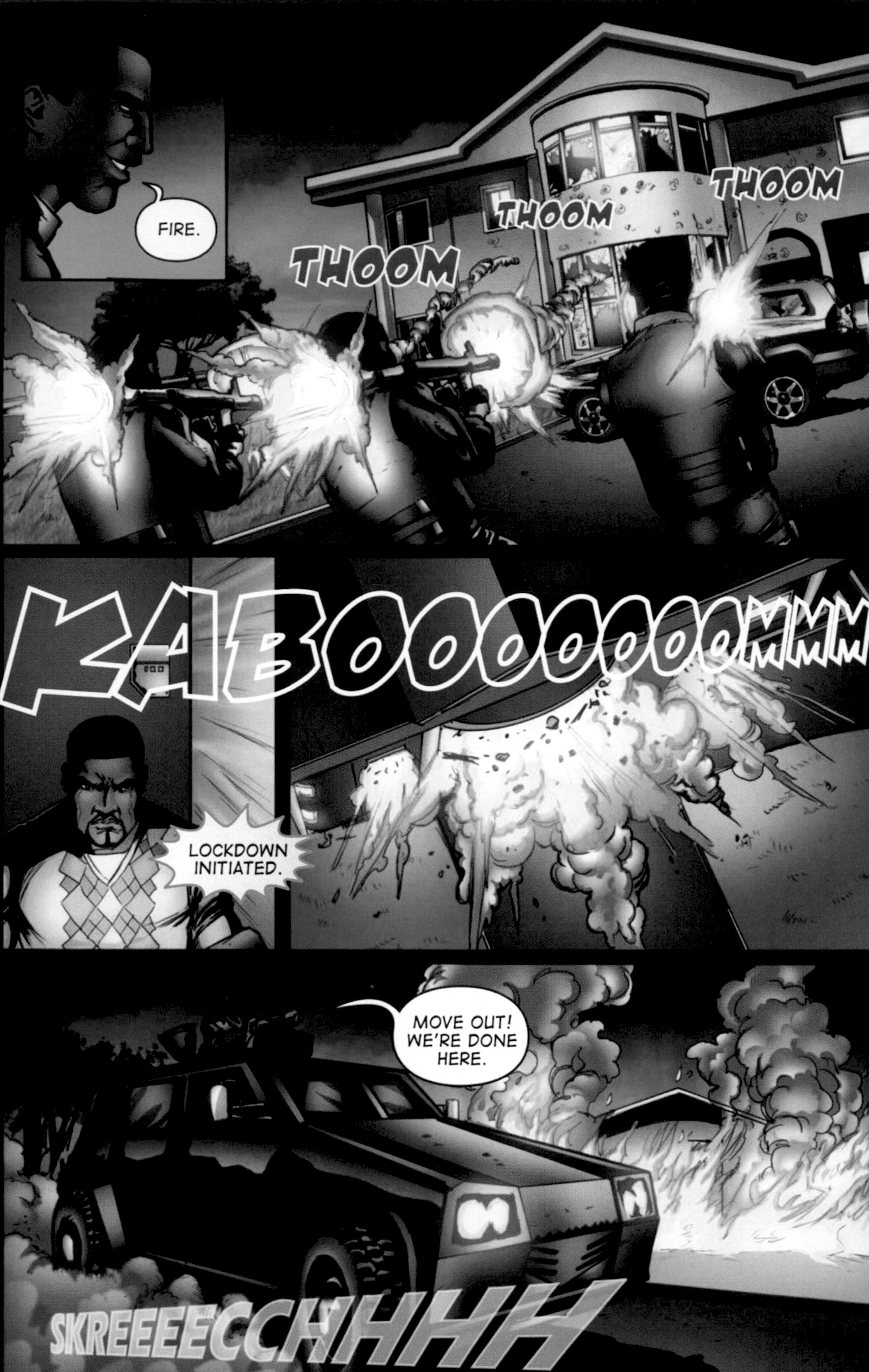
FIRE.
THOOM
THOOM
THOOM
KABOOOOOOOOMMM
LOCKDOWN INITIATED.
MOVE OUT! WE'RE DONE HERE.
SKREEEEECHHHHH

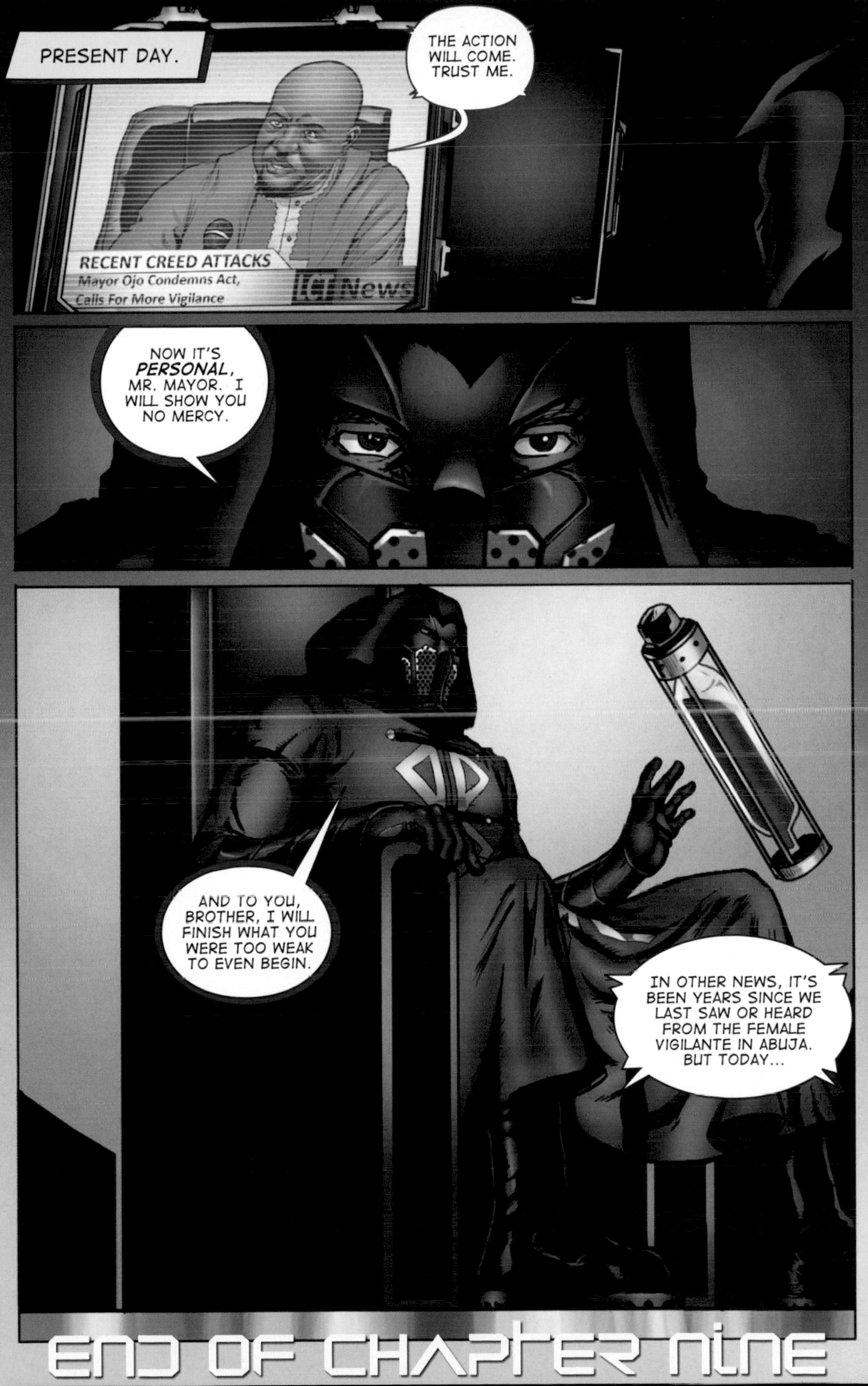
PRESENT DAY.
THE ACTION WILL COME. TRUST ME.
RECENT CREED ATTACKS
Mayor Ojo Condemns Act, Calls For More Vigilance
LCT News
NOW IT'S ***PERSONAL***, MR. MAYOR. I WILL SHOW YOU NO MERCY.
AND TO YOU, BROTHER, I WILL FINISH WHAT YOU WERE TOO WEAK TO EVEN BEGIN.
IN OTHER NEWS, IT'S BEEN YEARS SINCE WE LAST SAW OR HEARD FROM THE FEMALE VIGILANTE IN ABUJA. BUT TODAY...
END OF CHAPTER NINE

- Fan Art by Ozo Michael Ezeogu

Fun Fact: Wale Williams (EXO) and Zahra Martins (Fury) have known each other since they were kids. Both attended the same secondary (high) school and karate classes where they constantly traded the number one and two spots over several years. They were high school sweethearts and stayed together until their relationship ended after Wale left Lagoon City.

CHAPTER
ten

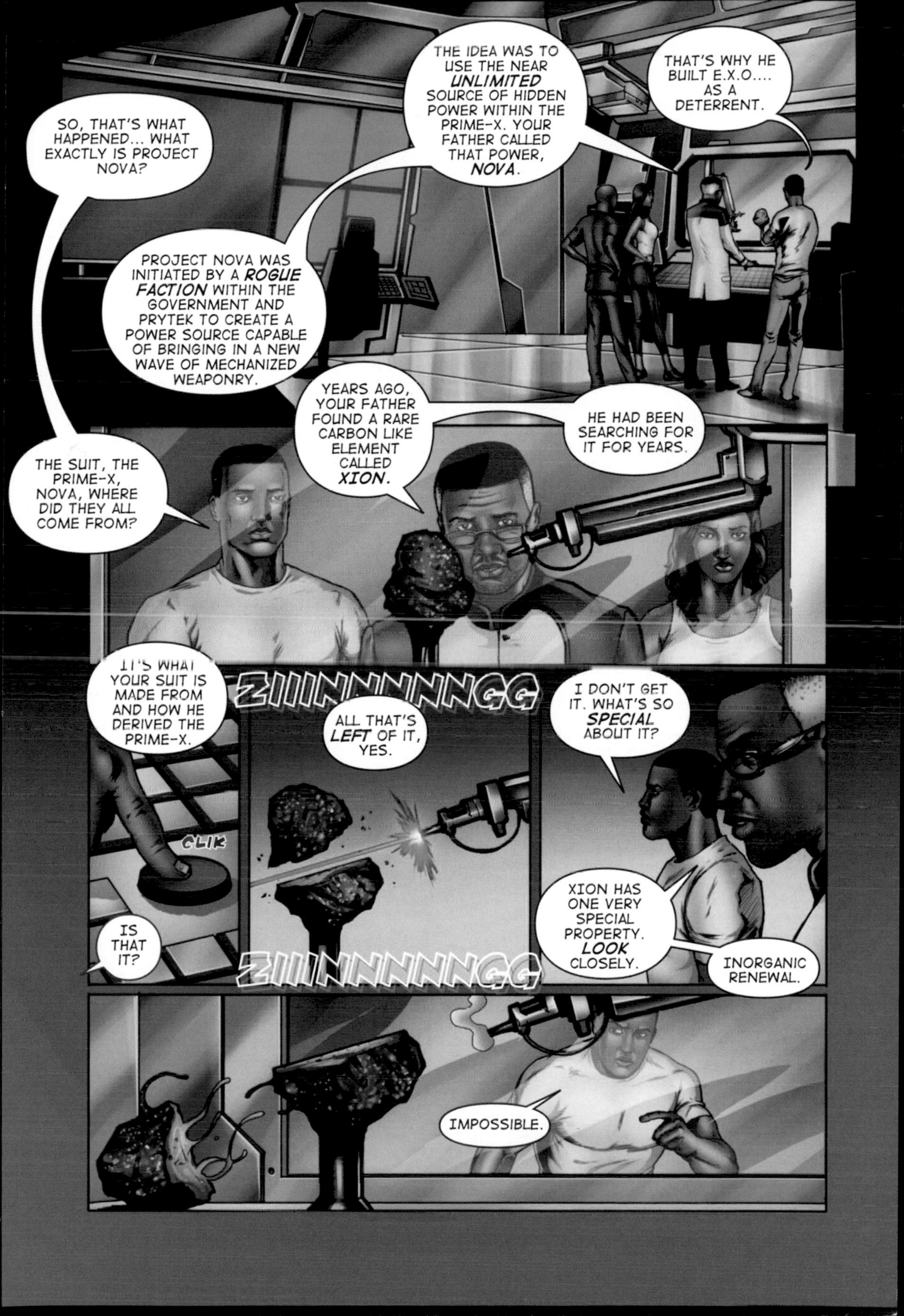
SO, THAT'S WHAT HAPPENED... WHAT EXACTLY IS PROJECT NOVA?
THE IDEA WAS TO USE THE NEAR UNLIMITED SOURCE OF HIDDEN POWER WITHIN THE PRIME-X. YOUR FATHER CALLED THAT POWER, NOVA.
THAT'S WHY HE BUILT E.X.O.... AS A DETERRENT.
PROJECT NOVA WAS INITIATED BY A ROGUE FACTION WITHIN THE GOVERNMENT AND PRYTEK TO CREATE A POWER SOURCE CAPABLE OF BRINGING IN A NEW WAVE OF MECHANIZED WEAPONRY.
THE SUIT, THE PRIME-X, NOVA, WHERE DID THEY ALL COME FROM?
YEARS AGO, YOUR FATHER FOUND A RARE CARBON LIKE ELEMENT CALLED XION.
HE HAD BEEN SEARCHING FOR IT FOR YEARS.
IT'S WHAT YOUR SUIT IS MADE FROM AND HOW HE DERIVED THE PRIME-X.
ZIIINNNNNNGG
CLIK
IS THAT IT?
ALL THAT'S LEFT OF IT, YES.
ZIIINNNNNNGG
I DON'T GET IT. WHAT'S SO SPECIAL ABOUT IT?
XION HAS ONE VERY SPECIAL PROPERTY. LOOK CLOSELY.
INORGANIC RENEWAL.
IMPOSSIBLE.

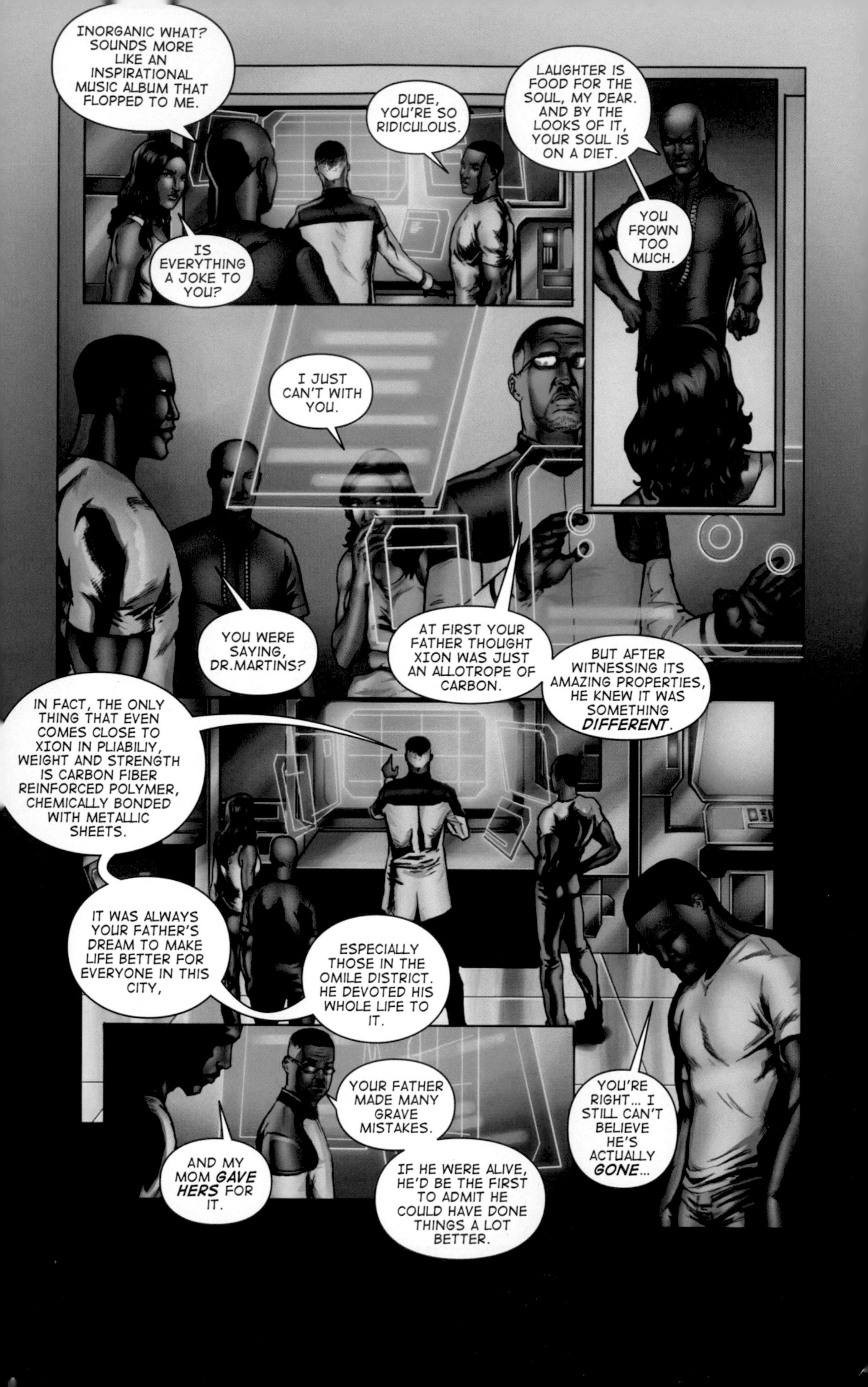
INORGANIC WHAT? SOUNDS MORE LIKE AN INSPIRATIONAL MUSIC ALBUM THAT FLOPPED TO ME.
DUDE, YOU'RE SO RIDICULOUS.
LAUGHTER IS FOOD FOR THE SOUL, MY DEAR. AND BY THE LOOKS OF IT, YOUR SOUL IS ON A DIET.
IS EVERYTHING A JOKE TO YOU?
YOU FROWN TOO MUCH.
I JUST CAN'T WITH YOU.
YOU WERE SAYING, DR.MARTINS?
AT FIRST YOUR FATHER THOUGHT XION WAS JUST AN ALLOTROPE OF CARBON.
BUT AFTER WITNESSING ITS AMAZING PROPERTIES, HE KNEW IT WAS SOMETHING *DIFFERENT*.
IN FACT, THE ONLY THING THAT EVEN COMES CLOSE TO XION IN PLIABILIY, WEIGHT AND STRENGTH IS CARBON FIBER REINFORCED POLYMER, CHEMICALLY BONDED WITH METALLIC SHEETS.
IT WAS ALWAYS YOUR FATHER'S DREAM TO MAKE LIFE BETTER FOR EVERYONE IN THIS CITY,
ESPECIALLY THOSE IN THE OMILE DISTRICT. HE DEVOTED HIS WHOLE LIFE TO IT.
AND MY MOM *GAVE HERS* FOR IT.
YOUR FATHER MADE MANY GRAVE MISTAKES.
IF HE WERE ALIVE, HE'D BE THE FIRST TO ADMIT HE COULD HAVE DONE THINGS A LOT BETTER.
YOU'RE RIGHT... I STILL CAN'T BELIEVE HE'S ACTUALLY *GONE*...

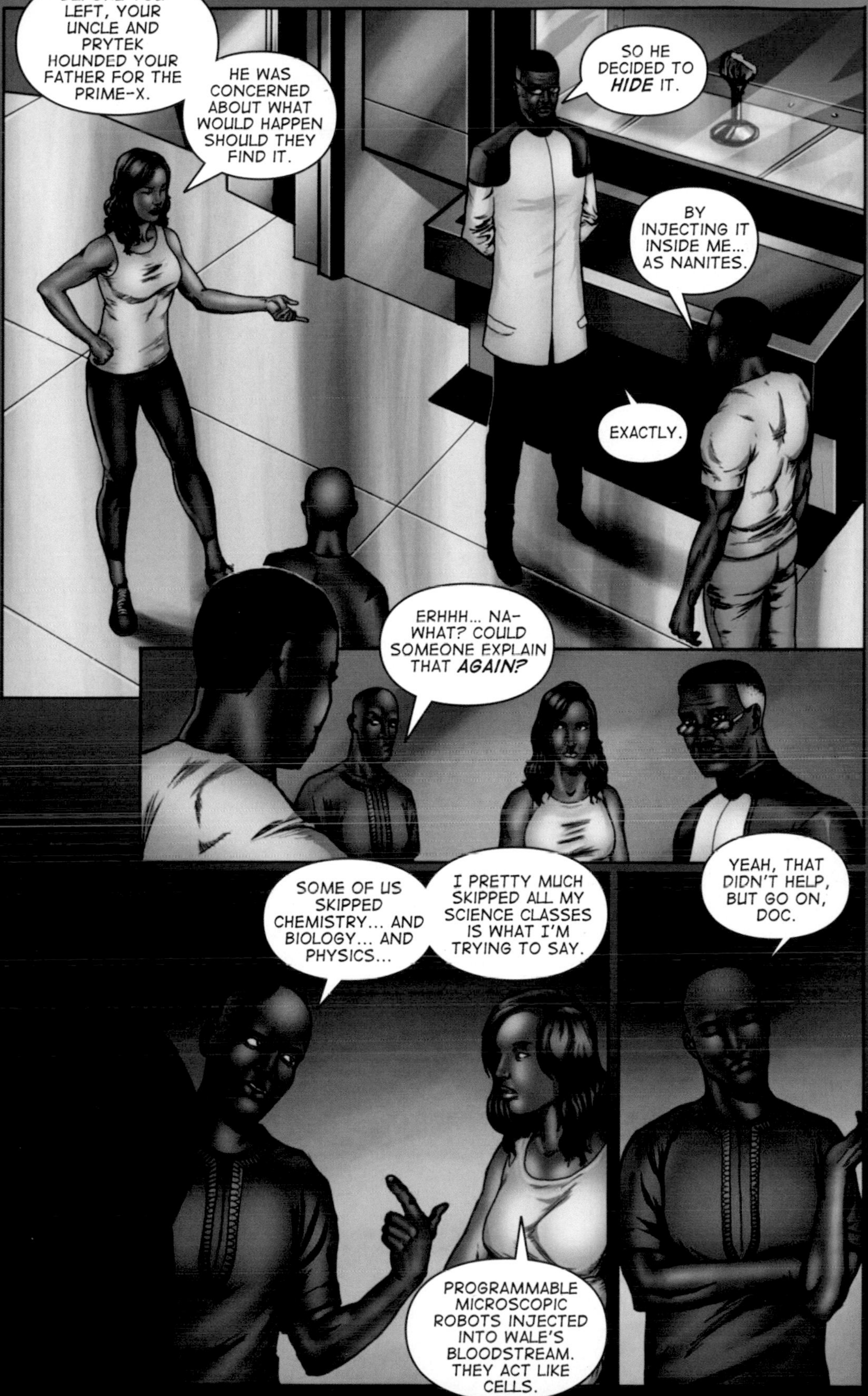

BEFORE YOU LEFT, YOUR UNCLE AND PRYTEK HOUNDED YOUR FATHER FOR THE PRIME-X.
HE WAS CONCERNED ABOUT WHAT WOULD HAPPEN SHOULD THEY FIND IT.
SO HE DECIDED TO *HIDE* IT.
BY INJECTING IT INSIDE ME... AS NANITES.
EXACTLY.
ERHHH... NA-WHAT? COULD SOMEONE EXPLAIN THAT *AGAIN?*
SOME OF US SKIPPED CHEMISTRY... AND BIOLOGY... AND PHYSICS...
I PRETTY MUCH SKIPPED ALL MY SCIENCE CLASSES IS WHAT I'M TRYING TO SAY.
YEAH, THAT DIDN'T HELP, BUT GO ON, DOC.
PROGRAMMABLE MICROSCOPIC ROBOTS INJECTED INTO WALE'S BLOODSTREAM. THEY ACT LIKE CELLS.

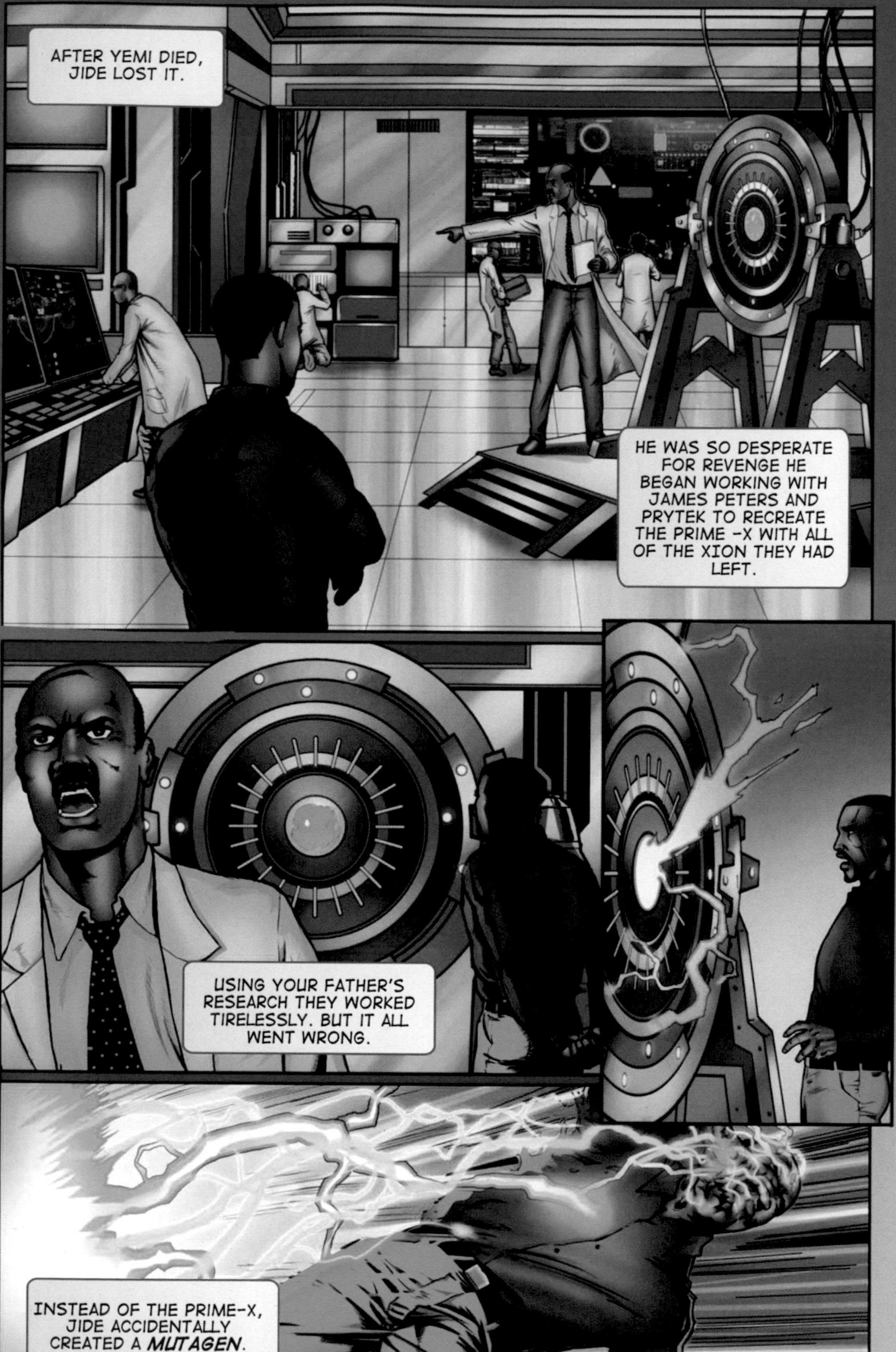
AFTER YEMI DIED, JIDE LOST IT.
HE WAS SO DESPERATE FOR REVENGE HE BEGAN WORKING WITH JAMES PETERS AND PRYTEK TO RECREATE THE PRIME -X WITH ALL OF THE XION THEY HAD LEFT.
USING YOUR FATHER'S RESEARCH THEY WORKED TIRELESSLY. BUT IT ALL WENT WRONG.
INSTEAD OF THE PRIME-X, JIDE ACCIDENTALLY CREATED A *MUTAGEN*.

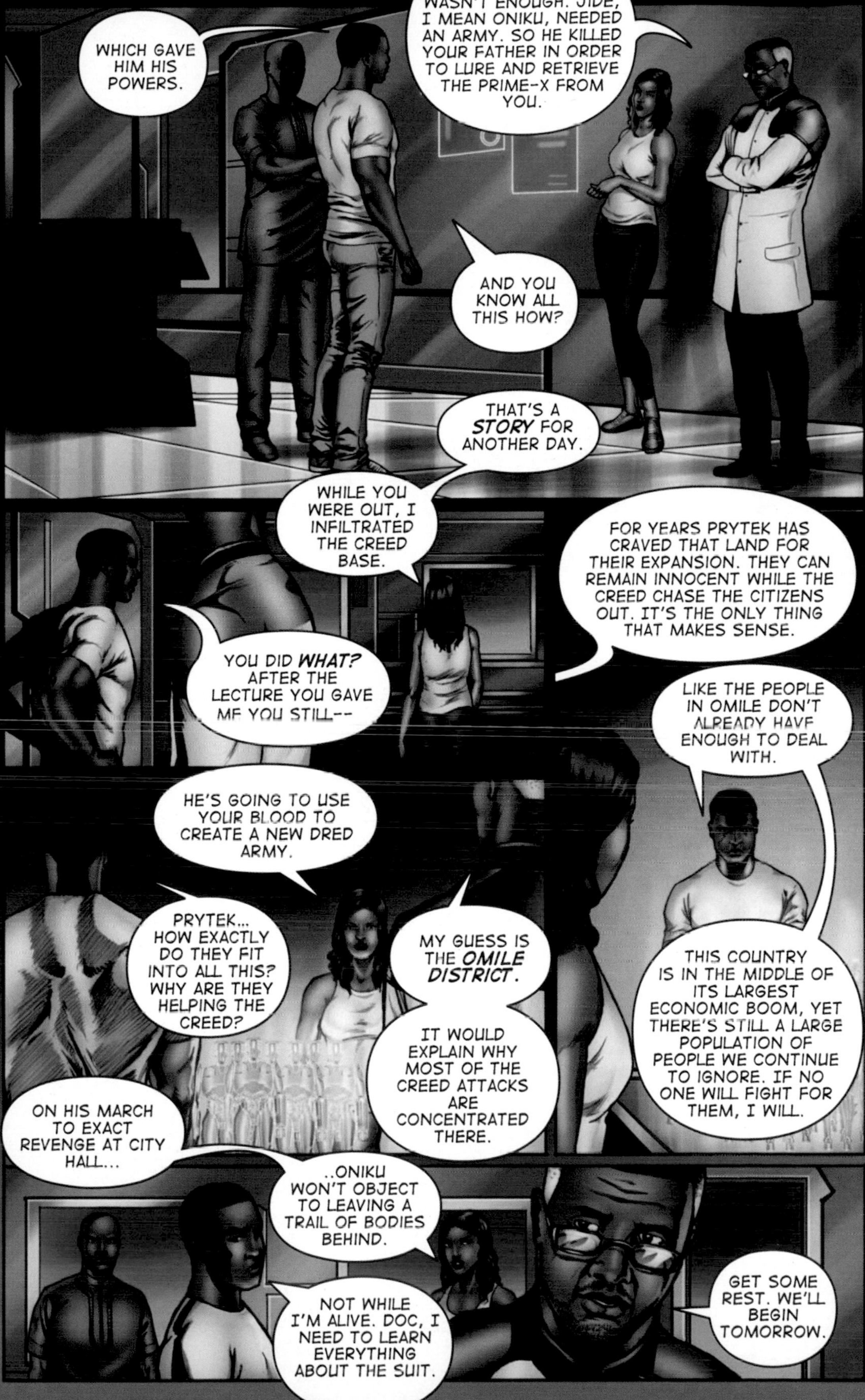
WHICH GAVE HIM HIS POWERS.
EXACTLY, BUT THAT WASN'T ENOUGH. JIDE, I MEAN ONIKU, NEEDED AN ARMY. SO HE KILLED YOUR FATHER IN ORDER TO LURE AND RETRIEVE THE PRIME-X FROM YOU.
AND YOU KNOW ALL THIS HOW?
THAT'S A *STORY* FOR ANOTHER DAY.
WHILE YOU WERE OUT, I INFILTRATED THE CREED BASE.
YOU DID *WHAT?* AFTER THE LECTURE YOU GAVE ME YOU STILL--
HE'S GOING TO USE YOUR BLOOD TO CREATE A NEW DRED ARMY.
PRYTEK... HOW EXACTLY DO THEY FIT INTO ALL THIS? WHY ARE THEY HELPING THE CREED?
MY GUESS IS THE *OMILE DISTRICT*.
IT WOULD EXPLAIN WHY MOST OF THE CREED ATTACKS ARE CONCENTRATED THERE.
FOR YEARS PRYTEK HAS CRAVED THAT LAND FOR THEIR EXPANSION. THEY CAN REMAIN INNOCENT WHILE THE CREED CHASE THE CITIZENS OUT. IT'S THE ONLY THING THAT MAKES SENSE.
LIKE THE PEOPLE IN OMILE DON'T ALREADY HAVE ENOUGH TO DEAL WITH.
THIS COUNTRY IS IN THE MIDDLE OF ITS LARGEST ECONOMIC BOOM, YET THERE'S STILL A LARGE POPULATION OF PEOPLE WE CONTINUE TO IGNORE. IF NO ONE WILL FIGHT FOR THEM, I WILL.
ON HIS MARCH TO EXACT REVENGE AT CITY HALL...
..ONIKU WON'T OBJECT TO LEAVING A TRAIL OF BODIES BEHIND.
NOT WHILE I'M ALIVE. DOC, I NEED TO LEARN EVERYTHING ABOUT THE SUIT.
GET SOME REST. WE'LL BEGIN TOMORROW.

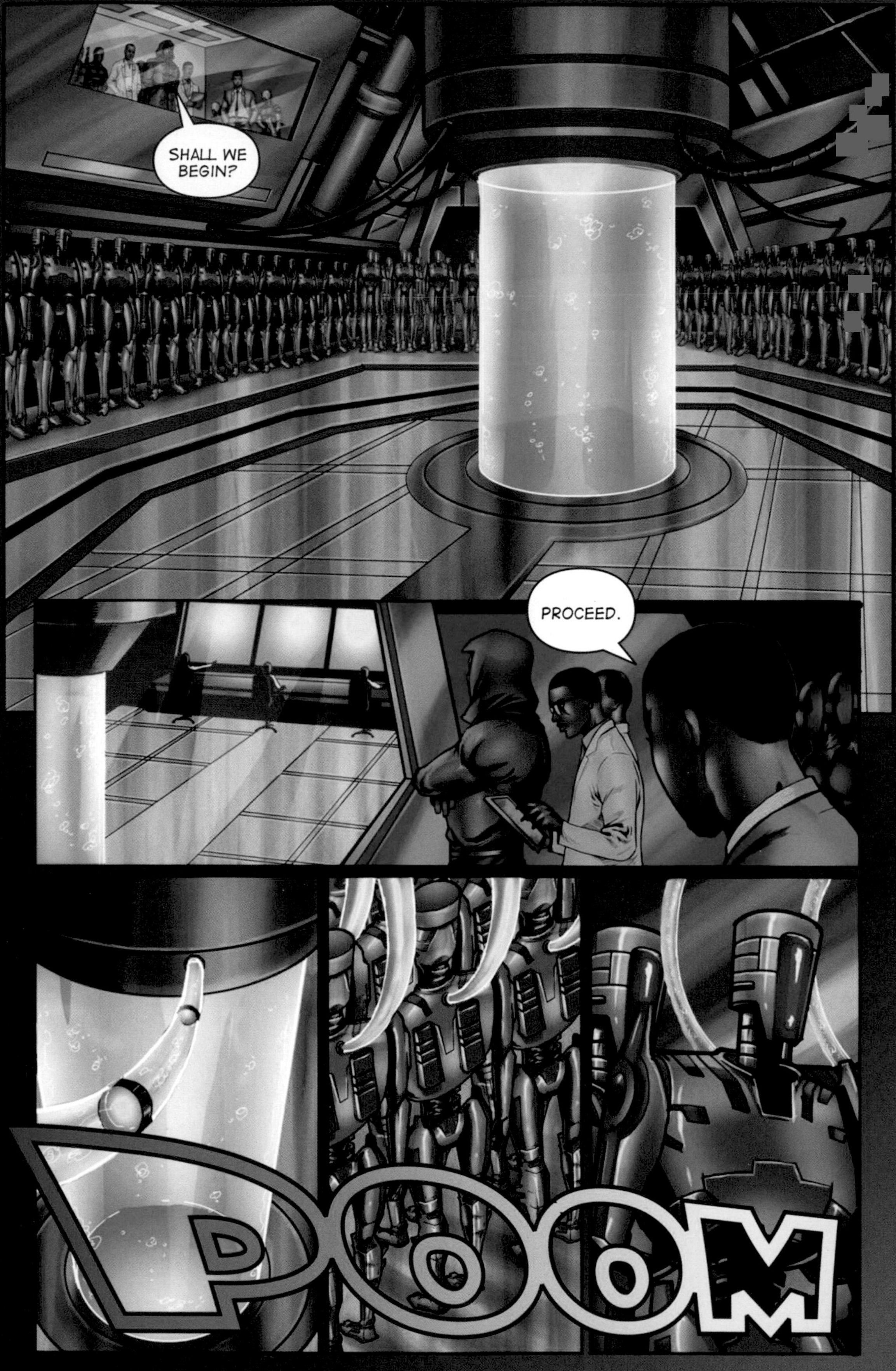
SHALL WE BEGIN?
PROCEED.
POOM

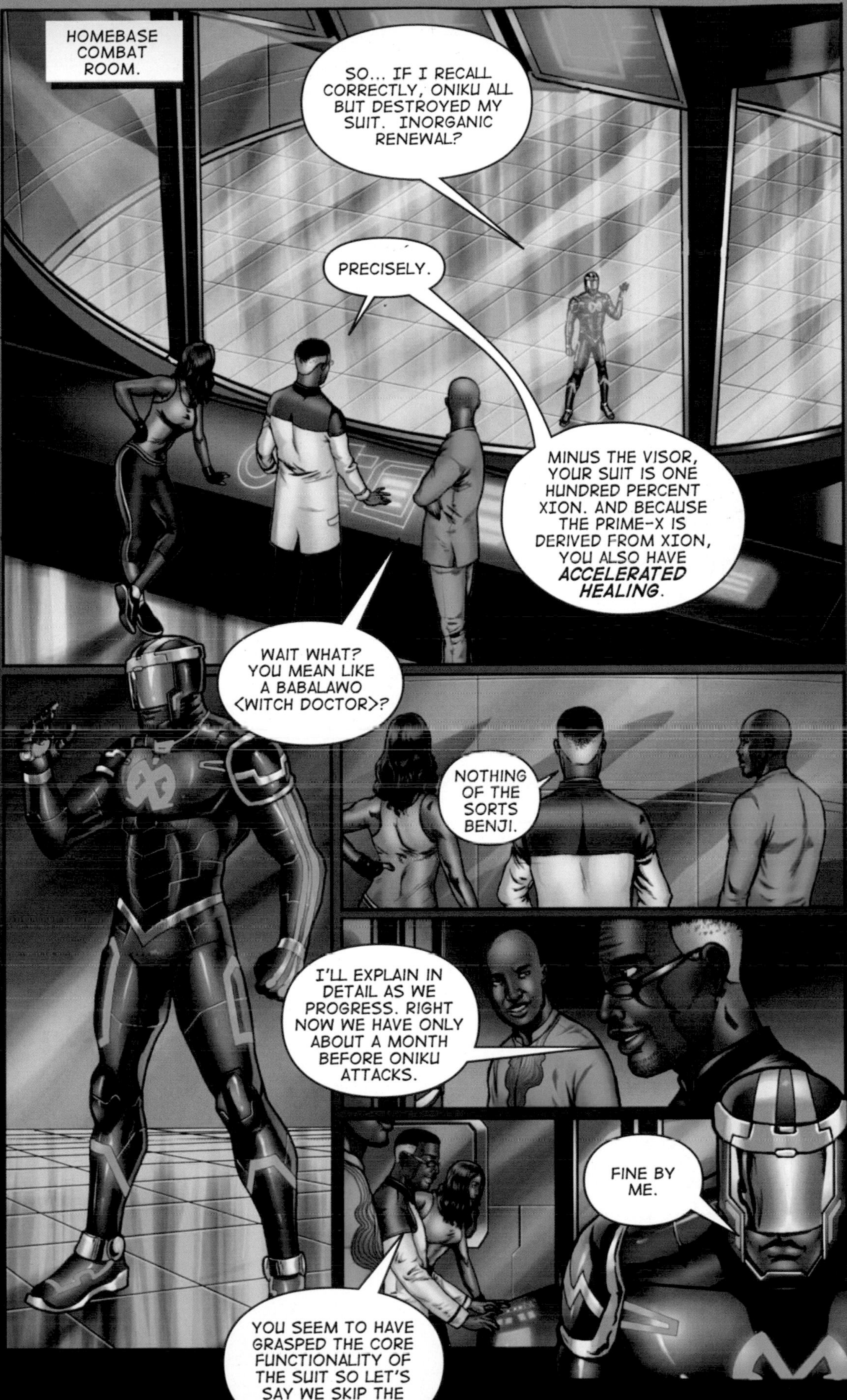
HOMEBASE COMBAT ROOM.
SO... IF I RECALL CORRECTLY, ONIKU ALL BUT DESTROYED MY SUIT. INORGANIC RENEWAL?
PRECISELY.
MINUS THE VISOR, YOUR SUIT IS ONE HUNDRED PERCENT XION. AND BECAUSE THE PRIME-X IS DERIVED FROM XION, YOU ALSO HAVE ***ACCELERATED HEALING***.
WAIT WHAT? YOU MEAN LIKE A BABALAWO <WITCH DOCTOR>?
NOTHING OF THE SORTS BENJI.
I'LL EXPLAIN IN DETAIL AS WE PROGRESS. RIGHT NOW WE HAVE ONLY ABOUT A MONTH BEFORE ONIKU ATTACKS.
FINE BY ME.
YOU SEEM TO HAVE GRASPED THE CORE FUNCTIONALITY OF THE SUIT SO LET'S SAY WE SKIP THE BASIC STUFF.

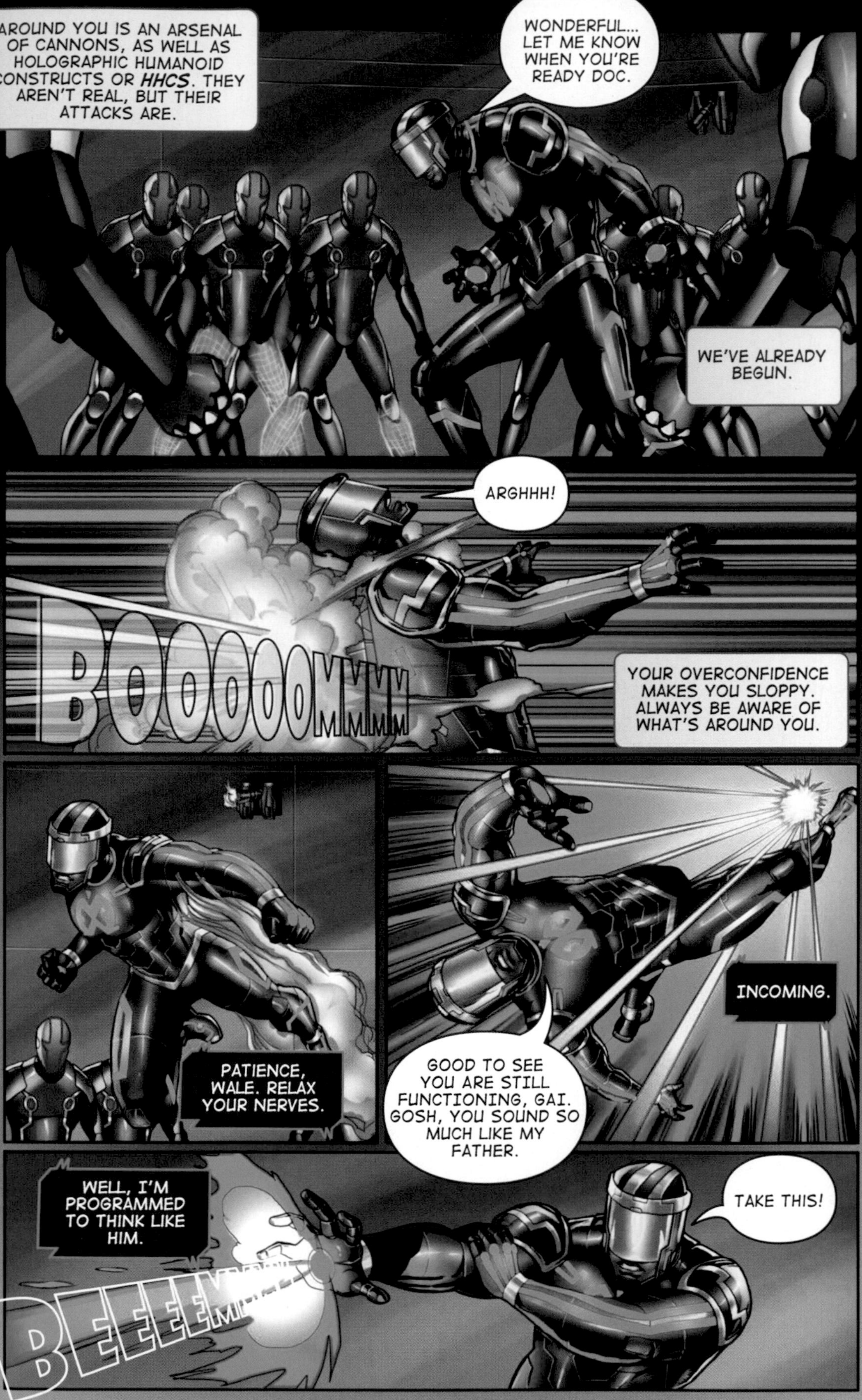
AROUND YOU IS AN ARSENAL OF CANNONS, AS WELL AS HOLOGRAPHIC HUMANOID CONSTRUCTS OR HHCS. THEY AREN'T REAL, BUT THEIR ATTACKS ARE.
WONDERFUL... LET ME KNOW WHEN YOU'RE READY DOC.
WE'VE ALREADY BEGUN.
ARGHHH!
BOOOOOMMMM
YOUR OVERCONFIDENCE MAKES YOU SLOPPY. ALWAYS BE AWARE OF WHAT'S AROUND YOU.
PATIENCE, WALE. RELAX YOUR NERVES.
INCOMING.
GOOD TO SEE YOU ARE STILL FUNCTIONING, GAI. GOSH, YOU SOUND SO MUCH LIKE MY FATHER.
WELL, I'M PROGRAMMED TO THINK LIKE HIM.
TAKE THIS!

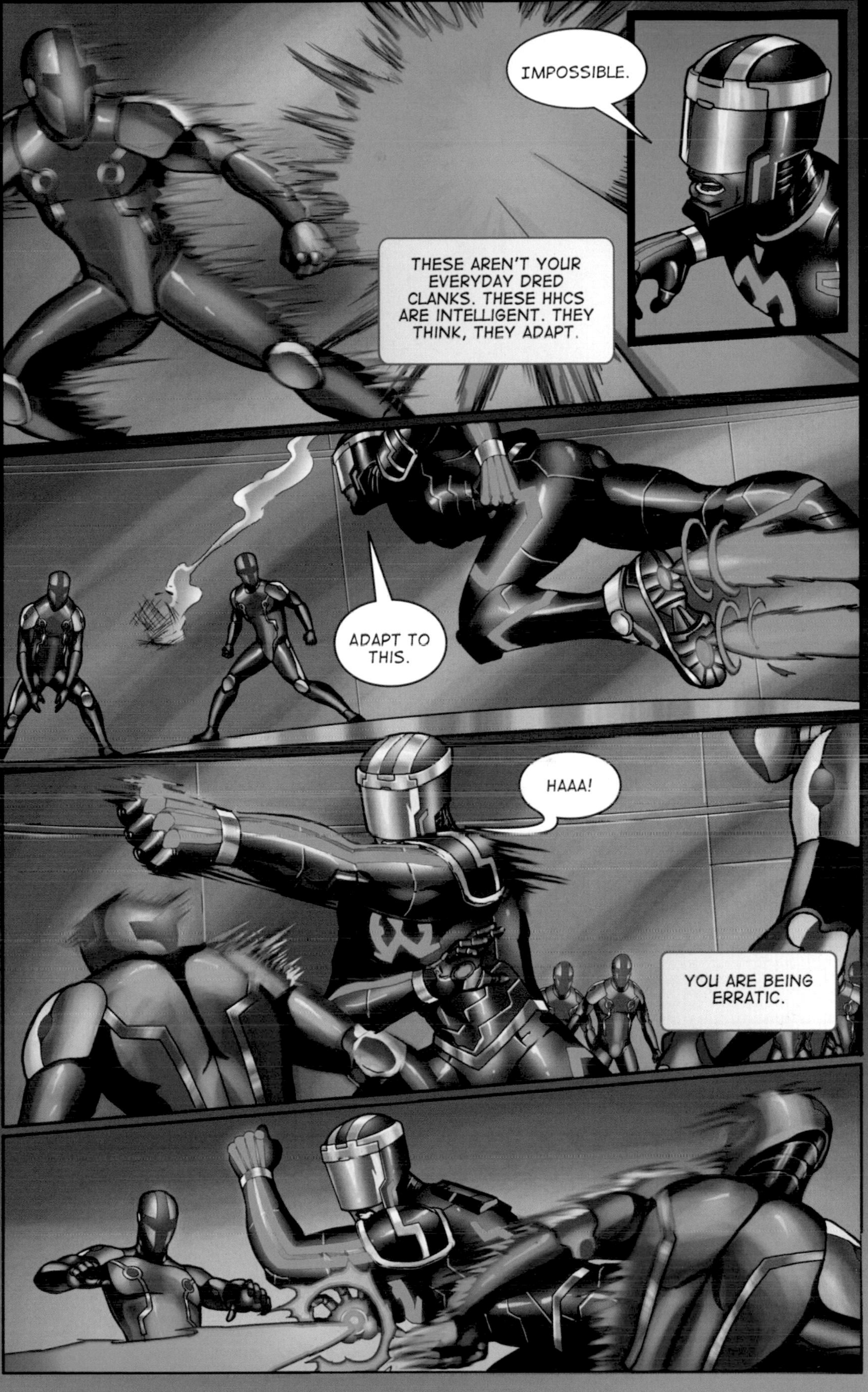
IMPOSSIBLE.
THESE AREN'T YOUR EVERYDAY DRED CLANKS. THESE HHCS ARE INTELLIGENT. THEY THINK, THEY ADAPT.
ADAPT TO THIS.
HAAA!
YOU ARE BEING ERRATIC.

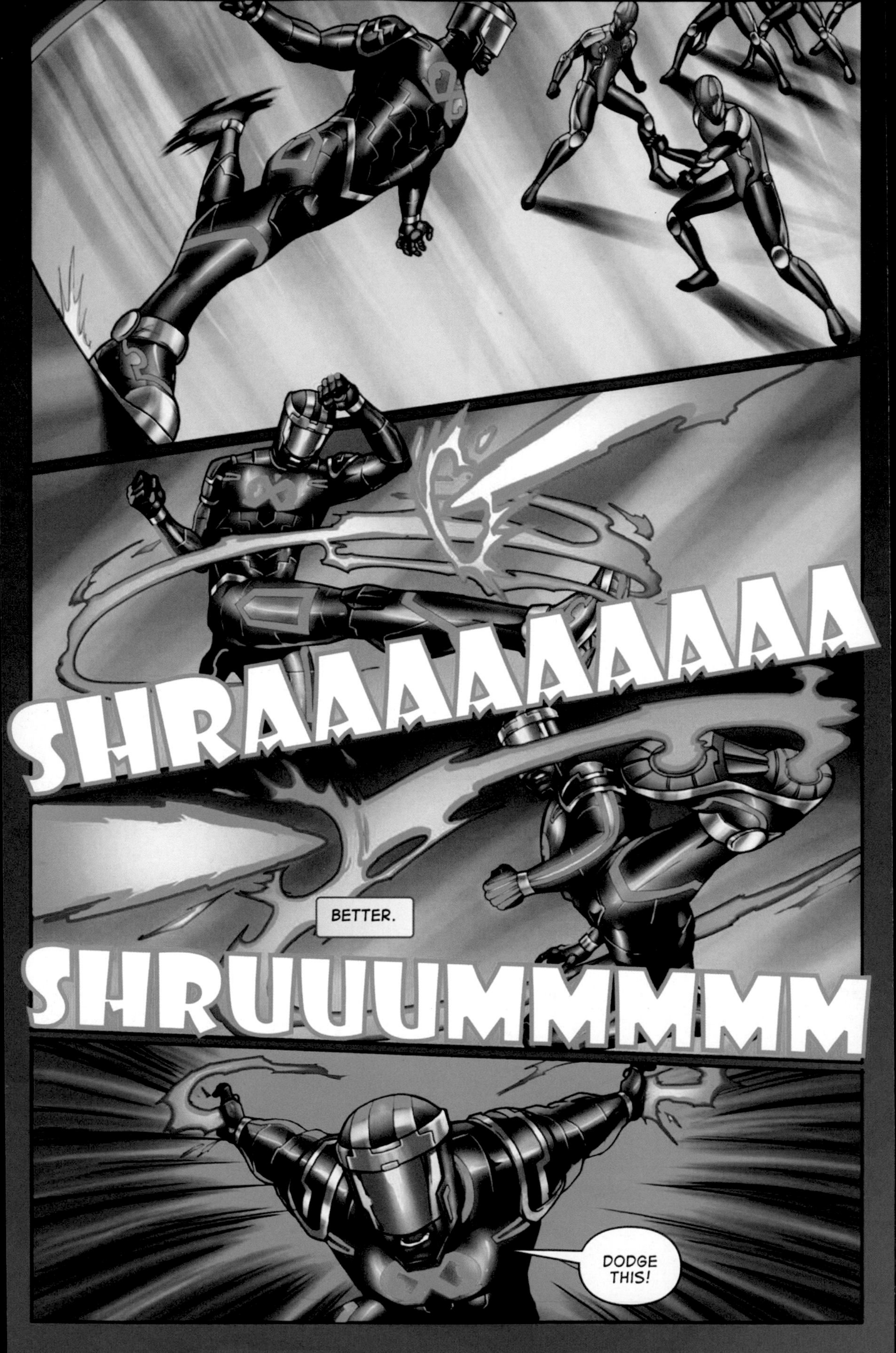
SHRAAAAAAAAAA
BETTER.
SHRUUUMMMMM
DODGE THIS!

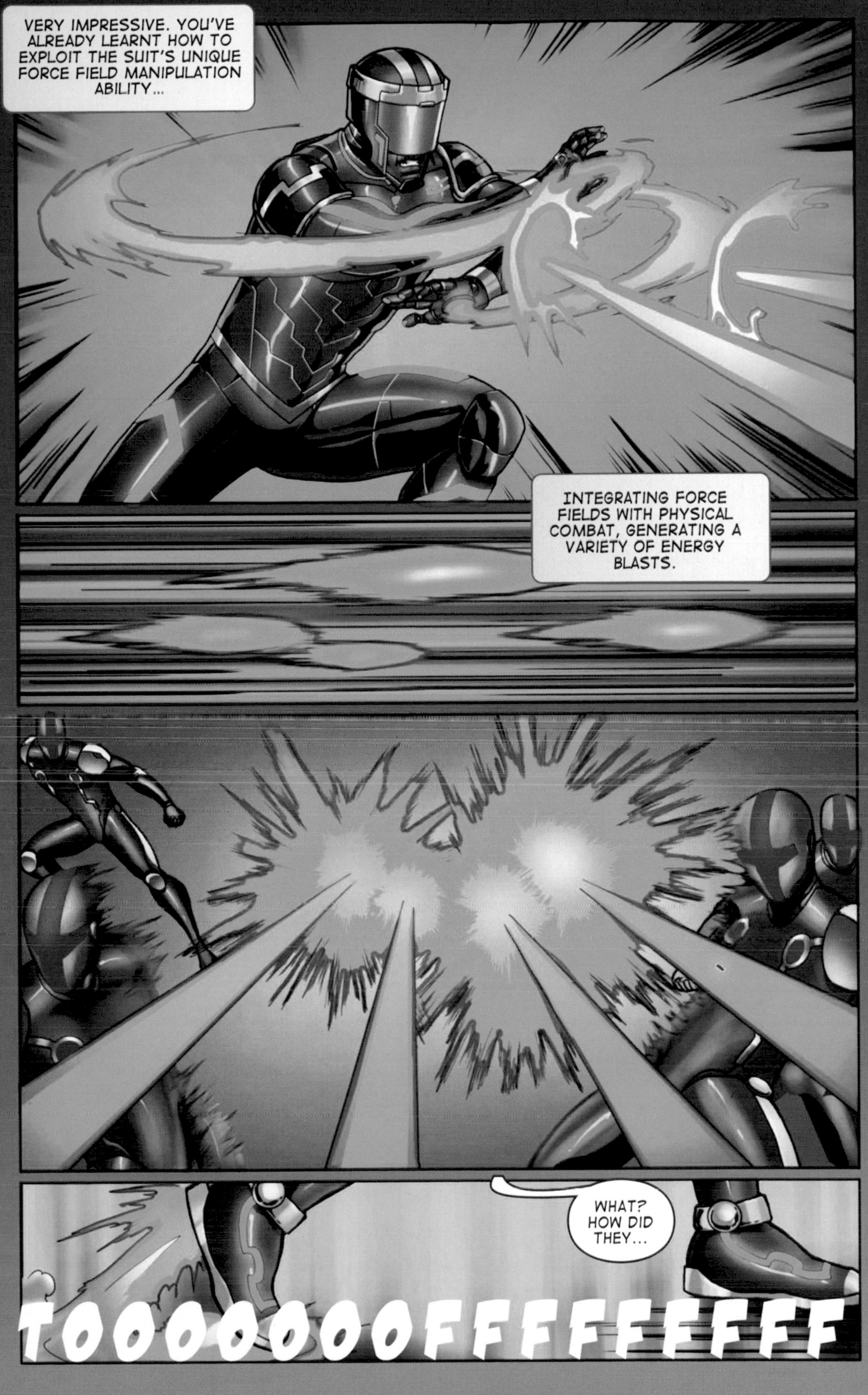
VERY IMPRESSIVE. YOU'VE ALREADY LEARNT HOW TO EXPLOIT THE SUIT'S UNIQUE FORCE FIELD MANIPULATION ABILITY...
INTEGRATING FORCE FIELDS WITH PHYSICAL COMBAT, GENERATING A VARIETY OF ENERGY BLASTS.
WHAT? HOW DID THEY...
TOOOOOOOFFFFFFFFFF

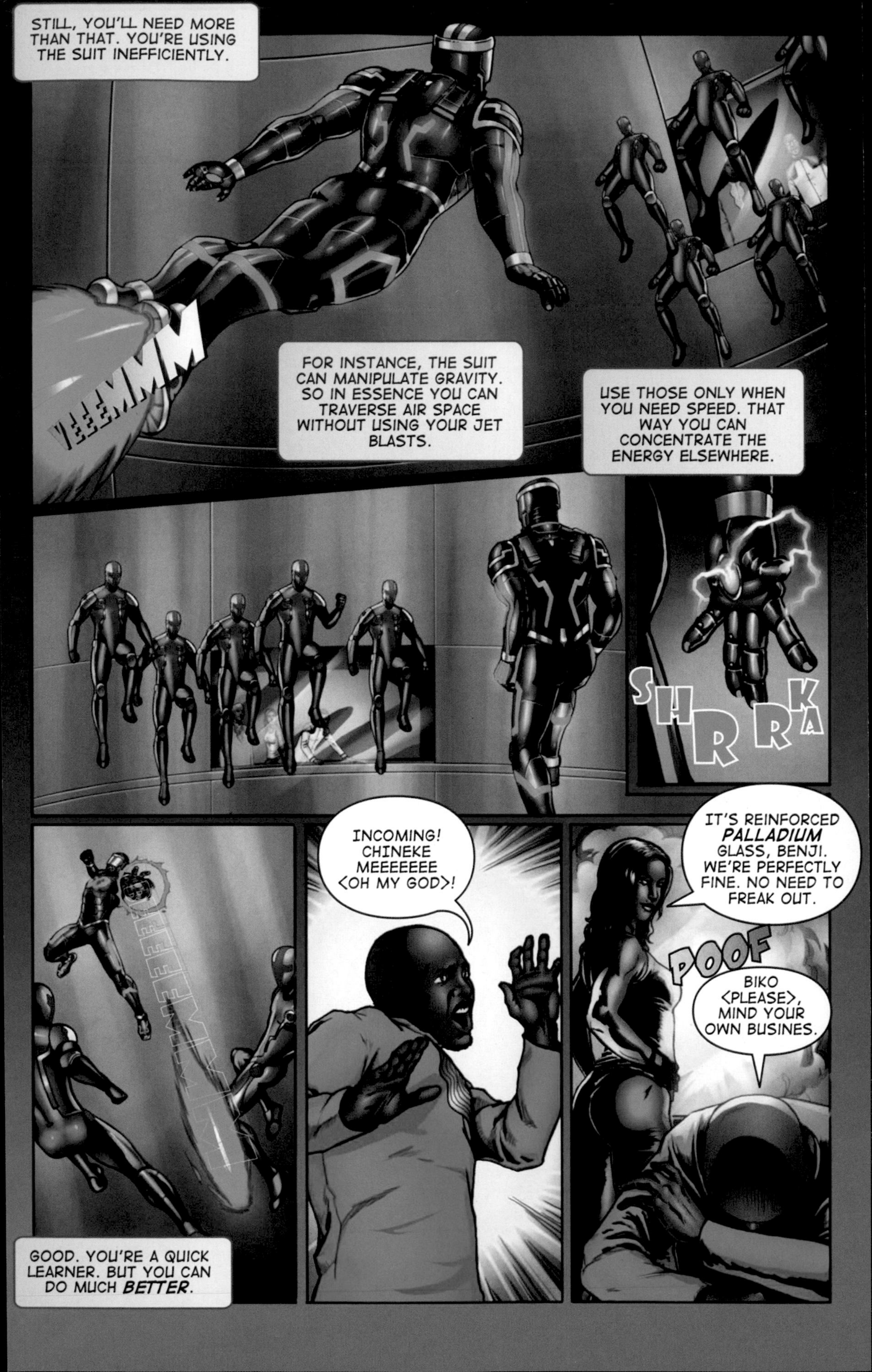
STILL, YOU'LL NEED MORE THAN THAT. YOU'RE USING THE SUIT INEFFICIENTLY.
VEEEMMM
FOR INSTANCE, THE SUIT CAN MANIPULATE GRAVITY. SO IN ESSENCE YOU CAN TRAVERSE AIR SPACE WITHOUT USING YOUR JET BLASTS.
USE THOSE ONLY WHEN YOU NEED SPEED. THAT WAY YOU CAN CONCENTRATE THE ENERGY ELSEWHERE.
SHRRKA
INCOMING! CHINEKE MEEEEEEE <OH MY GOD>!
IT'S REINFORCED ***PALLADIUM*** GLASS, BENJI. WE'RE PERFECTLY FINE. NO NEED TO FREAK OUT.
POOF
BIKO <PLEASE>, MIND YOUR OWN BUSINES.
GOOD. YOU'RE A QUICK LEARNER. BUT YOU CAN DO MUCH ***BETTER***.

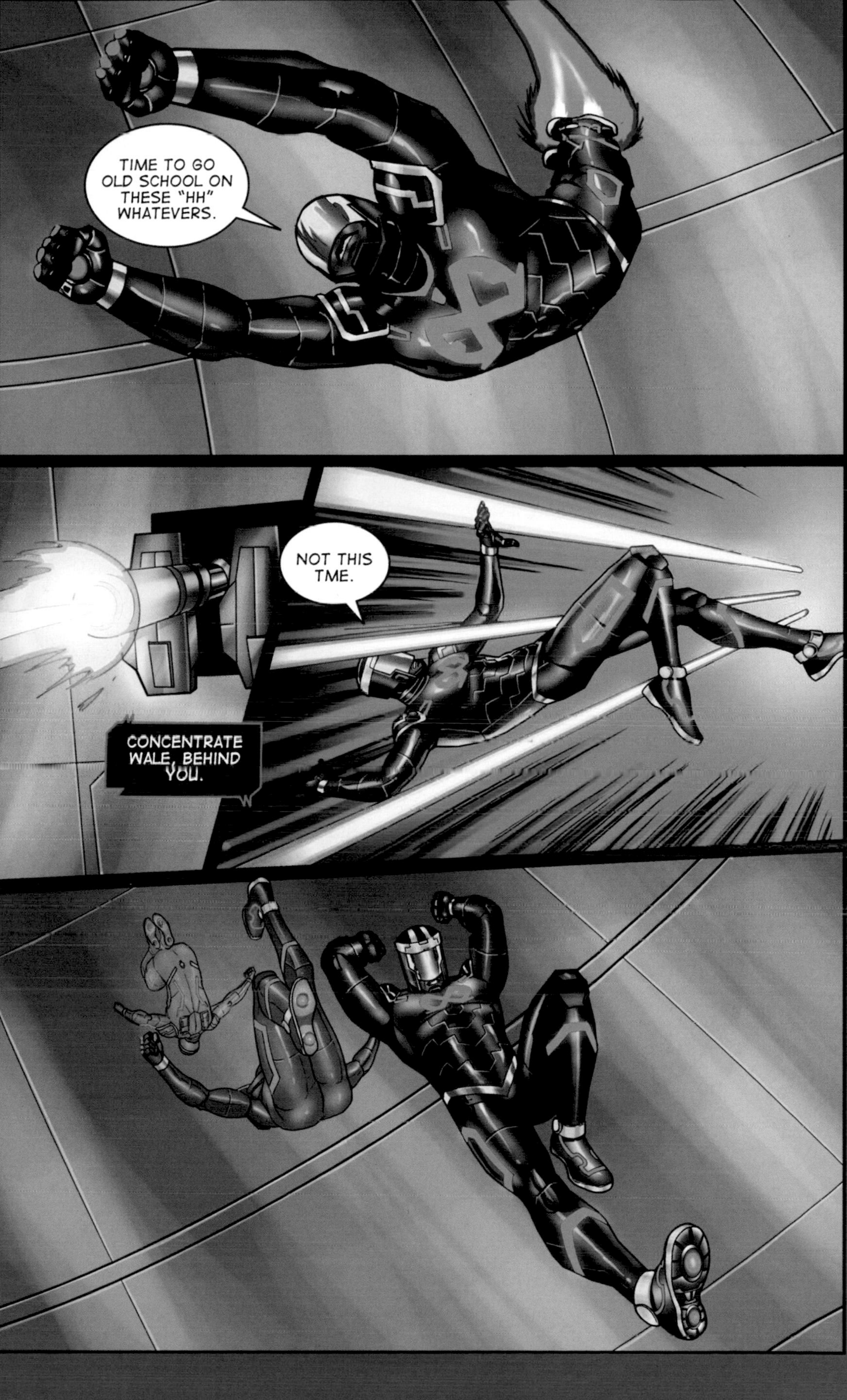
TIME TO GO OLD SCHOOL ON THESE "HH" WHATEVERS.
NOT THIS TME.
CONCENTRATE WALE, BEHIND YOU.

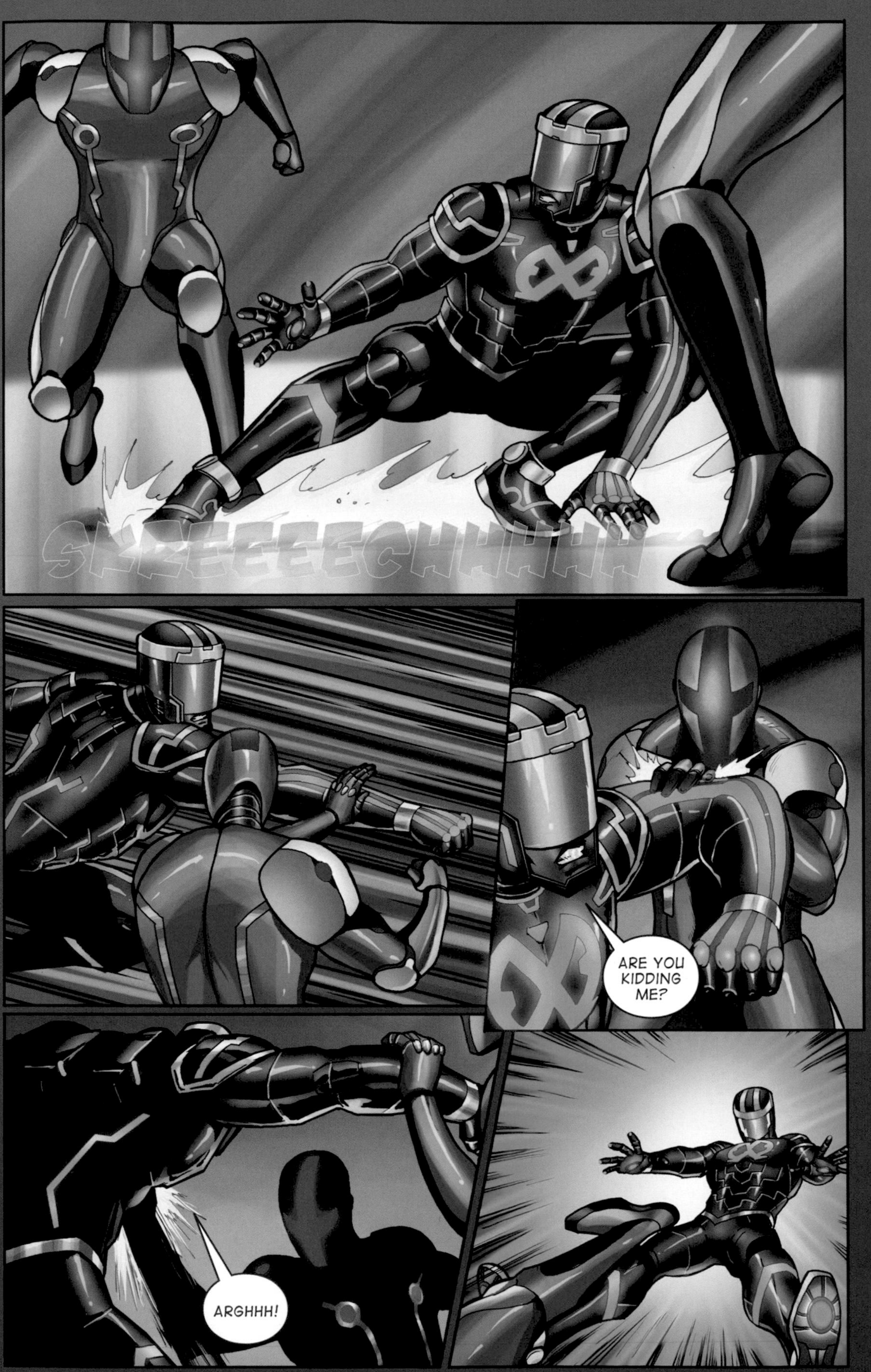
SKREEEEECHHHHH
ARE YOU KIDDING ME?
ARGHHH!

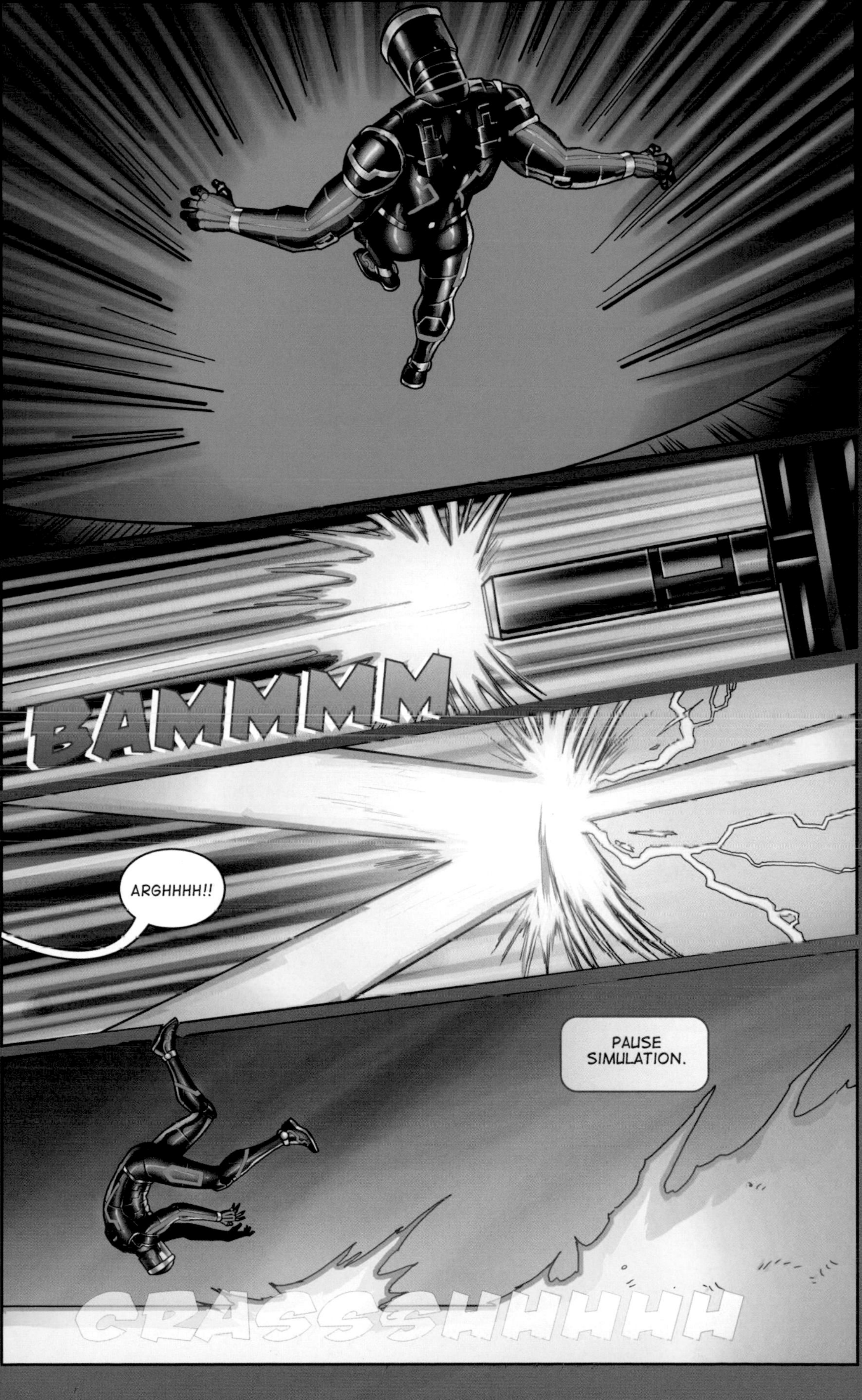
BAMMMM
ARGHHHH!!
PAUSE SIMULATION.
CRASSSHHHHH

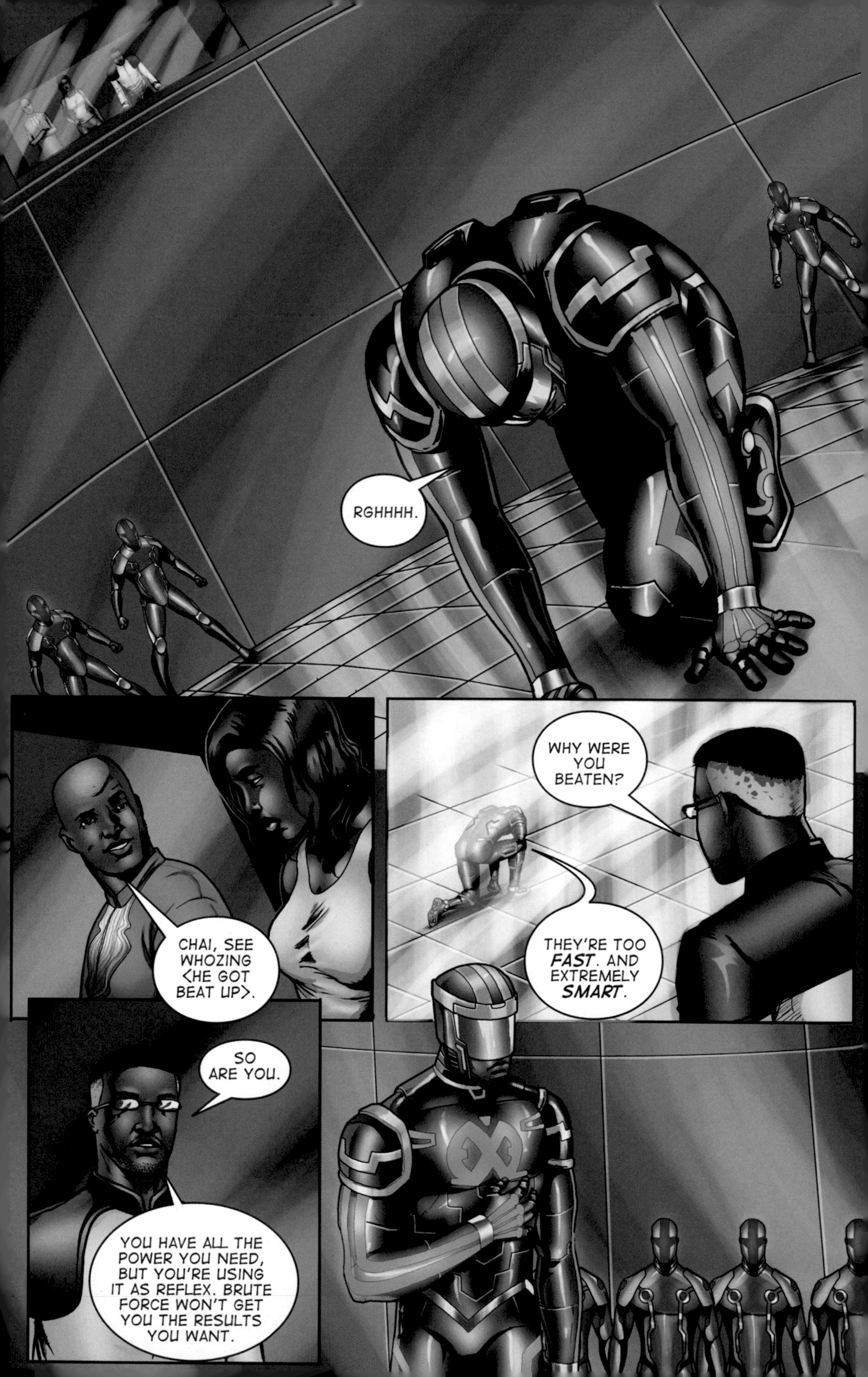
RGHHHH.
CHAI, SEE WHOZING <HE GOT BEAT UP>.
WHY WERE YOU BEATEN?
THEY'RE TOO *FAST*. AND EXTREMELY *SMART*.
SO ARE YOU.
YOU HAVE ALL THE POWER YOU NEED, BUT YOU'RE USING IT AS REFLEX. BRUTE FORCE WON'T GET YOU THE RESULTS YOU WANT.

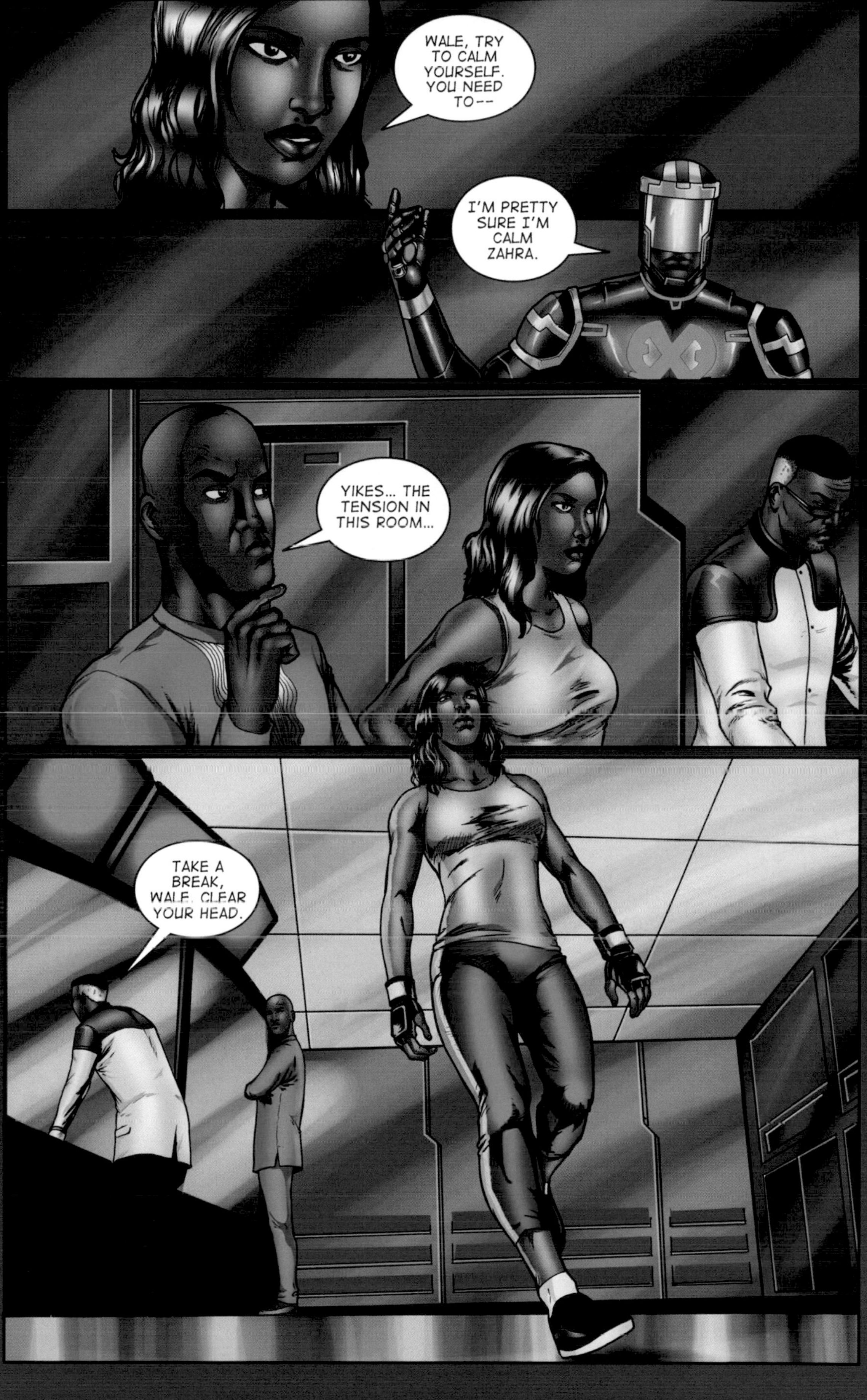
WALE, TRY TO CALM YOURSELF. YOU NEED TO--
I'M PRETTY SURE I'M CALM ZAHRA.
YIKES... THE TENSION IN THIS ROOM...
TAKE A BREAK, WALE. CLEAR YOUR HEAD.

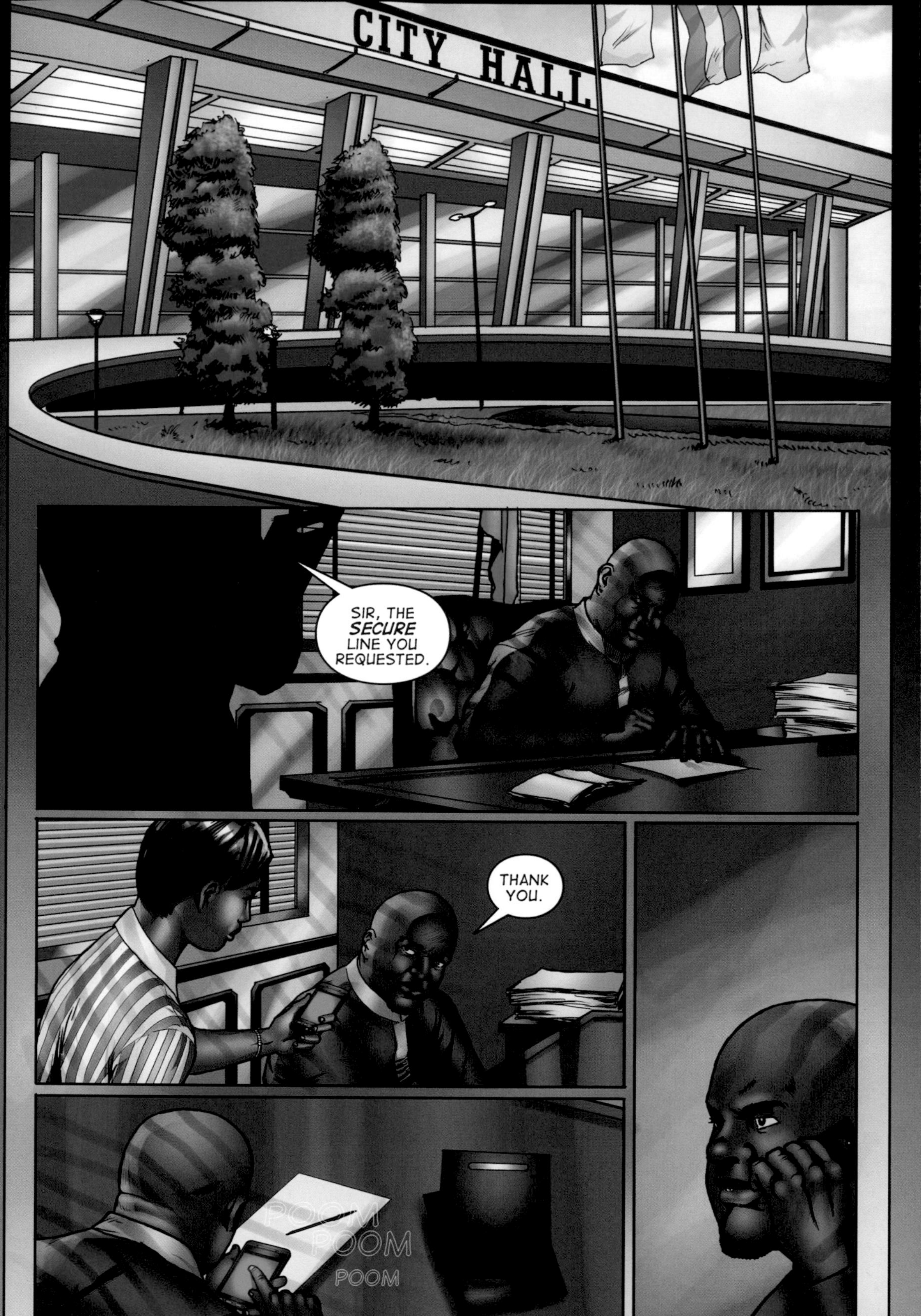
CITY HALL
SIR, THE SECURE LINE YOU REQUESTED.
THANK YOU.
POOM
POOM
POOM

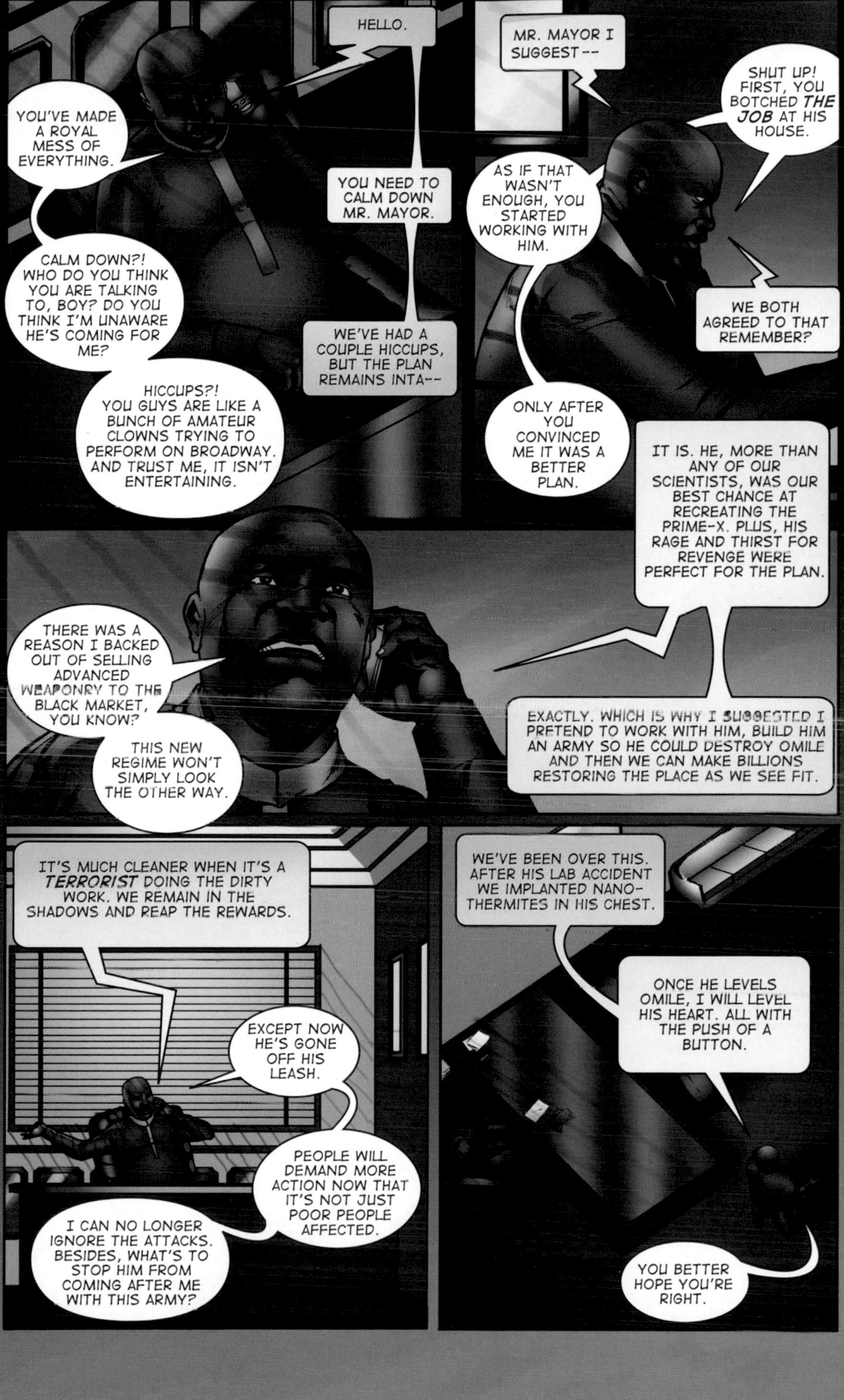
HELLO.
YOU'VE MADE A ROYAL MESS OF EVERYTHING.
YOU NEED TO CALM DOWN MR. MAYOR.
CALM DOWN?! WHO DO YOU THINK YOU ARE TALKING TO, BOY? DO YOU THINK I'M UNAWARE HE'S COMING FOR ME?
WE'VE HAD A COUPLE HICCUPS, BUT THE PLAN REMAINS INTA--
HICCUPS?! YOU GUYS ARE LIKE A BUNCH OF AMATEUR CLOWNS TRYING TO PERFORM ON BROADWAY. AND TRUST ME, IT ISN'T ENTERTAINING.
MR. MAYOR I SUGGEST--
SHUT UP! FIRST, YOU BOTCHED THE JOB AT HIS HOUSE.
AS IF THAT WASN'T ENOUGH, YOU STARTED WORKING WITH HIM.
WE BOTH AGREED TO THAT REMEMBER?
ONLY AFTER YOU CONVINCED ME IT WAS A BETTER PLAN.
IT IS. HE, MORE THAN ANY OF OUR SCIENTISTS, WAS OUR BEST CHANCE AT RECREATING THE PRIME-X. PLUS, HIS RAGE AND THIRST FOR REVENGE WERE PERFECT FOR THE PLAN.
THERE WAS A REASON I BACKED OUT OF SELLING ADVANCED WEAPONRY TO THE BLACK MARKET, YOU KNOW?
THIS NEW REGIME WON'T SIMPLY LOOK THE OTHER WAY.
EXACTLY. WHICH IS WHY I SUGGESTED I PRETEND TO WORK WITH HIM, BUILD HIM AN ARMY SO HE COULD DESTROY OMILE AND THEN WE CAN MAKE BILLIONS RESTORING THE PLACE AS WE SEE FIT.
IT'S MUCH CLEANER WHEN IT'S A TERRORIST DOING THE DIRTY WORK. WE REMAIN IN THE SHADOWS AND REAP THE REWARDS.
EXCEPT NOW HE'S GONE OFF HIS LEASH.
PEOPLE WILL DEMAND MORE ACTION NOW THAT IT'S NOT JUST POOR PEOPLE AFFECTED.
I CAN NO LONGER IGNORE THE ATTACKS. BESIDES, WHAT'S TO STOP HIM FROM COMING AFTER ME WITH THIS ARMY?
WE'VE BEEN OVER THIS. AFTER HIS LAB ACCIDENT WE IMPLANTED NANO-THERMITES IN HIS CHEST.
ONCE HE LEVELS OMILE, I WILL LEVEL HIS HEART. ALL WITH THE PUSH OF A BUTTON.
YOU BETTER HOPE YOU'RE RIGHT.

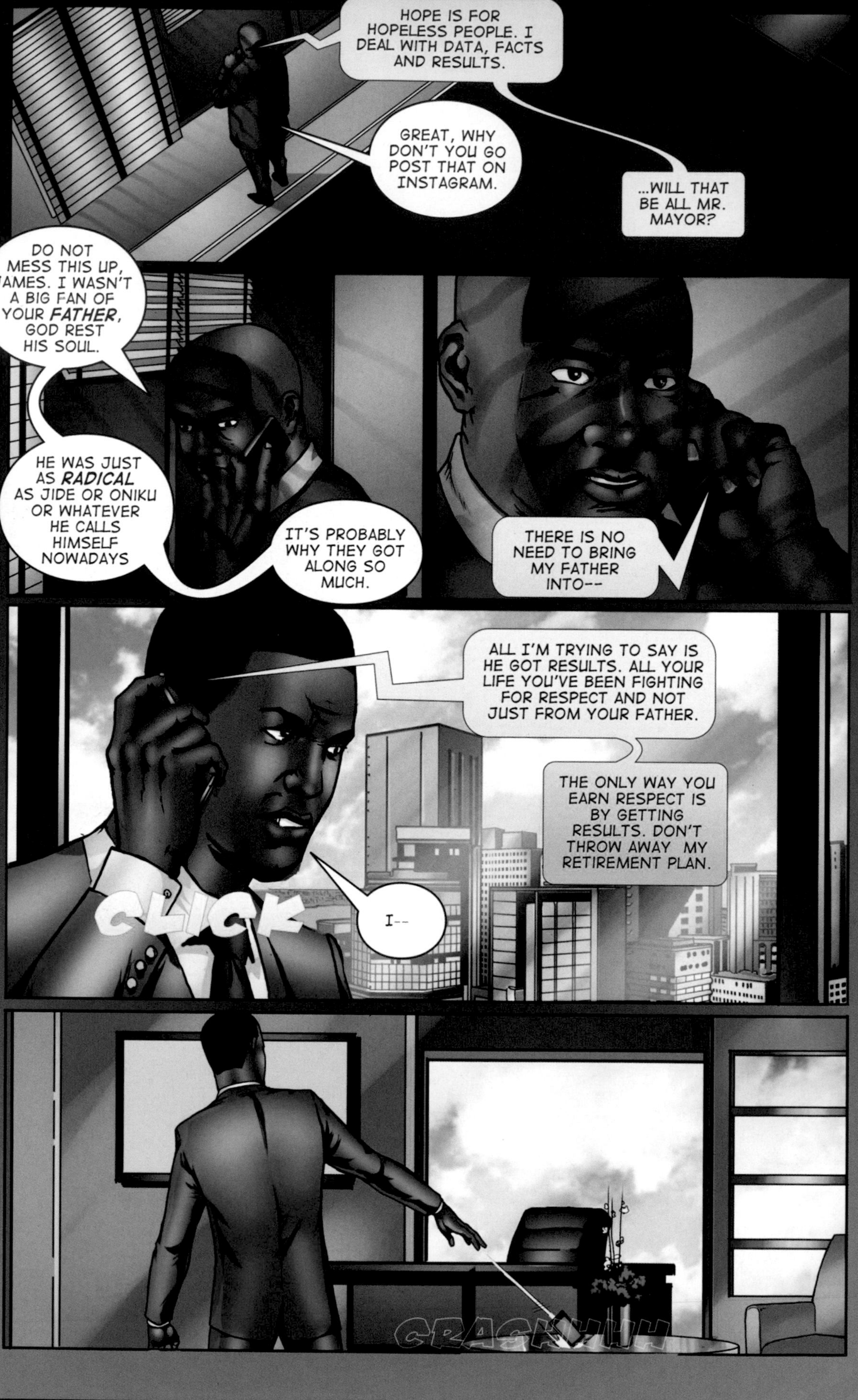
HOPE IS FOR HOPELESS PEOPLE. I DEAL WITH DATA, FACTS AND RESULTS.
GREAT, WHY DON'T YOU GO POST THAT ON INSTAGRAM.
...WILL THAT BE ALL MR. MAYOR?
DO NOT MESS THIS UP, JAMES. I WASN'T A BIG FAN OF YOUR FATHER, GOD REST HIS SOUL.
HE WAS JUST AS RADICAL AS JIDE OR ONIKU OR WHATEVER HE CALLS HIMSELF NOWADAYS
IT'S PROBABLY WHY THEY GOT ALONG SO MUCH.
THERE IS NO NEED TO BRING MY FATHER INTO--
ALL I'M TRYING TO SAY IS HE GOT RESULTS. ALL YOUR LIFE YOU'VE BEEN FIGHTING FOR RESPECT AND NOT JUST FROM YOUR FATHER.
THE ONLY WAY YOU EARN RESPECT IS BY GETTING RESULTS. DON'T THROW AWAY MY RETIREMENT PLAN.
CLICK
I--
CRASHHHH

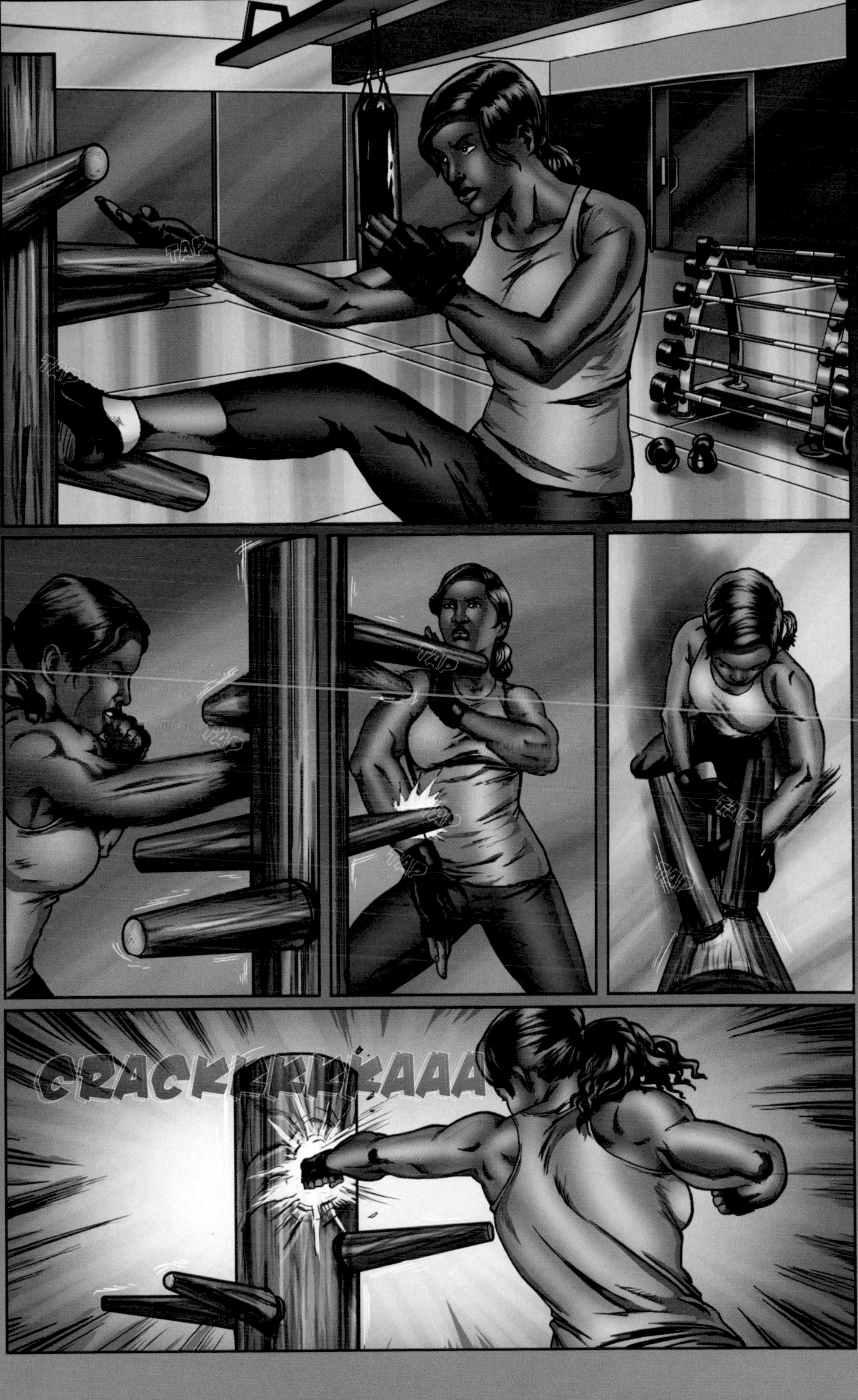
TAP
TAP
TAP
TAP
TAP
TAP
TAP
TAP
CRACKKKKKAAA

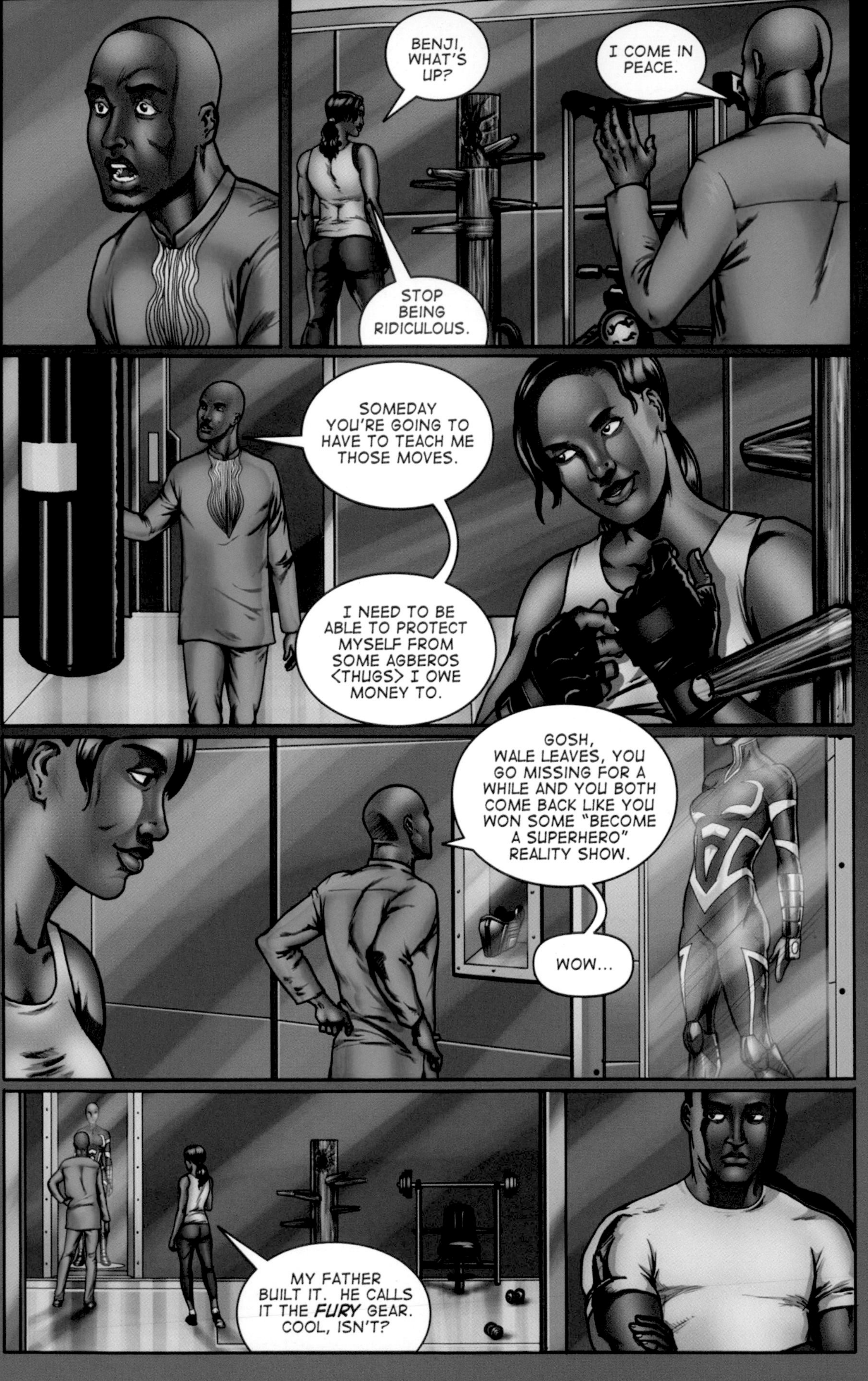
BENJI, WHAT'S UP?
STOP BEING RIDICULOUS.
I COME IN PEACE.
SOMEDAY YOU'RE GOING TO HAVE TO TEACH ME THOSE MOVES.
I NEED TO BE ABLE TO PROTECT MYSELF FROM SOME AGBEROS <THUGS> I OWE MONEY TO.
GOSH, WALE LEAVES, YOU GO MISSING FOR A WHILE AND YOU BOTH COME BACK LIKE YOU WON SOME "BECOME A SUPERHERO" REALITY SHOW.
WOW...
MY FATHER BUILT IT. HE CALLS IT THE *FURY* GEAR. COOL, ISN'T?

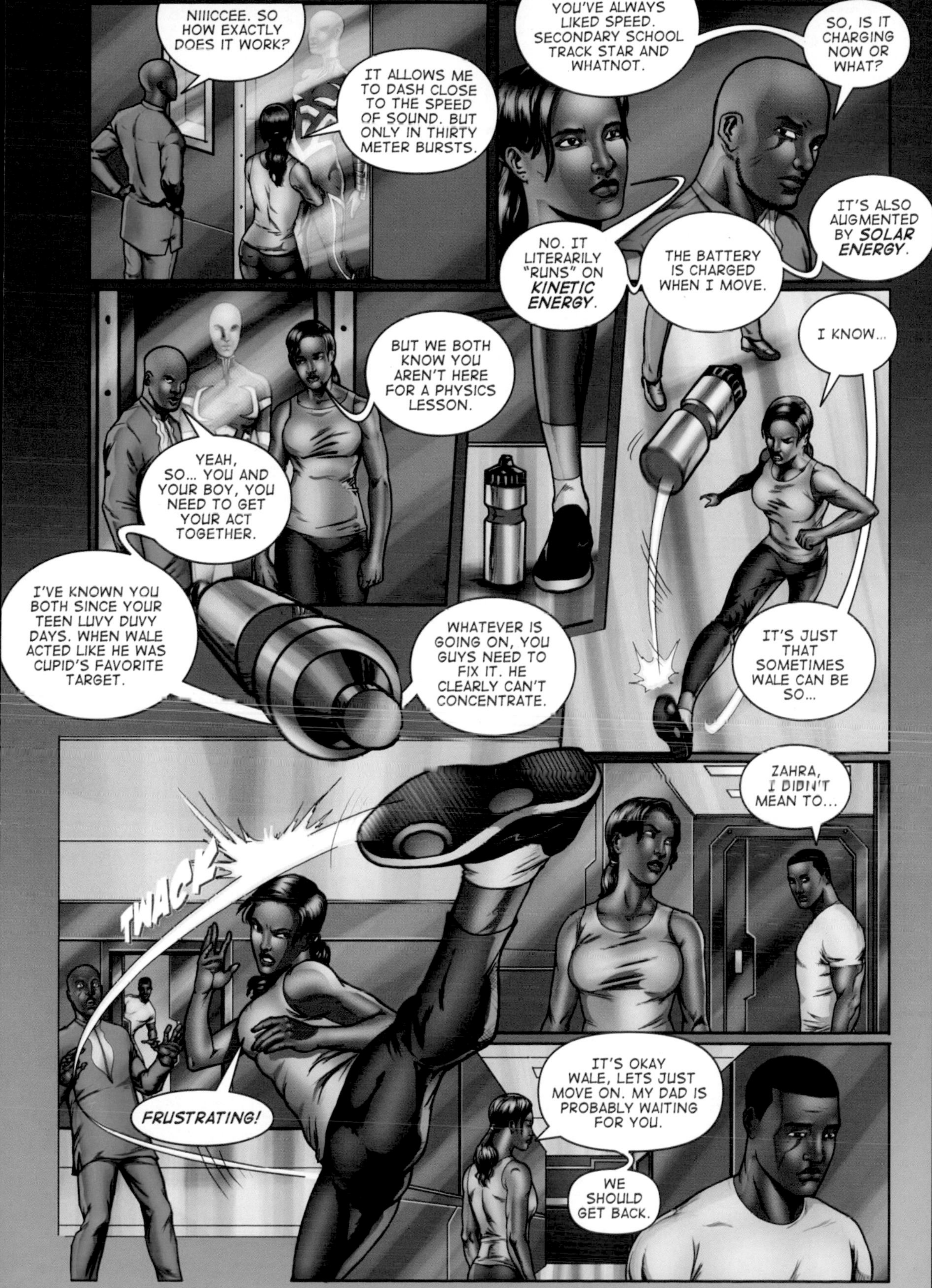
NIIICCEE. SO HOW EXACTLY DOES IT WORK?
IT ALLOWS ME TO DASH CLOSE TO THE SPEED OF SOUND. BUT ONLY IN THIRTY METER BURSTS.
MAKES SENSE. YOU'VE ALWAYS LIKED SPEED. SECONDARY SCHOOL TRACK STAR AND WHATNOT.
SO, IS IT CHARGING NOW OR WHAT?
NO. IT LITERARILY "RUNS" ON KINETIC ENERGY.
THE BATTERY IS CHARGED WHEN I MOVE.
IT'S ALSO AUGMENTED BY SOLAR ENERGY.
BUT WE BOTH KNOW YOU AREN'T HERE FOR A PHYSICS LESSON.
YEAH, SO... YOU AND YOUR BOY, YOU NEED TO GET YOUR ACT TOGETHER.
I KNOW...
I'VE KNOWN YOU BOTH SINCE YOUR TEEN LUVY DUVY DAYS. WHEN WALE ACTED LIKE HE WAS CUPID'S FAVORITE TARGET.
WHATEVER IS GOING ON, YOU GUYS NEED TO FIX IT. HE CLEARLY CAN'T CONCENTRATE.
IT'S JUST THAT SOMETIMES WALE CAN BE SO...
TWACK
FRUSTRATING!
ZAHRA, I DIDN'T MEAN TO...
IT'S OKAY WALE, LETS JUST MOVE ON. MY DAD IS PROBABLY WAITING FOR YOU.
WE SHOULD GET BACK.

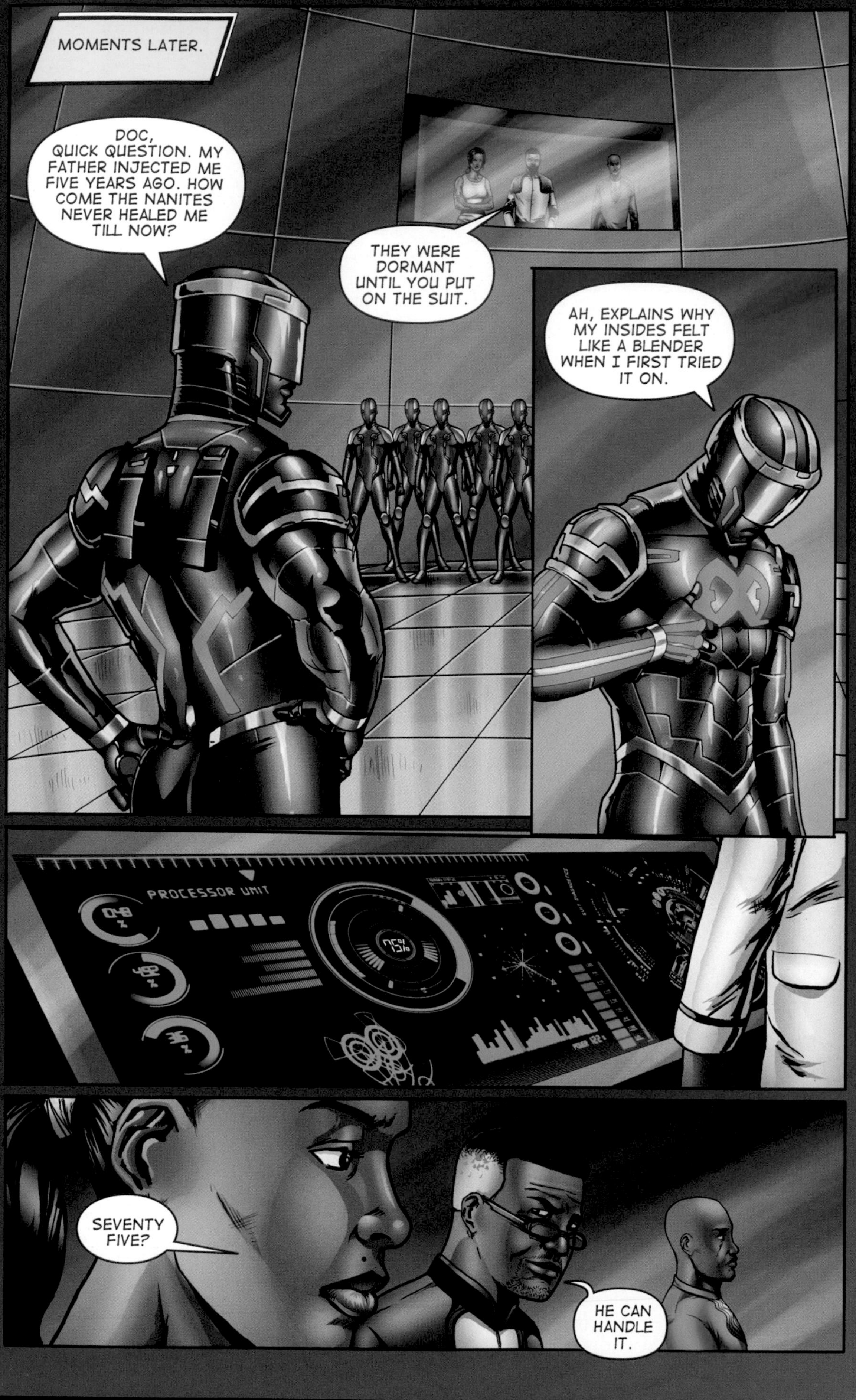
MOMENTS LATER.
DOC, QUICK QUESTION. MY FATHER INJECTED ME FIVE YEARS AGO. HOW COME THE NANITES NEVER HEALED ME TILL NOW?
THEY WERE DORMANT UNTIL YOU PUT ON THE SUIT.
AH, EXPLAINS WHY MY INSIDES FELT LIKE A BLENDER WHEN I FIRST TRIED IT ON.
PROCESSOR UNIT
SEVENTY FIVE?
HE CAN HANDLE IT.

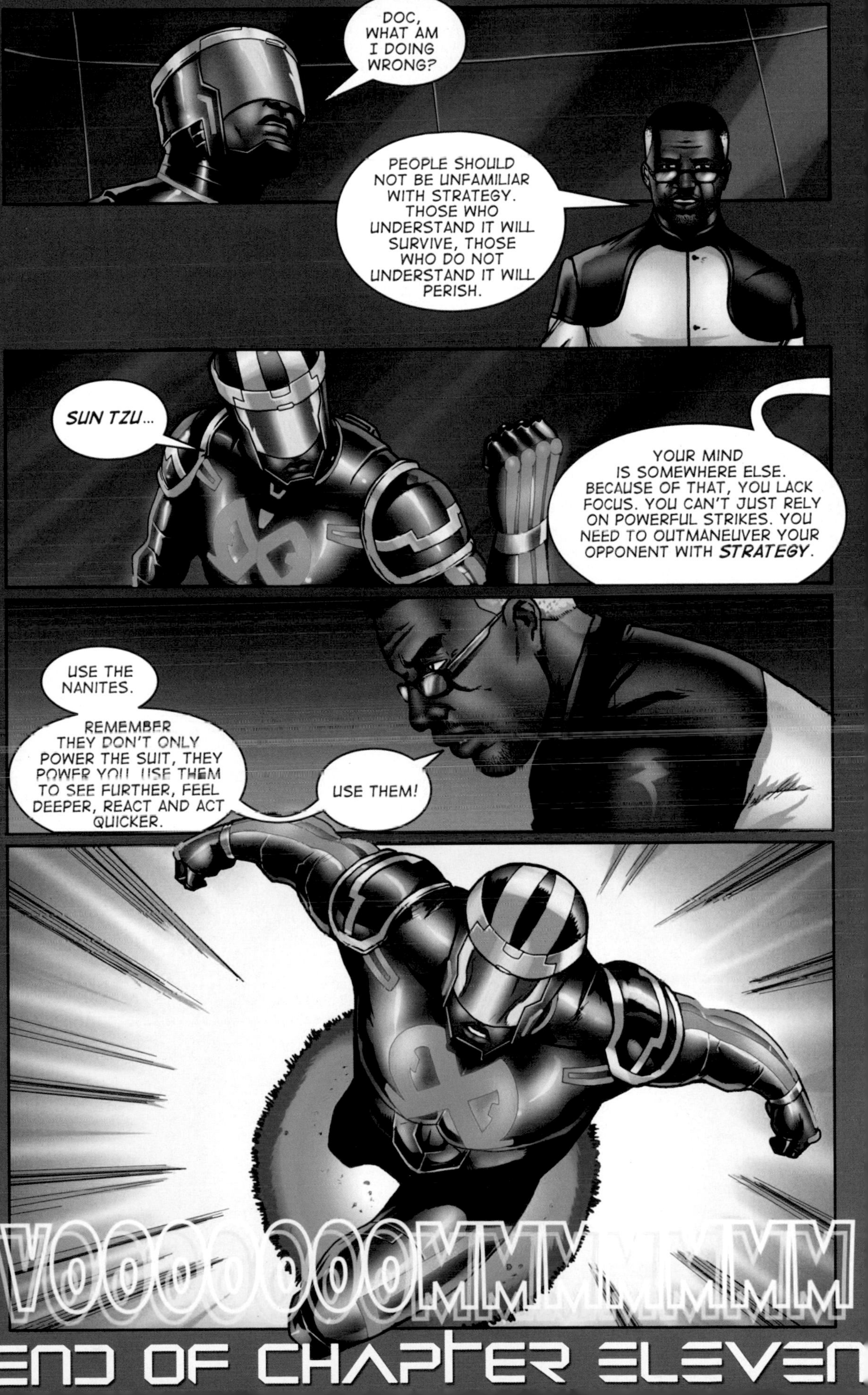
DOC, WHAT AM I DOING WRONG?
PEOPLE SHOULD NOT BE UNFAMILIAR WITH STRATEGY. THOSE WHO UNDERSTAND IT WILL SURVIVE, THOSE WHO DO NOT UNDERSTAND IT WILL PERISH.
SUN TZU...
YOUR MIND IS SOMEWHERE ELSE. BECAUSE OF THAT, YOU LACK FOCUS. YOU CAN'T JUST RELY ON POWERFUL STRIKES. YOU NEED TO OUTMANEUVER YOUR OPPONENT WITH STRATEGY.
USE THE NANITES.
REMEMBER THEY DON'T ONLY POWER THE SUIT, THEY POWER YOU. USE THEM TO SEE FURTHER, FEEL DEEPER, REACT AND ACT QUICKER.
USE THEM!
VOOOOOOOOMMMMMMMMM
END OF CHAPTER ELEVEN

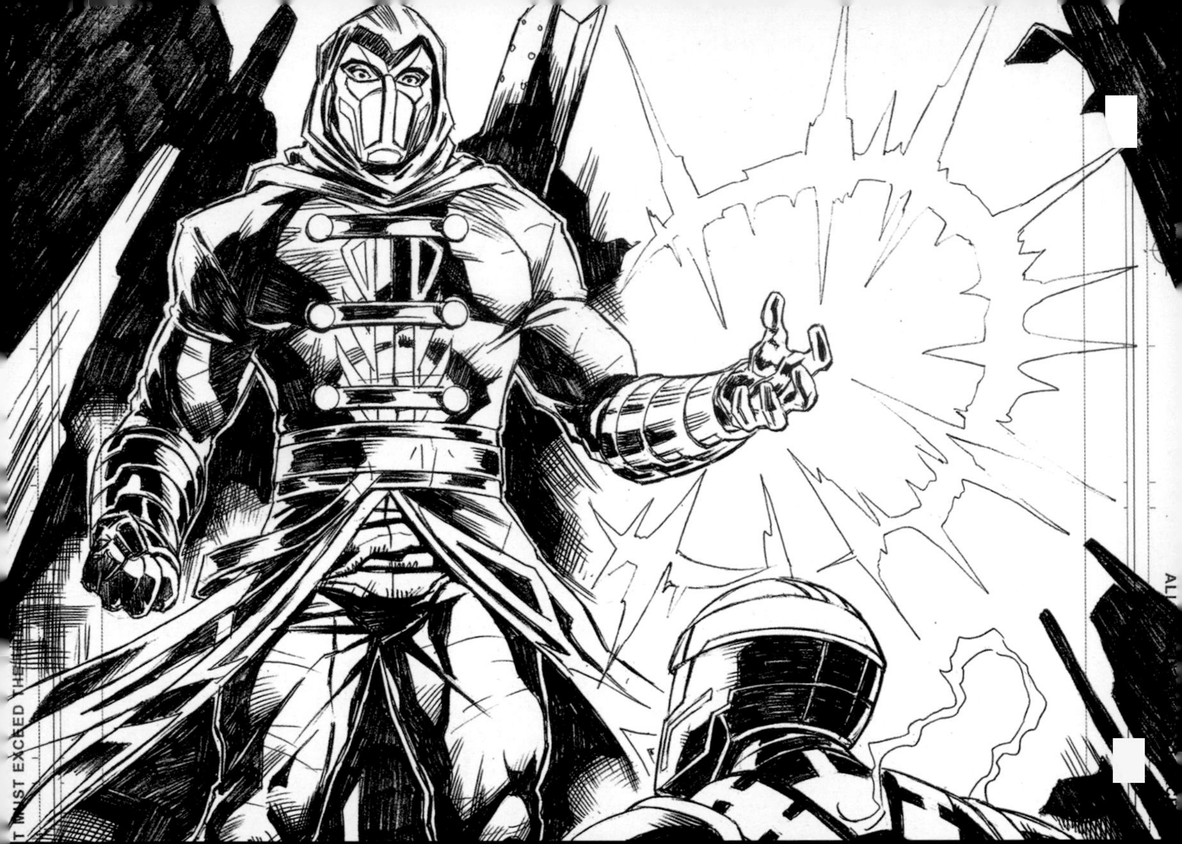

- Fan Art by Cyrus Mesarcia

Fun Fact: The name Oniku is a play on two words from the Yoruba (one of the three major tribes in Nigeria) language. "Oni" roughly translates to "Bringer" while the word "Iku" means "death". In essence, Oni-Iku would roughly translate to "Bringer of Death". A Grim Reaper so to speak.

CHAPTER TWELVE

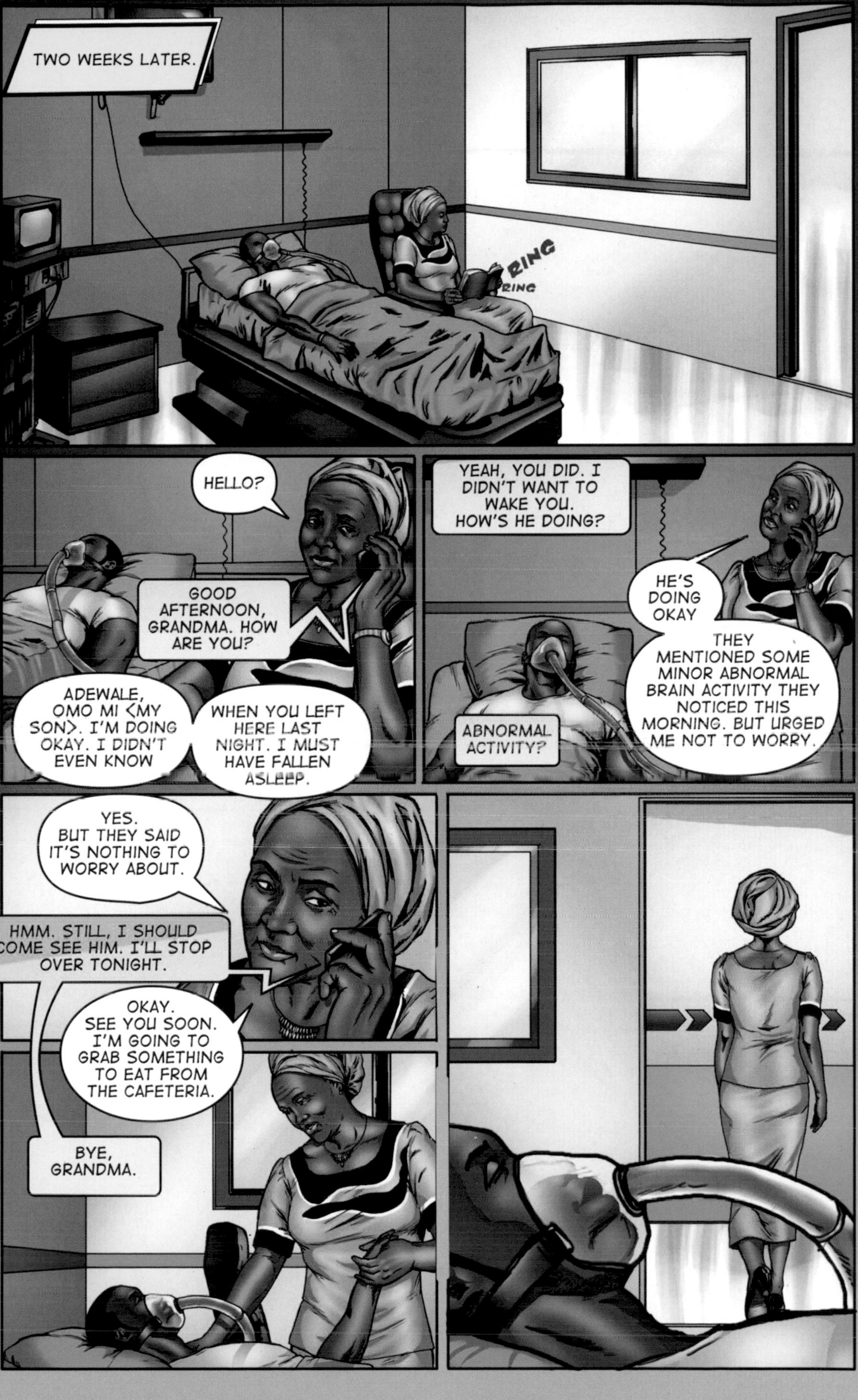
TWO WEEKS LATER.
RING
RING
HELLO?
GOOD AFTERNOON, GRANDMA. HOW ARE YOU?
ADEWALE, OMO MI <MY SON>. I'M DOING OKAY. I DIDN'T EVEN KNOW
WHEN YOU LEFT HERE LAST NIGHT. I MUST HAVE FALLEN ASLEEP.
YEAH, YOU DID. I DIDN'T WANT TO WAKE YOU. HOW'S HE DOING?
HE'S DOING OKAY
THEY MENTIONED SOME MINOR ABNORMAL BRAIN ACTIVITY THEY NOTICED THIS MORNING. BUT URGED ME NOT TO WORRY.
ABNORMAL ACTIVITY?
YES. BUT THEY SAID IT'S NOTHING TO WORRY ABOUT.
HMM. STILL, I SHOULD COME SEE HIM. I'LL STOP OVER TONIGHT.
OKAY. SEE YOU SOON. I'M GOING TO GRAB SOMETHING TO EAT FROM THE CAFETERIA.
BYE, GRANDMA.

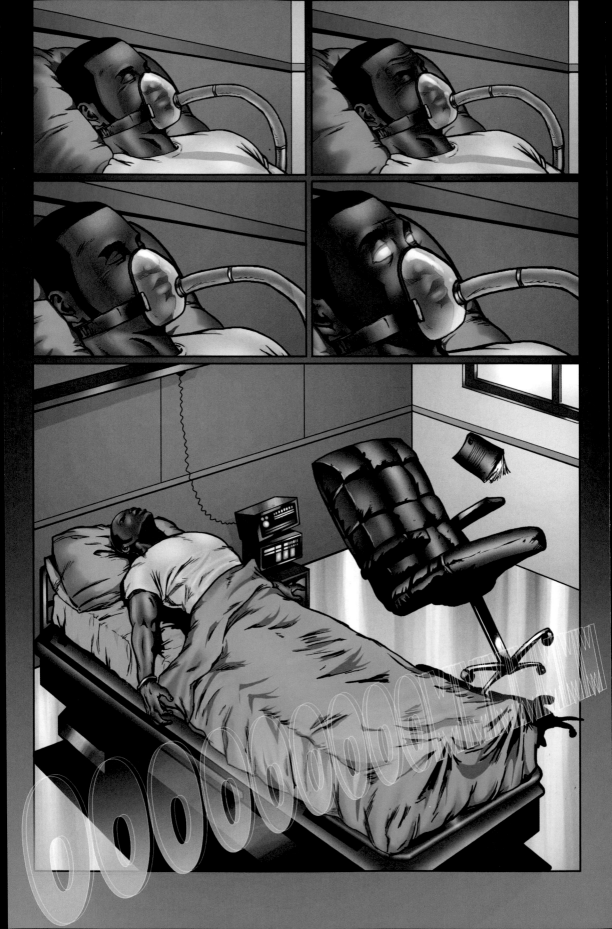

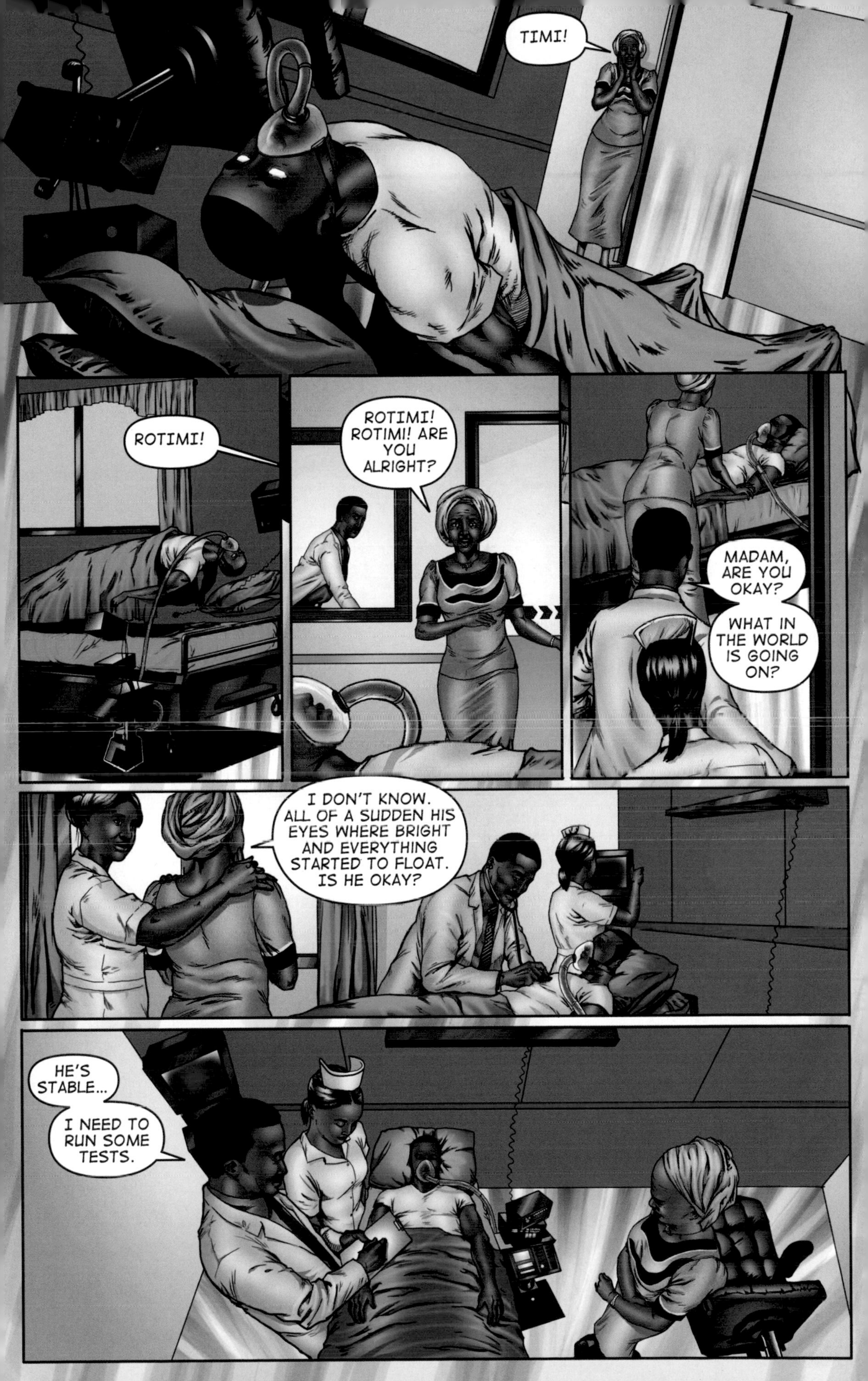
TIMI!
ROTIMI!
ROTIMI! ROTIMI! ARE YOU ALRIGHT?
MADAM, ARE YOU OKAY?
WHAT IN THE WORLD IS GOING ON?
I DON'T KNOW. ALL OF A SUDDEN HIS EYES WHERE BRIGHT AND EVERYTHING STARTED TO FLOAT. IS HE OKAY?
HE'S STABLE...
I NEED TO RUN SOME TESTS.

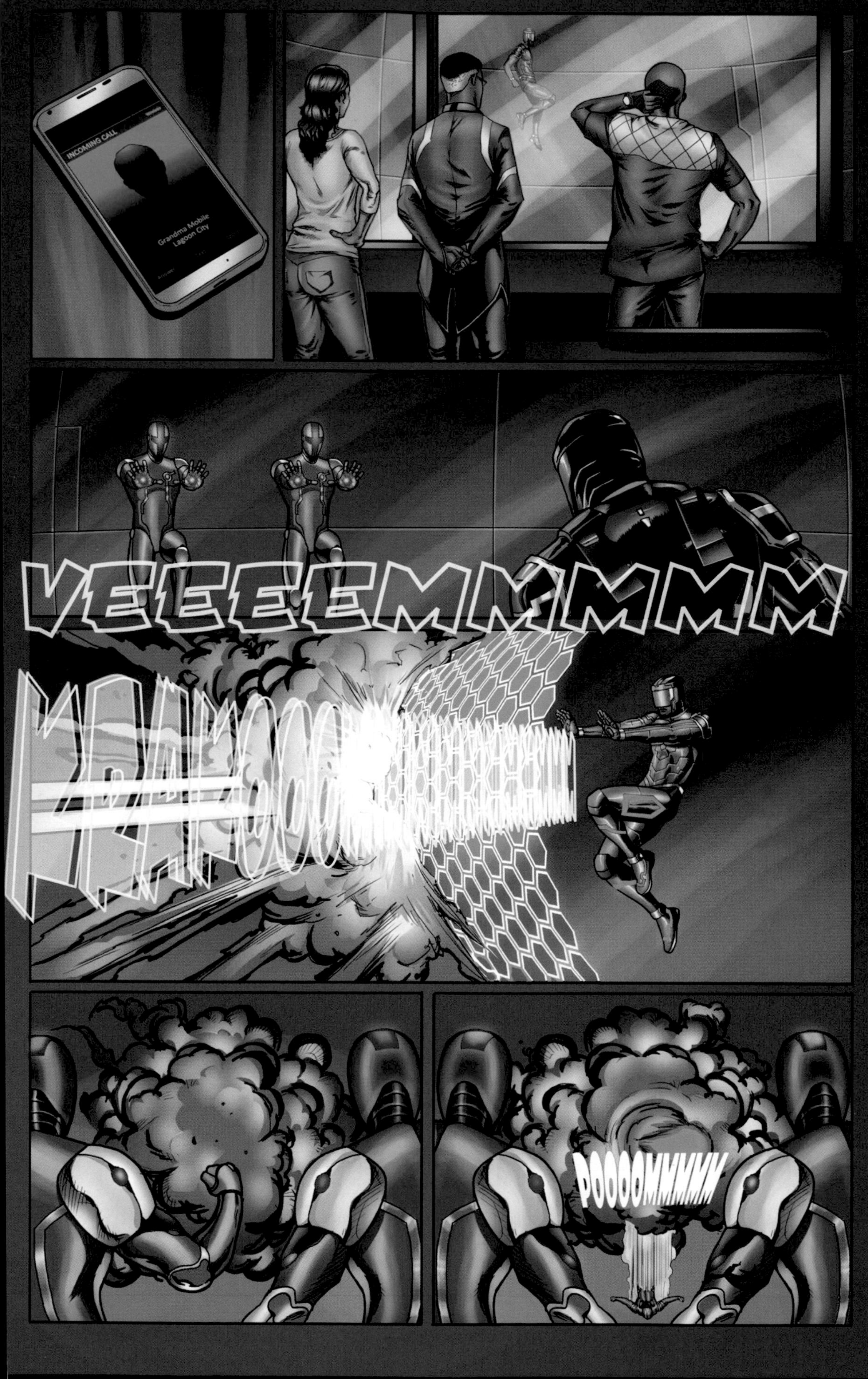
INCOMING CALL
Grandma Mobile
Lagoon City
VEEEMMMMMM
POOOOMMMMM

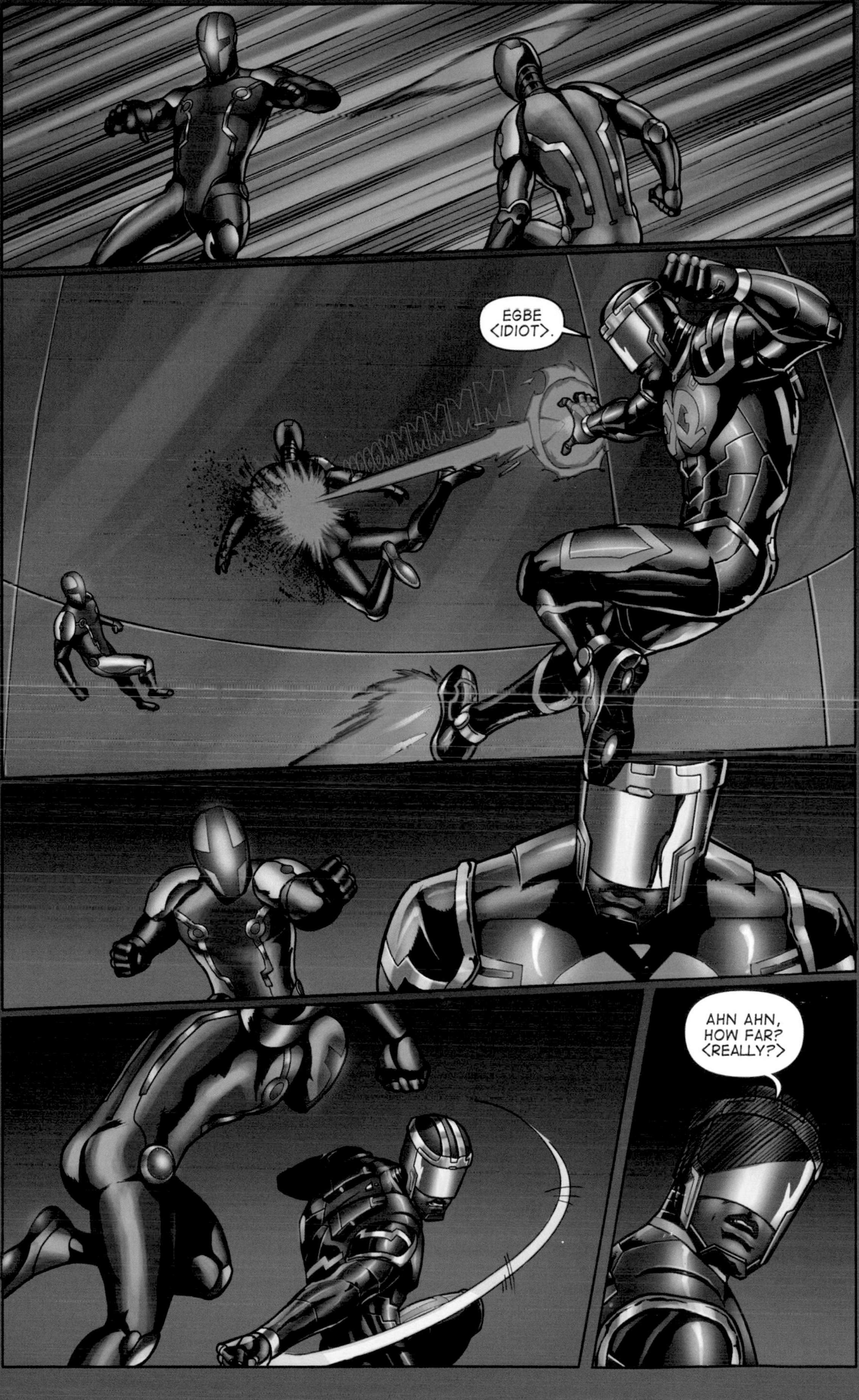
EGBE <IDIOT>.
AHN AHN, HOW FAR? <REALLY?>

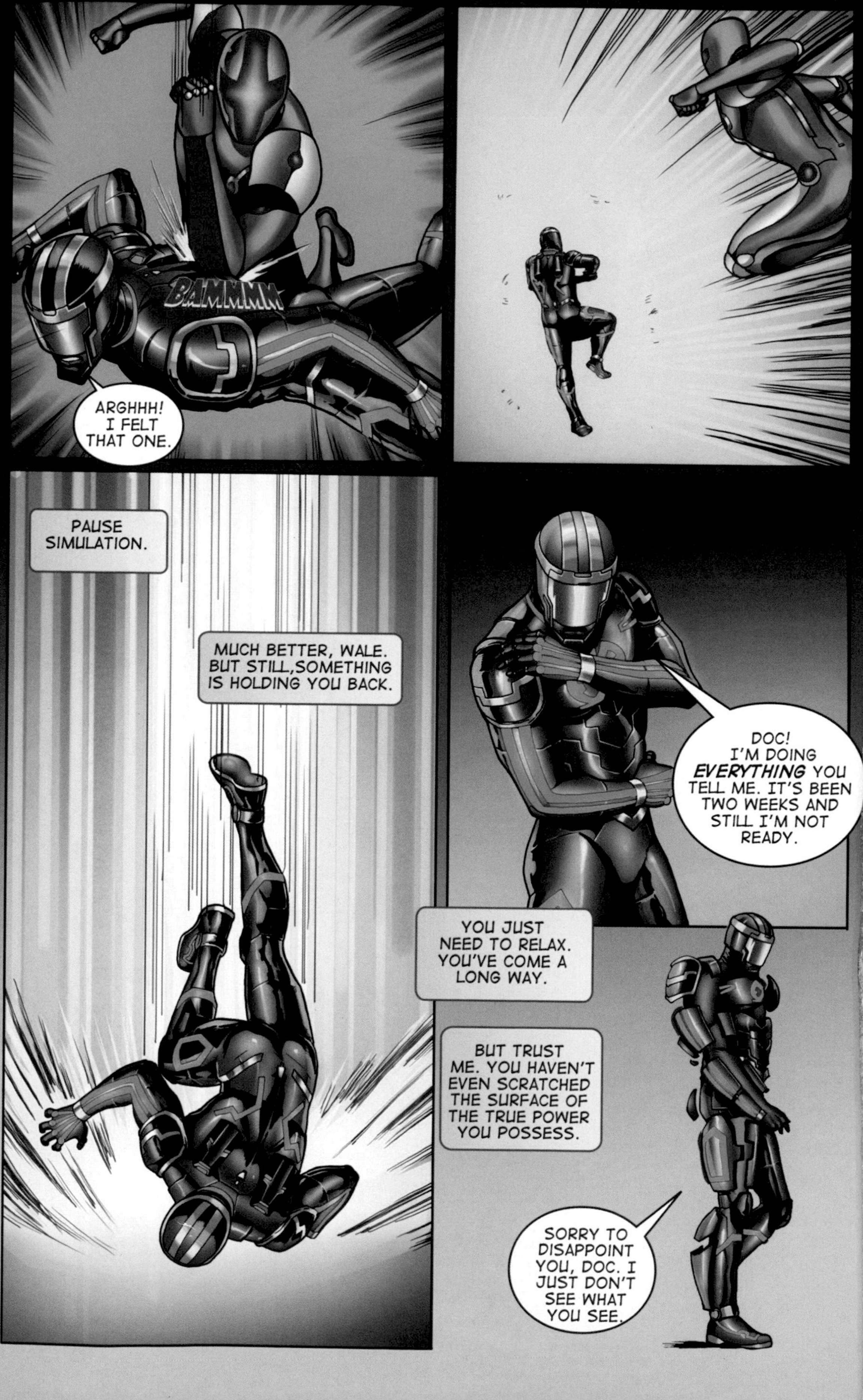
BAMMMM
ARGHHH! I FELT THAT ONE.
PAUSE SIMULATION.
MUCH BETTER, WALE. BUT STILL,SOMETHING IS HOLDING YOU BACK.
DOC! I'M DOING EVERYTHING YOU TELL ME. IT'S BEEN TWO WEEKS AND STILL I'M NOT READY.
YOU JUST NEED TO RELAX. YOU'VE COME A LONG WAY.
BUT TRUST ME. YOU HAVEN'T EVEN SCRATCHED THE SURFACE OF THE TRUE POWER YOU POSSESS.
SORRY TO DISAPPOINT YOU, DOC. I JUST DON'T SEE WHAT YOU SEE.

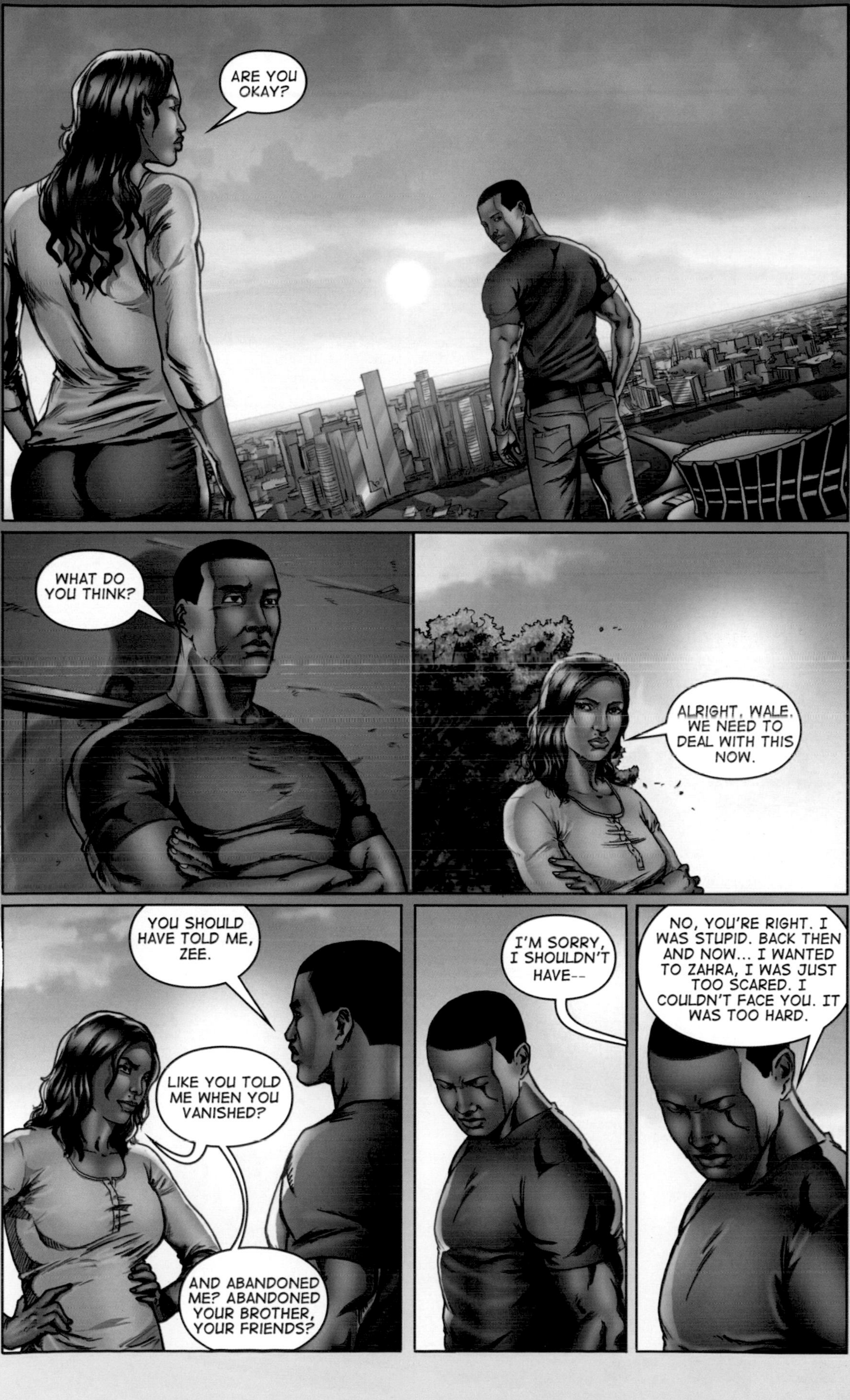

ARE YOU OKAY?
WHAT DO YOU THINK?
ALRIGHT, WALE. WE NEED TO DEAL WITH THIS NOW.
YOU SHOULD HAVE TOLD ME, ZEE.
LIKE YOU TOLD ME WHEN YOU VANISHED?
AND ABANDONED ME? ABANDONED YOUR BROTHER, YOUR FRIENDS?
I'M SORRY, I SHOULDN'T HAVE--
NO, YOU'RE RIGHT. I WAS STUPID. BACK THEN AND NOW... I WANTED TO ZAHRA, I WAS JUST TOO SCARED. I COULDN'T FACE YOU. IT WAS TOO HARD.

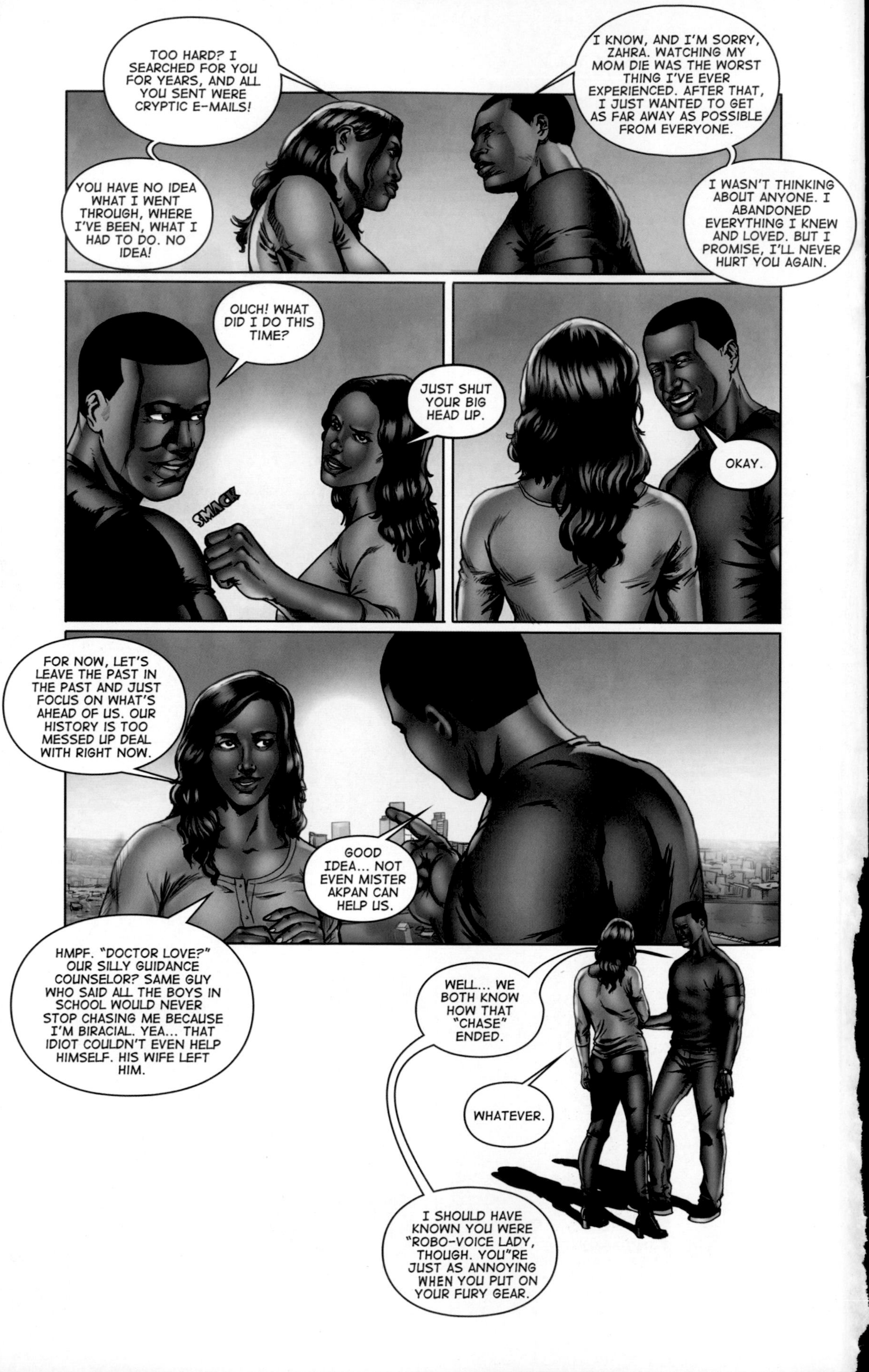
TOO HARD? I SEARCHED FOR YOU FOR YEARS, AND ALL YOU SENT WERE CRYPTIC E-MAILS!
YOU HAVE NO IDEA WHAT I WENT THROUGH, WHERE I'VE BEEN, WHAT I HAD TO DO. NO IDEA!
I KNOW, AND I'M SORRY, ZAHRA. WATCHING MY MOM DIE WAS THE WORST THING I'VE EVER EXPERIENCED. AFTER THAT, I JUST WANTED TO GET AS FAR AWAY AS POSSIBLE FROM EVERYONE.
I WASN'T THINKING ABOUT ANYONE. I ABANDONED EVERYTHING I KNEW AND LOVED. BUT I PROMISE, I'LL NEVER HURT YOU AGAIN.
SMACK
OUCH! WHAT DID I DO THIS TIME?
JUST SHUT YOUR BIG HEAD UP.
OKAY.
FOR NOW, LET'S LEAVE THE PAST IN THE PAST AND JUST FOCUS ON WHAT'S AHEAD OF US. OUR HISTORY IS TOO MESSED UP DEAL WITH RIGHT NOW.
GOOD IDEA... NOT EVEN MISTER AKPAN CAN HELP US.
HMPF. "DOCTOR LOVE?" OUR SILLY GUIDANCE COUNSELOR? SAME GUY WHO SAID ALL THE BOYS IN SCHOOL WOULD NEVER STOP CHASING ME BECAUSE I'M BIRACIAL. YEA... THAT IDIOT COULDN'T EVEN HELP HIMSELF. HIS WIFE LEFT HIM.
WELL... WE BOTH KNOW HOW THAT "CHASE" ENDED.
WHATEVER.
I SHOULD HAVE KNOWN YOU WERE "ROBO-VOICE LADY, THOUGH. YOU"RE JUST AS ANNOYING WHEN YOU PUT ON YOUR FURY GEAR.

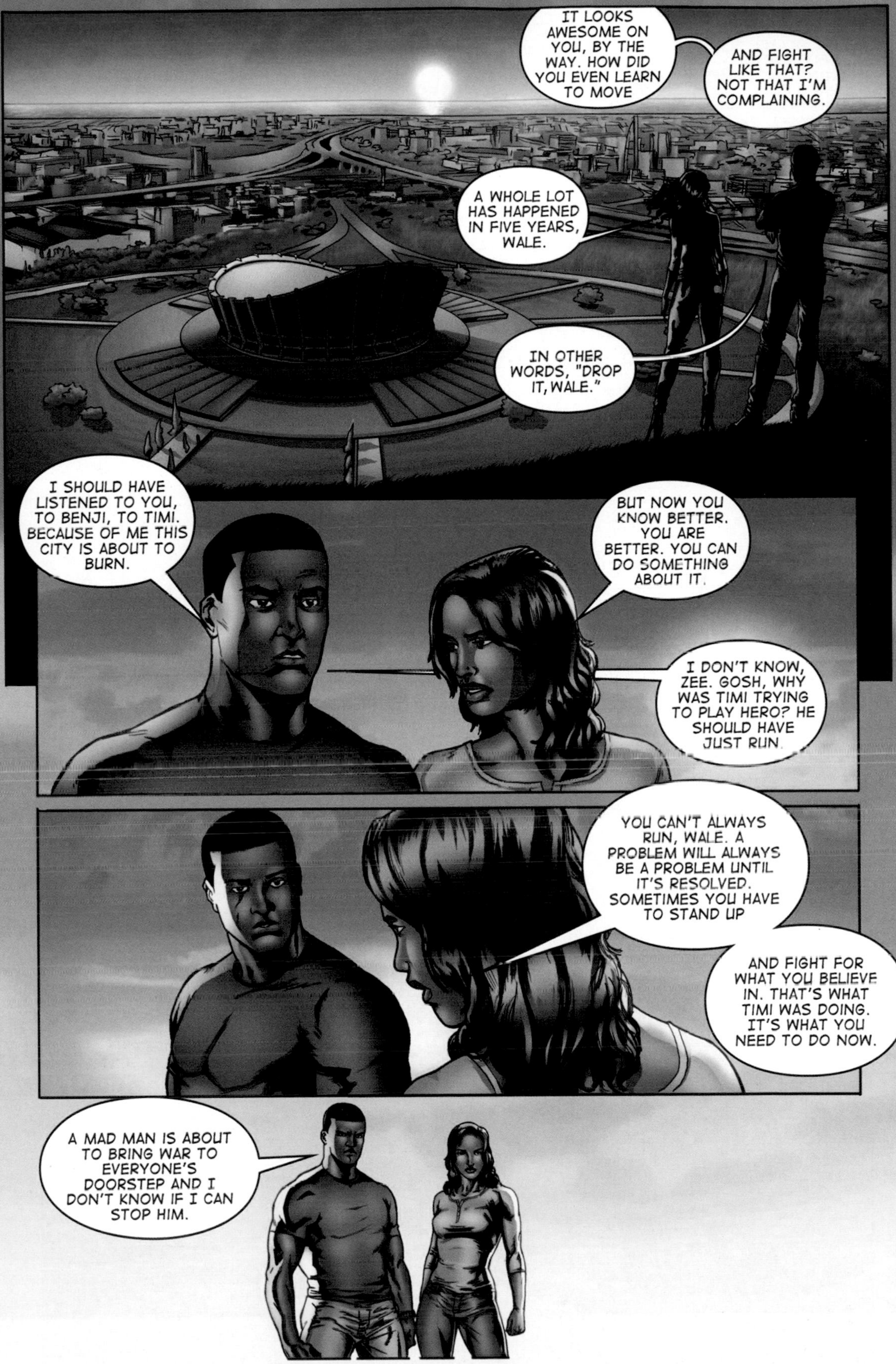
IT LOOKS AWESOME ON YOU, BY THE WAY. HOW DID YOU EVEN LEARN TO MOVE
AND FIGHT LIKE THAT? NOT THAT I'M COMPLAINING.
A WHOLE LOT HAS HAPPENED IN FIVE YEARS, WALE.
IN OTHER WORDS, "DROP IT, WALE."
I SHOULD HAVE LISTENED TO YOU, TO BENJI, TO TIMI. BECAUSE OF ME THIS CITY IS ABOUT TO BURN.
BUT NOW YOU KNOW BETTER. YOU ARE BETTER. YOU CAN DO SOMETHING ABOUT IT.
I DON'T KNOW, ZEE. GOSH, WHY WAS TIMI TRYING TO PLAY HERO? HE SHOULD HAVE JUST RUN.
YOU CAN'T ALWAYS RUN, WALE. A PROBLEM WILL ALWAYS BE A PROBLEM UNTIL IT'S RESOLVED. SOMETIMES YOU HAVE TO STAND UP
AND FIGHT FOR WHAT YOU BELIEVE IN. THAT'S WHAT TIMI WAS DOING. IT'S WHAT YOU NEED TO DO NOW.
A MAD MAN IS ABOUT TO BRING WAR TO EVERYONE'S DOORSTEP AND I DON'T KNOW IF I CAN STOP HIM.

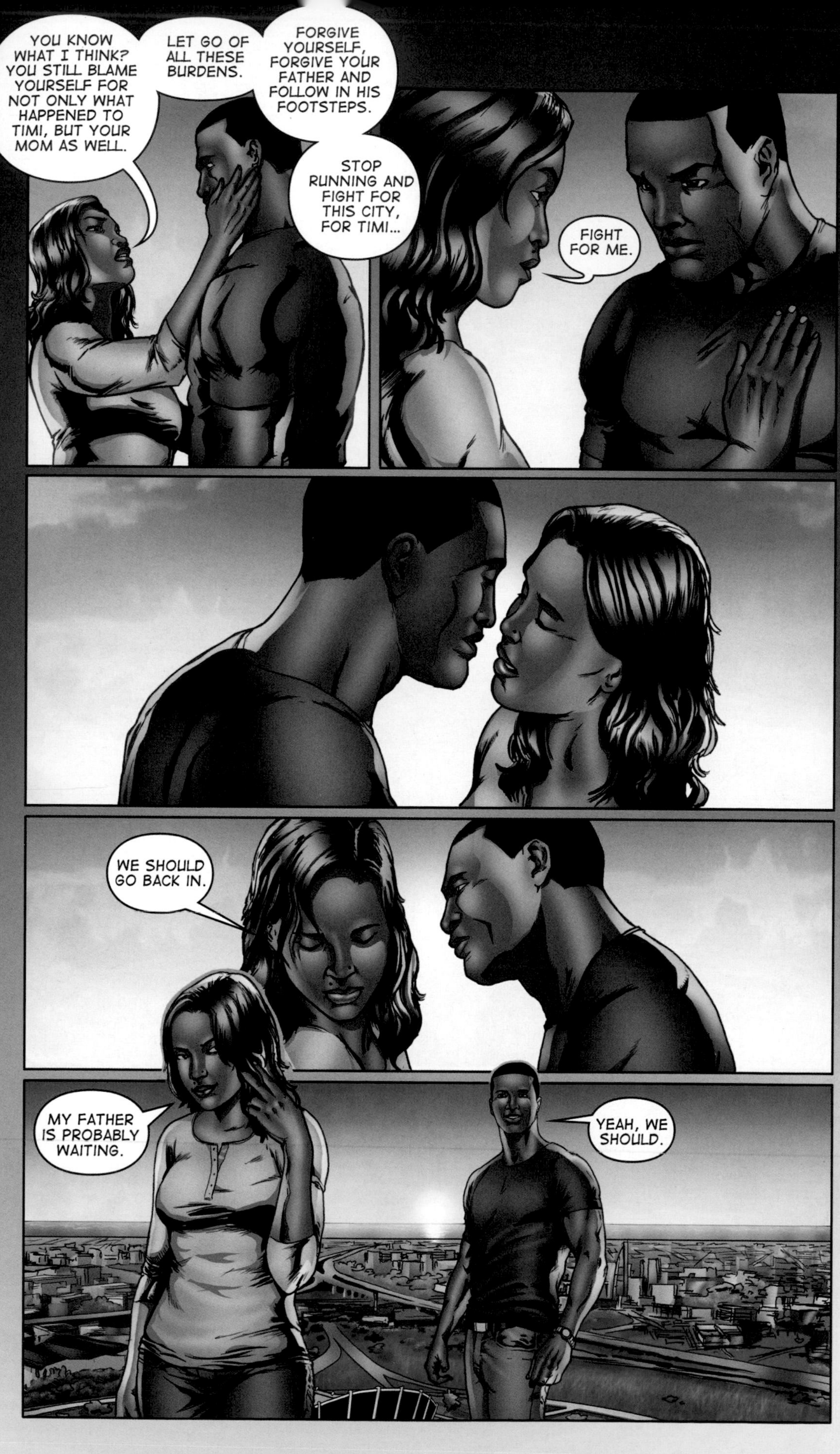
YOU KNOW WHAT I THINK? YOU STILL BLAME YOURSELF FOR NOT ONLY WHAT HAPPENED TO TIMI, BUT YOUR MOM AS WELL.
LET GO OF ALL THESE BURDENS.
FORGIVE YOURSELF, FORGIVE YOUR FATHER AND FOLLOW IN HIS FOOTSTEPS.
STOP RUNNING AND FIGHT FOR THIS CITY, FOR TIMI...
FIGHT FOR ME.
WE SHOULD GO BACK IN.
MY FATHER IS PROBABLY WAITING.
YEAH, WE SHOULD.

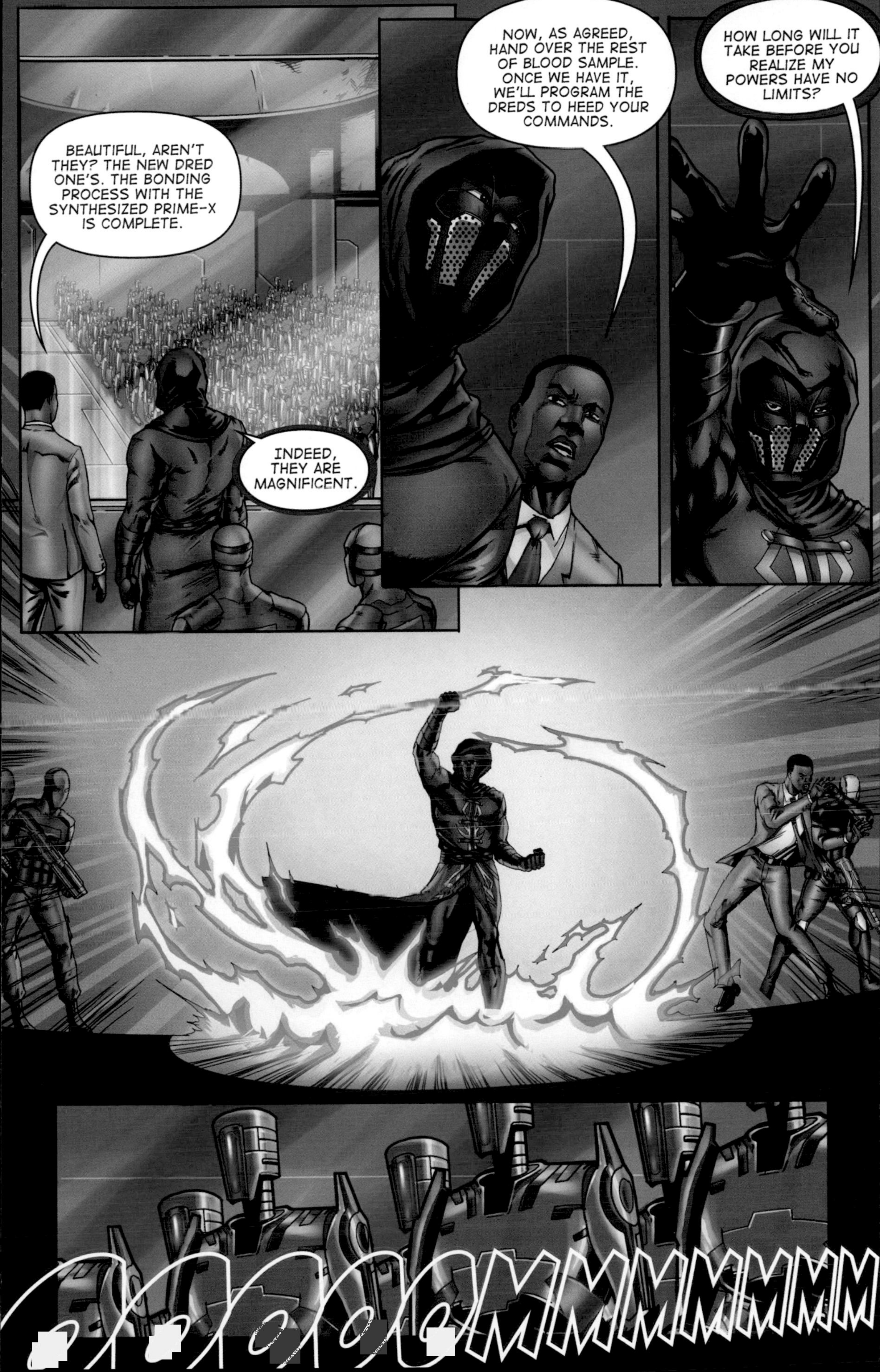
BEAUTIFUL, AREN'T THEY? THE NEW DRED ONE'S. THE BONDING PROCESS WITH THE SYNTHESIZED PRIME-X IS COMPLETE.
INDEED, THEY ARE MAGNIFICENT.
NOW, AS AGREED, HAND OVER THE REST OF BLOOD SAMPLE. ONCE WE HAVE IT, WE'LL PROGRAM THE DREDS TO HEED YOUR COMMANDS.
HOW LONG WILL IT TAKE BEFORE YOU REALIZE MY POWERS HAVE NO LIMITS?

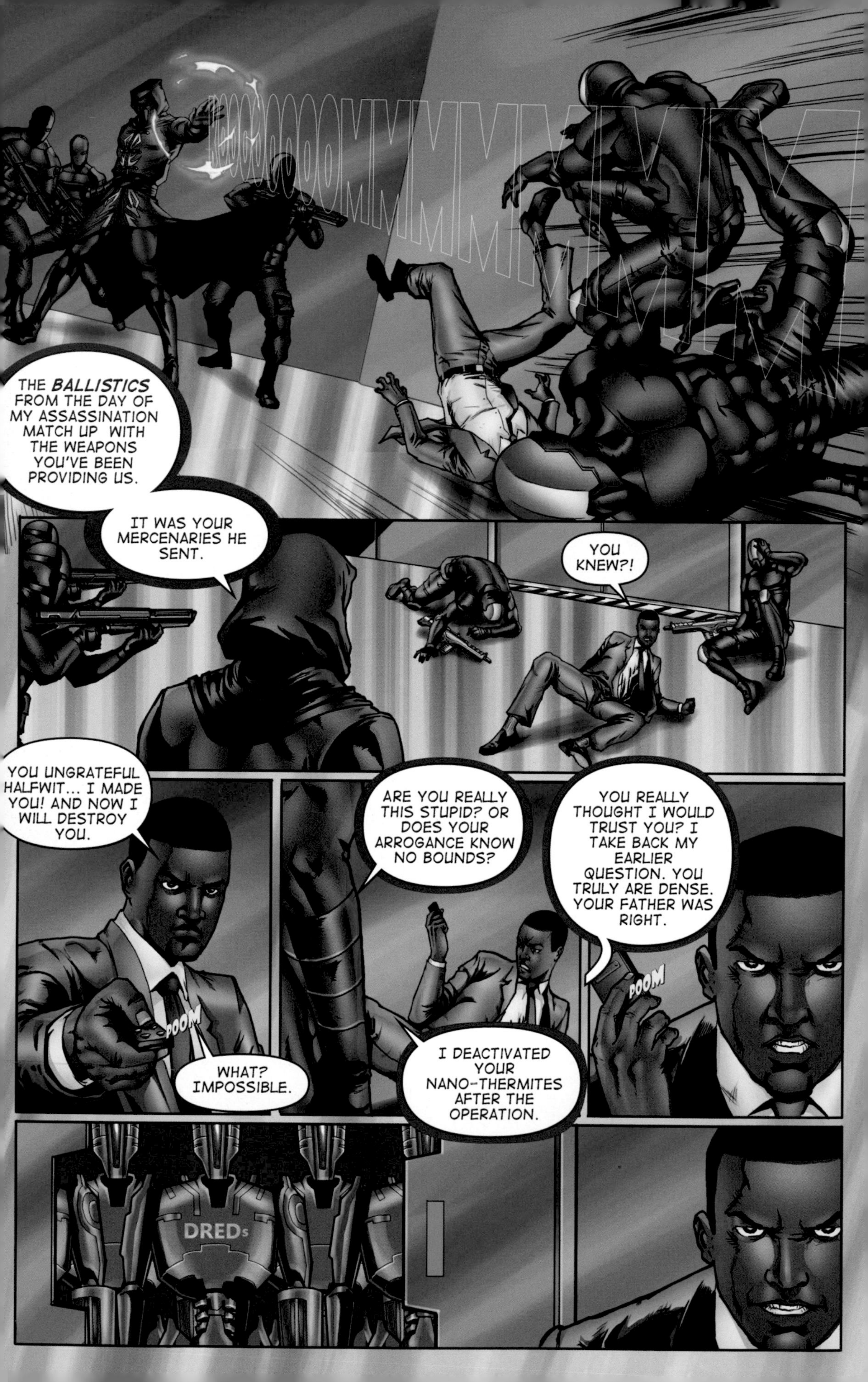
KOOOOOOOOMMMMMMMMMMM
THE BALLISTICS FROM THE DAY OF MY ASSASSINATION MATCH UP WITH THE WEAPONS YOU'VE BEEN PROVIDING US.
IT WAS YOUR MERCENARIES HE SENT.
YOU KNEW?!
YOU UNGRATEFUL HALFWIT... I MADE YOU! AND NOW I WILL DESTROY YOU.
POOM
WHAT? IMPOSSIBLE.
ARE YOU REALLY THIS STUPID? OR DOES YOUR ARROGANCE KNOW NO BOUNDS?
I DEACTIVATED YOUR NANO-THERMITES AFTER THE OPERATION.
YOU REALLY THOUGHT I WOULD TRUST YOU? I TAKE BACK MY EARLIER QUESTION. YOU TRULY ARE DENSE. YOUR FATHER WAS RIGHT.
POOM
DREDs

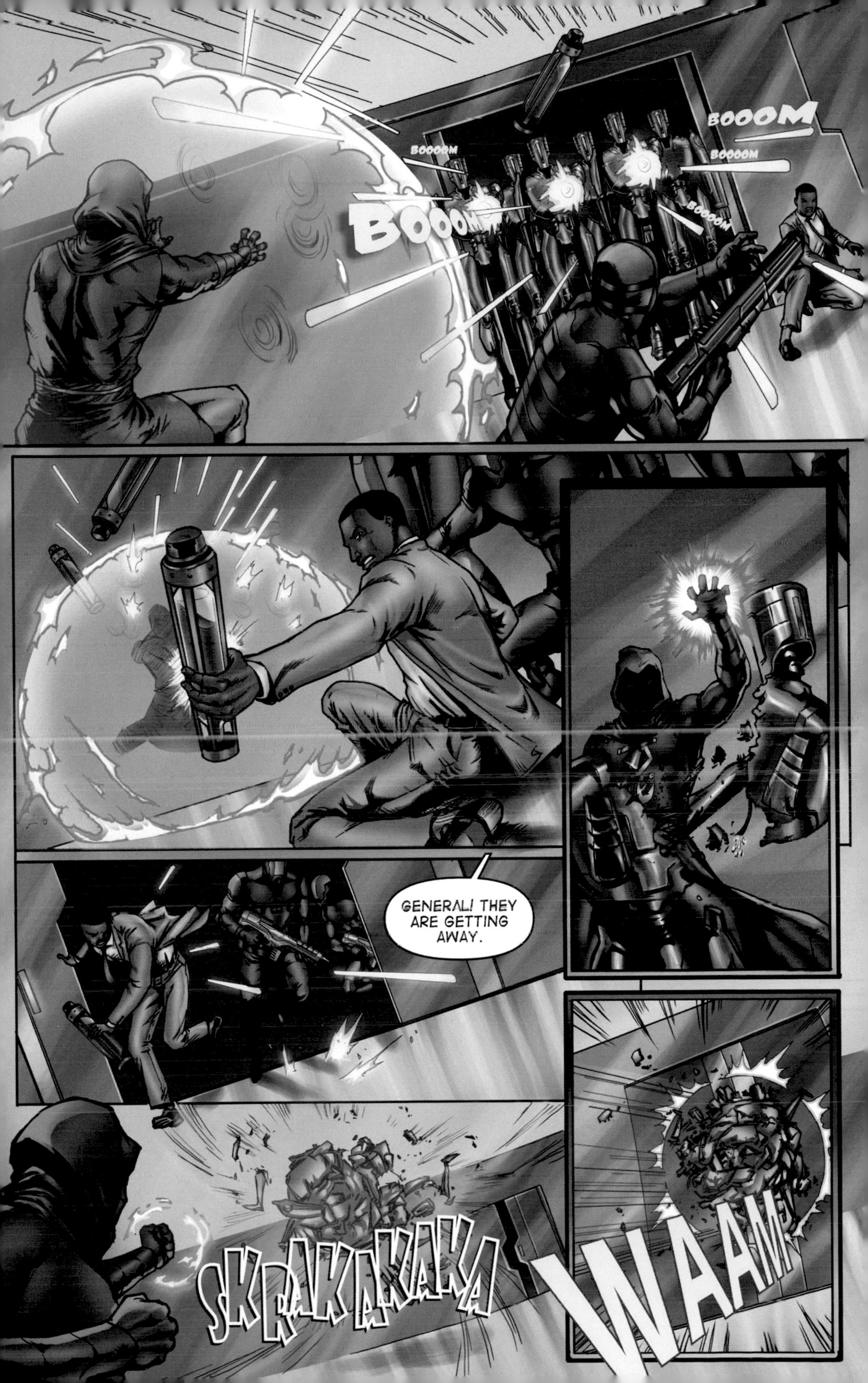
BOOOOM
BOOOM
BOOOOM
BOOOM
BOOOOM
GENERAL! THEY ARE GETTING AWAY.
SKRAKAKAKAKA
WAAM

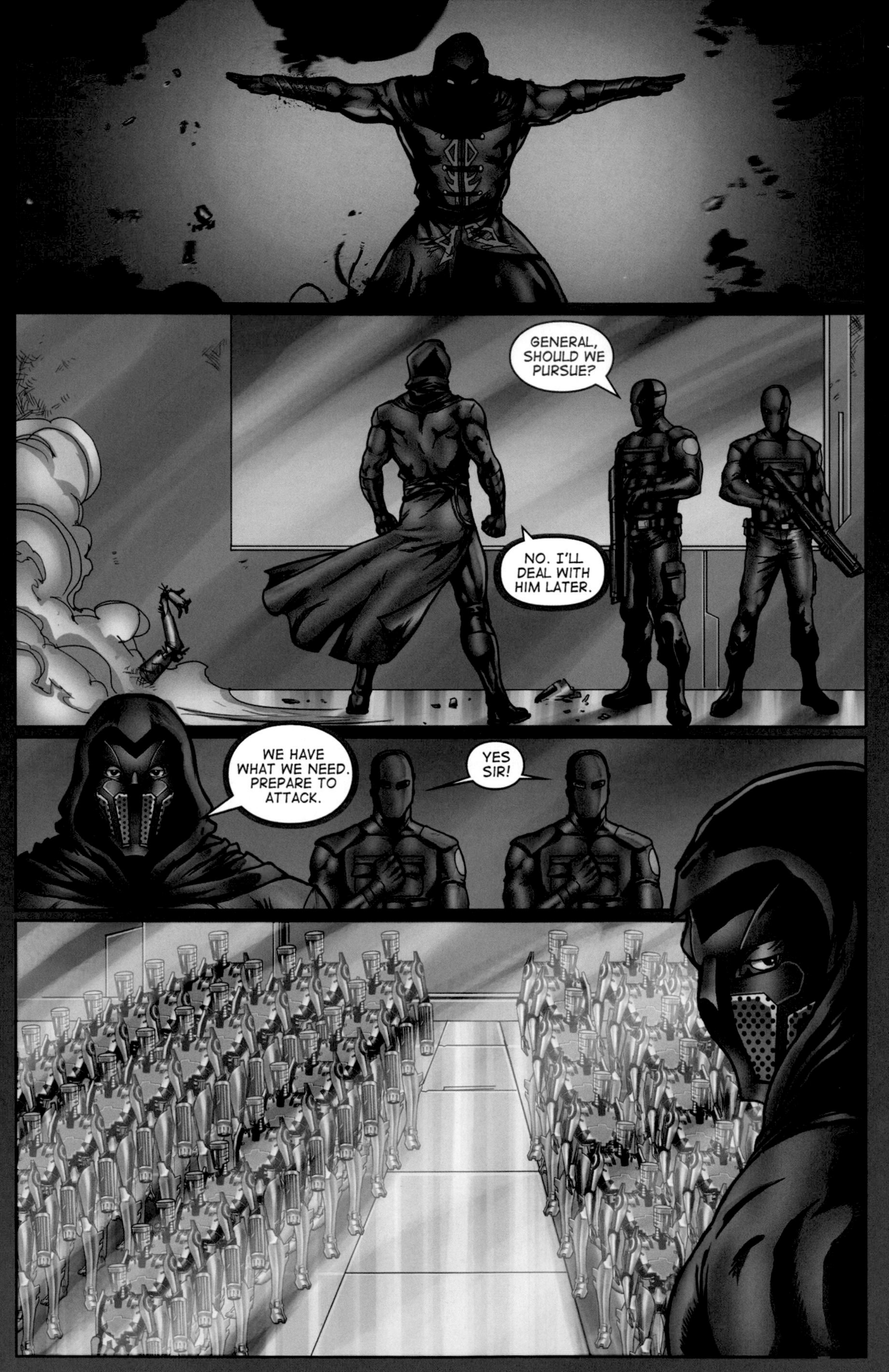
GENERAL, SHOULD WE PURSUE?
NO. I'LL DEAL WITH HIM LATER.
WE HAVE WHAT WE NEED. PREPARE TO ATTACK.
YES SIR!

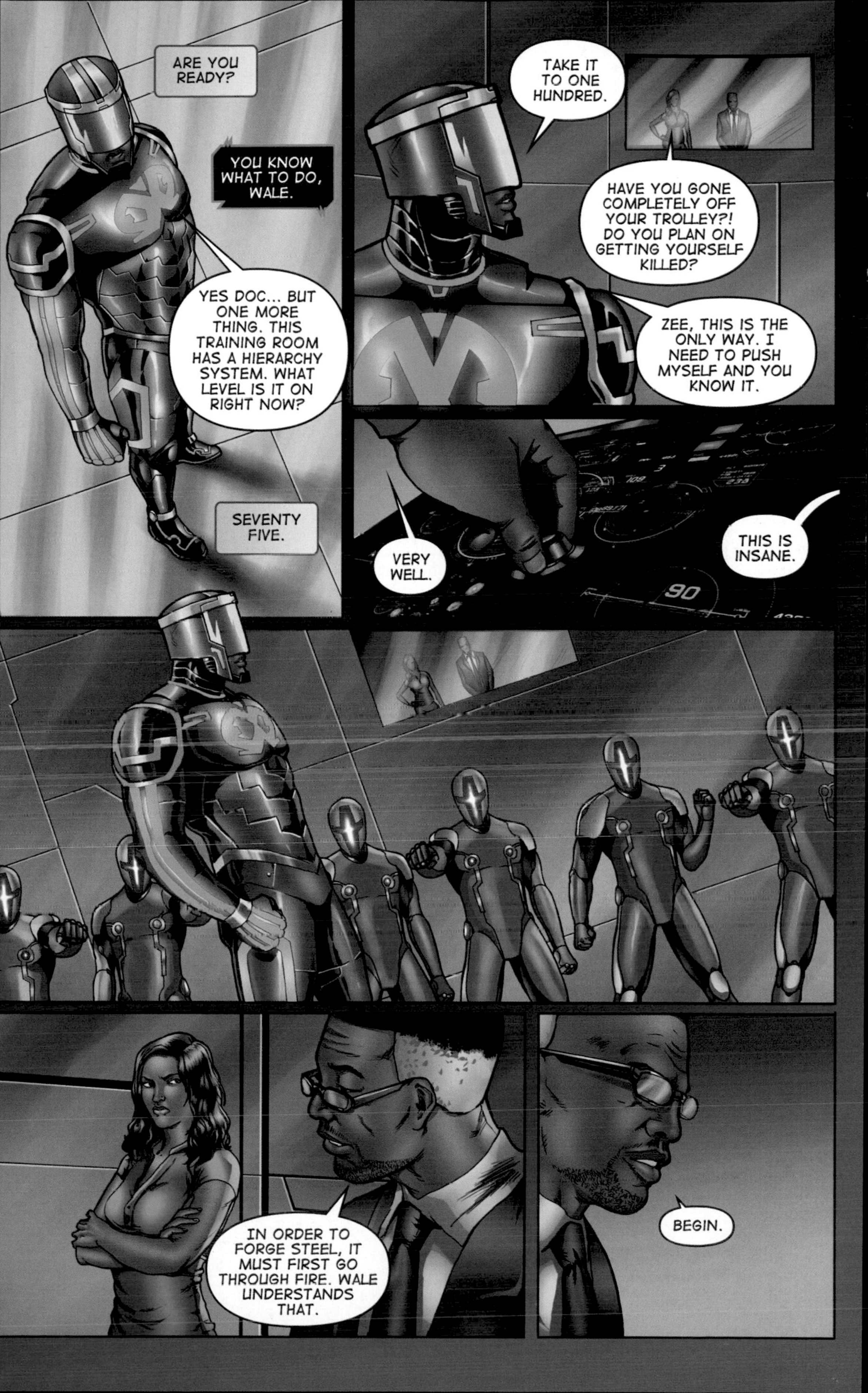
ARE YOU READY?
YOU KNOW WHAT TO DO, WALE.
YES DOC... BUT ONE MORE THING. THIS TRAINING ROOM HAS A HIERARCHY SYSTEM. WHAT LEVEL IS IT ON RIGHT NOW?
SEVENTY FIVE.
TAKE IT TO ONE HUNDRED.
HAVE YOU GONE COMPLETELY OFF YOUR TROLLEY?! DO YOU PLAN ON GETTING YOURSELF KILLED?
ZEE, THIS IS THE ONLY WAY. I NEED TO PUSH MYSELF AND YOU KNOW IT.
VERY WELL.
THIS IS INSANE.
IN ORDER TO FORGE STEEL, IT MUST FIRST GO THROUGH FIRE. WALE UNDERSTANDS THAT.
BEGIN.

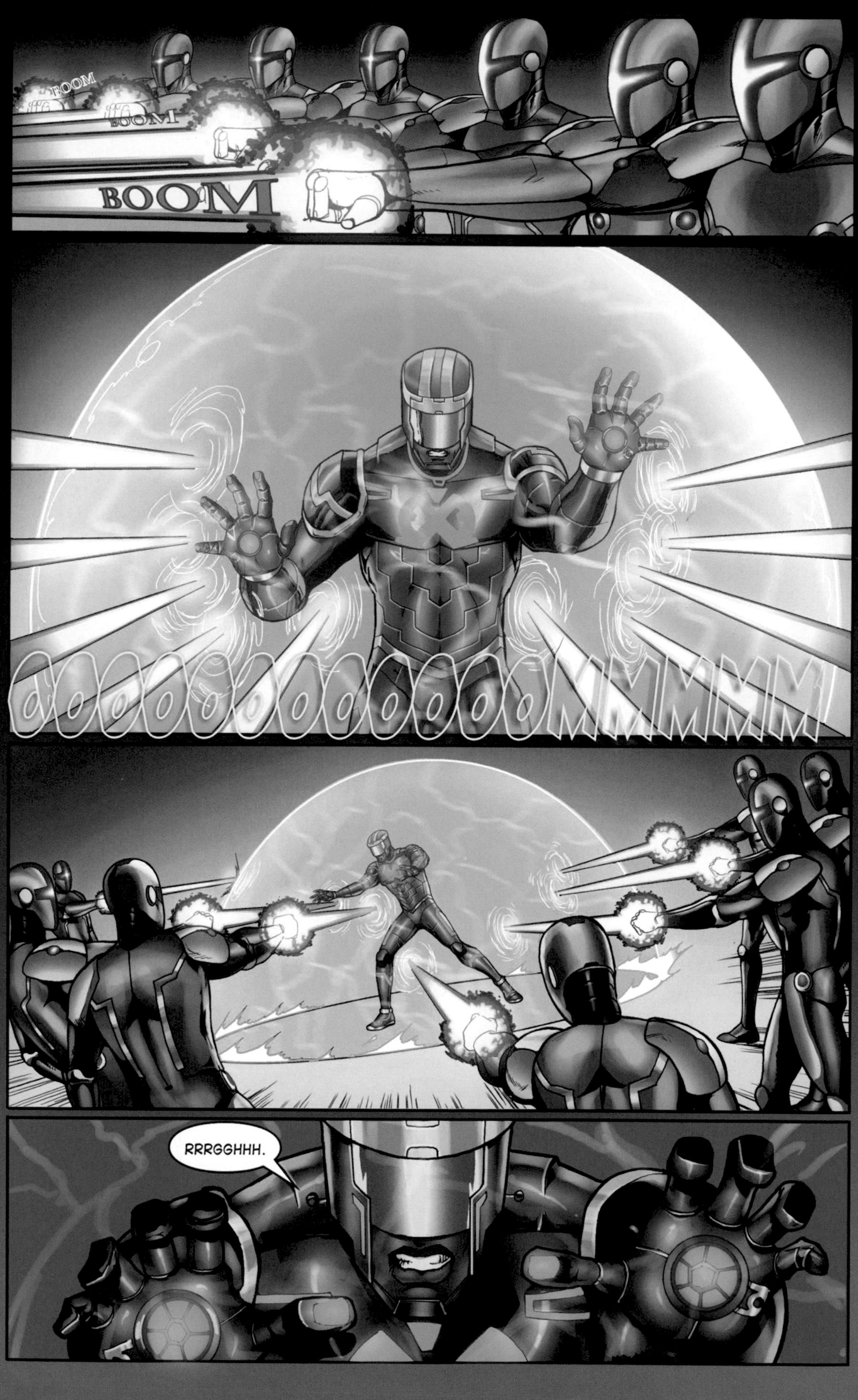
BOOM
BOOM
BOOM
OOOOOOOOOOOOOOOOMMMMMM
RRRGGHHH.

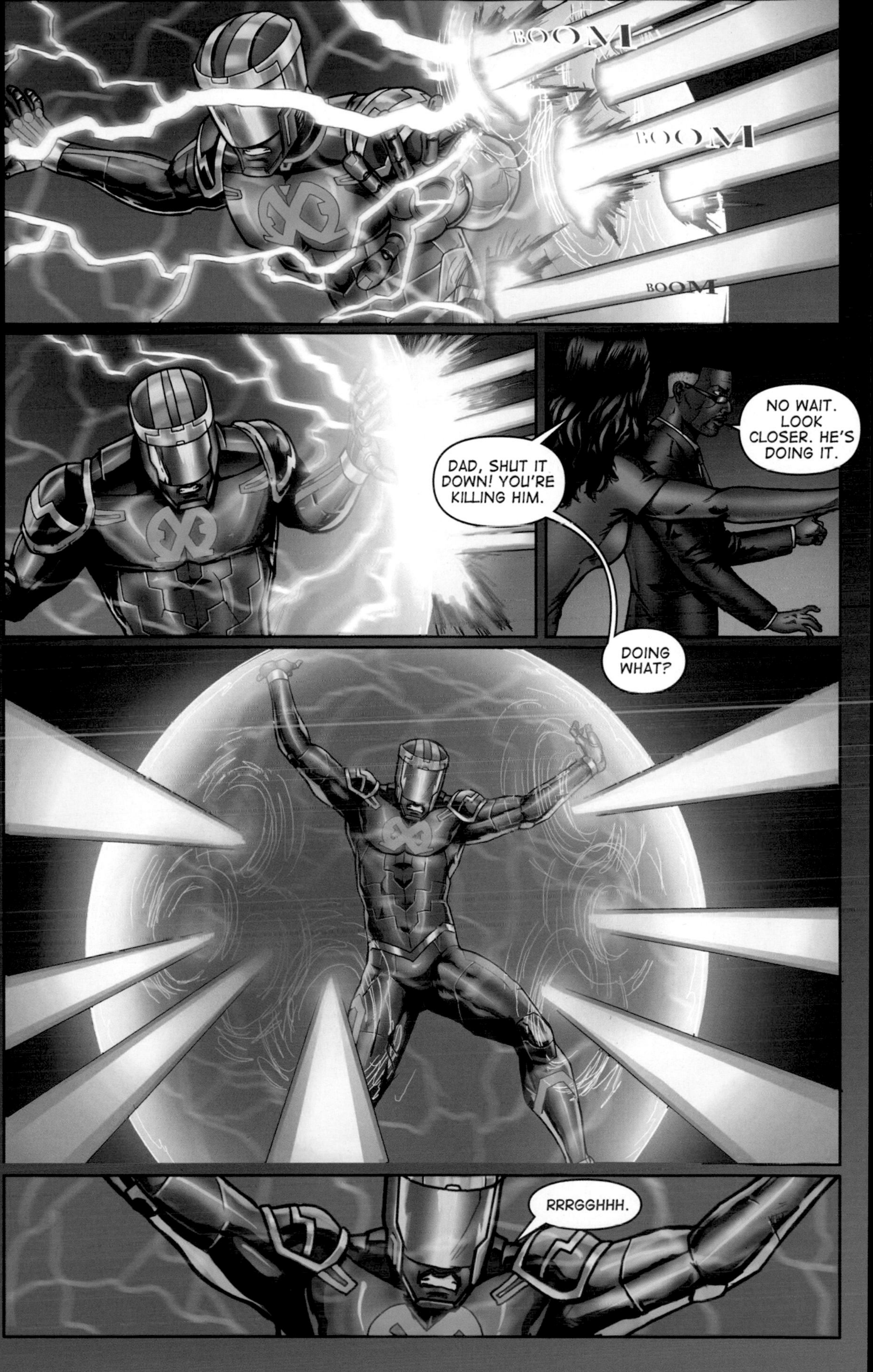
BOOM
BOOM
BOOM
DAD, SHUT IT DOWN! YOU'RE KILLING HIM.
NO WAIT. LOOK CLOSER. HE'S DOING IT.
DOING WHAT?
RRRGGHHH.

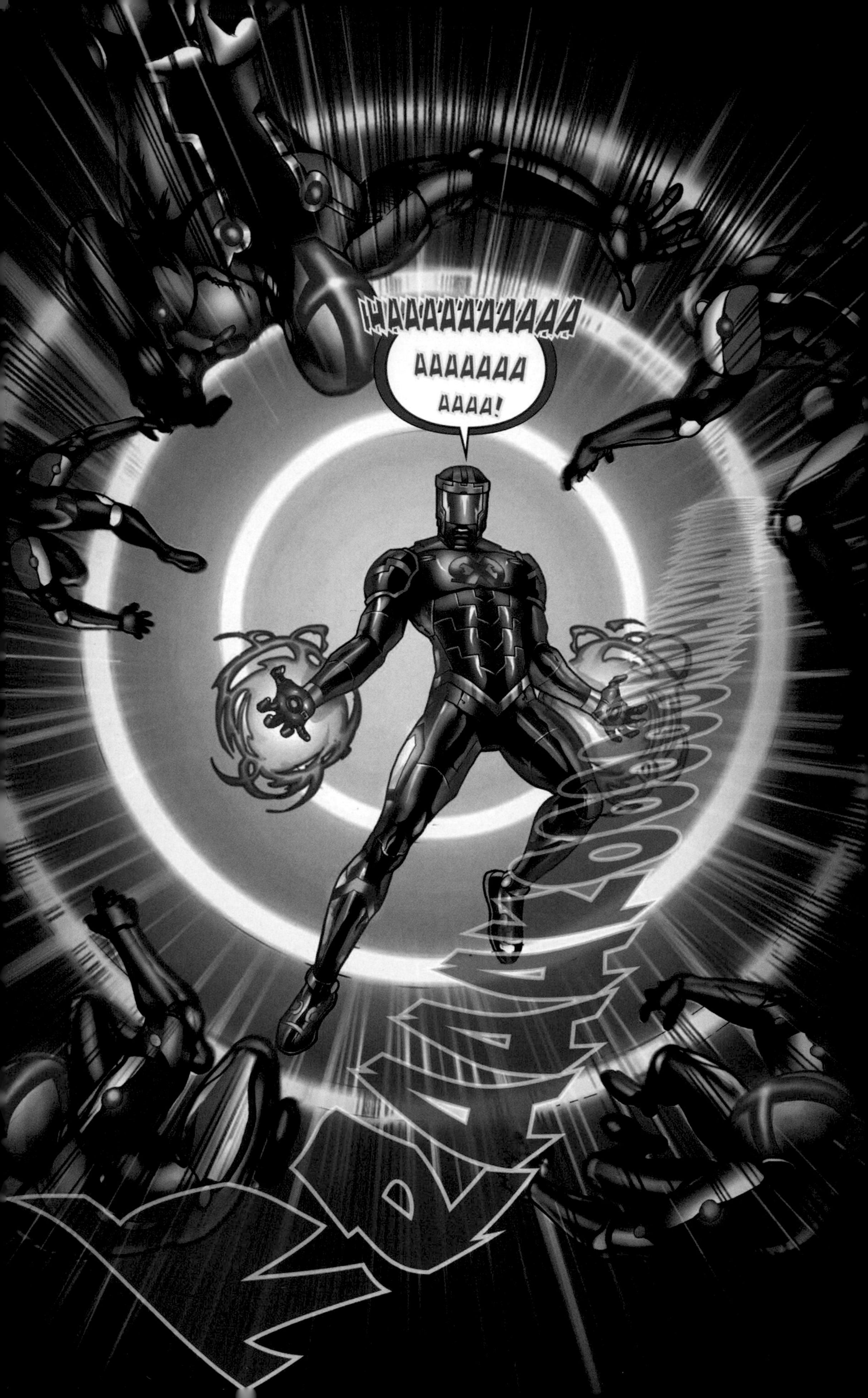
HAAAAAAAAAA
AAAAAAA
AAAA!

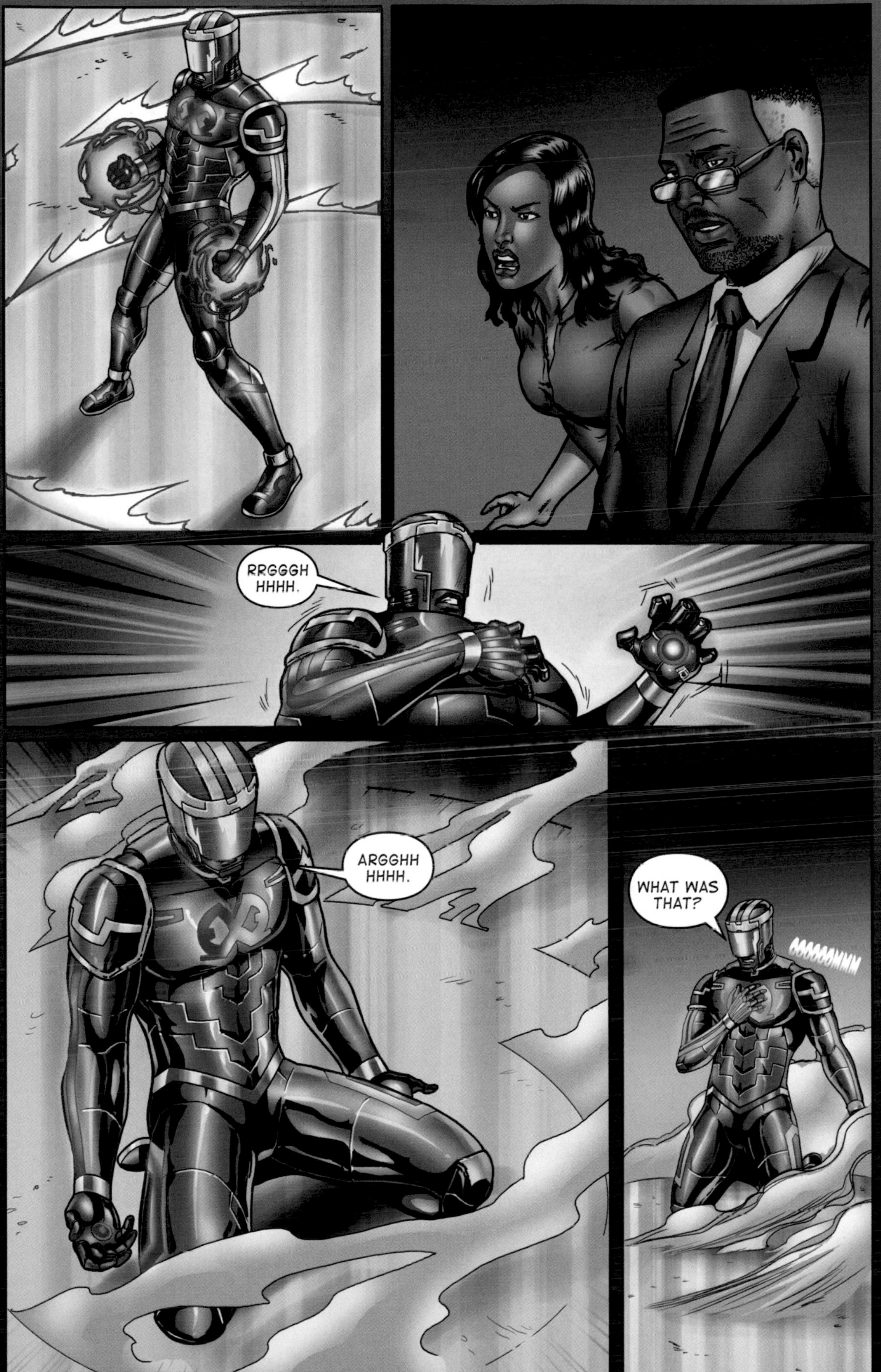
RRGGGH HHHH.
ARGGHH HHHH.
WHAT WAS THAT?
GGGGGMMM

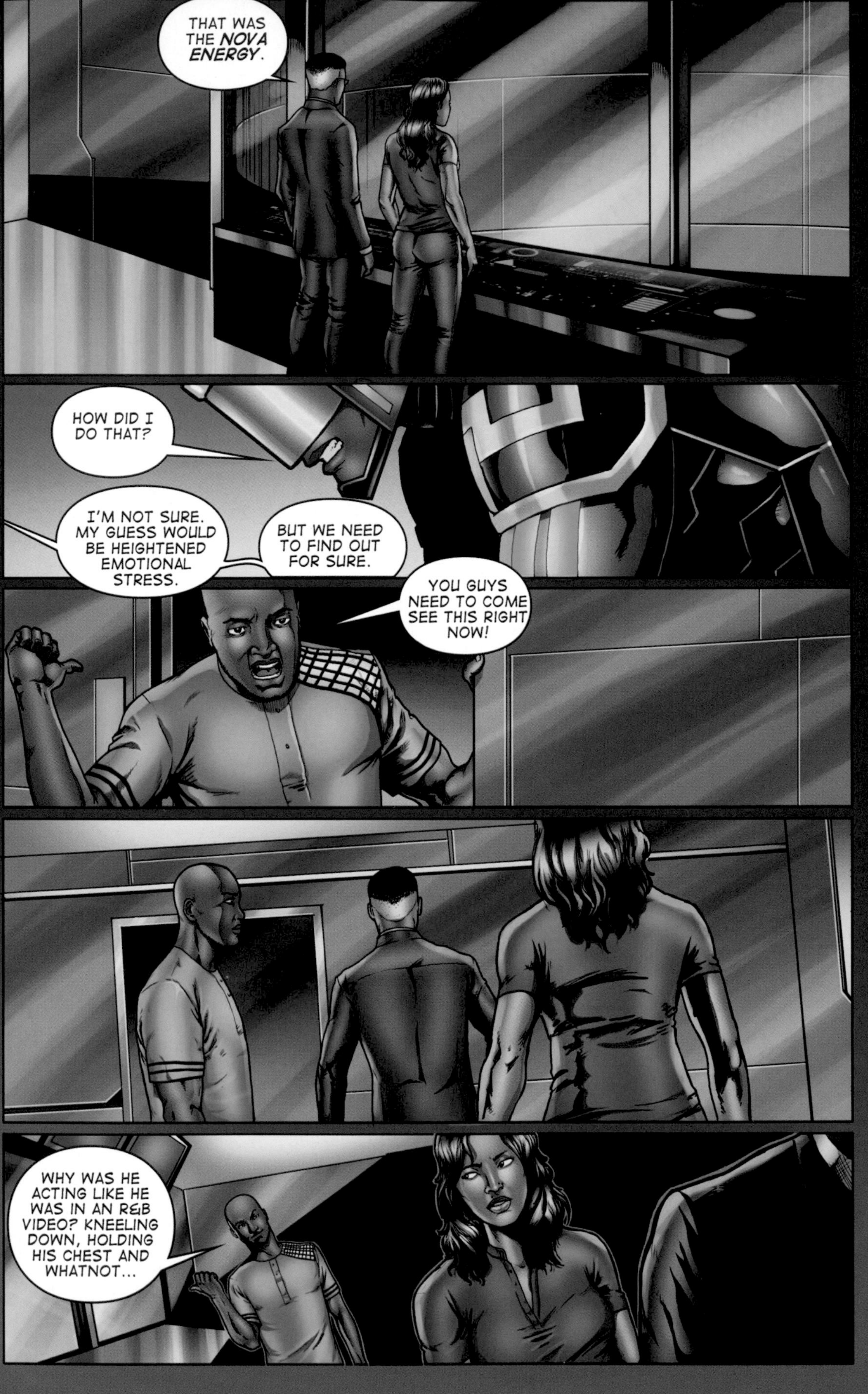
THAT WAS THE NOVA ENERGY.
HOW DID I DO THAT?
I'M NOT SURE. MY GUESS WOULD BE HEIGHTENED EMOTIONAL STRESS.
BUT WE NEED TO FIND OUT FOR SURE.
YOU GUYS NEED TO COME SEE THIS RIGHT NOW!
WHY WAS HE ACTING LIKE HE WAS IN AN R&B VIDEO? KNEELING DOWN, HOLDING HIS CHEST AND WHATNOT...

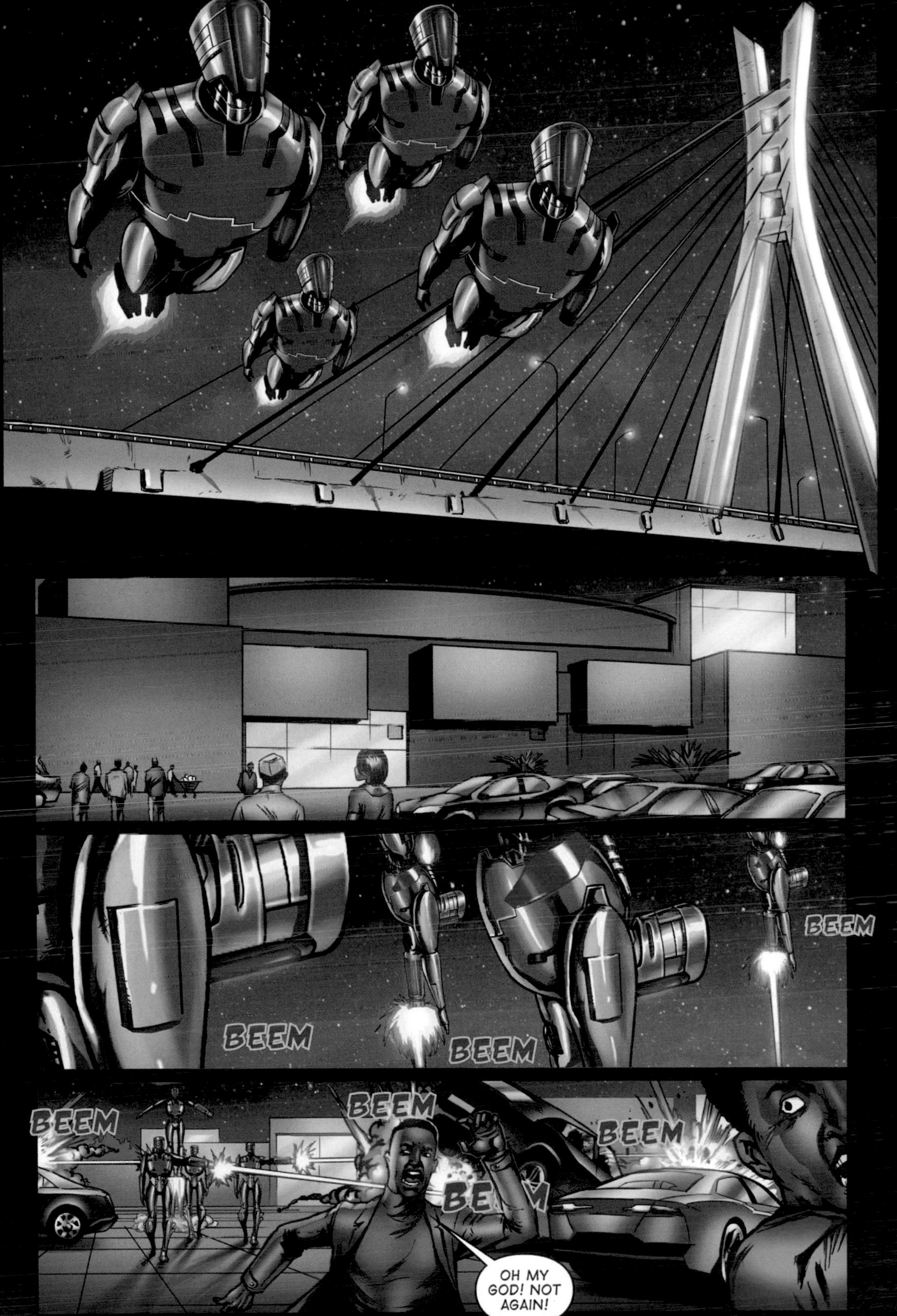
BEEM
BEEM
BEEM
BEEM
BEEM
BEEM
BEEM
OH MY GOD! NOT AGAIN!

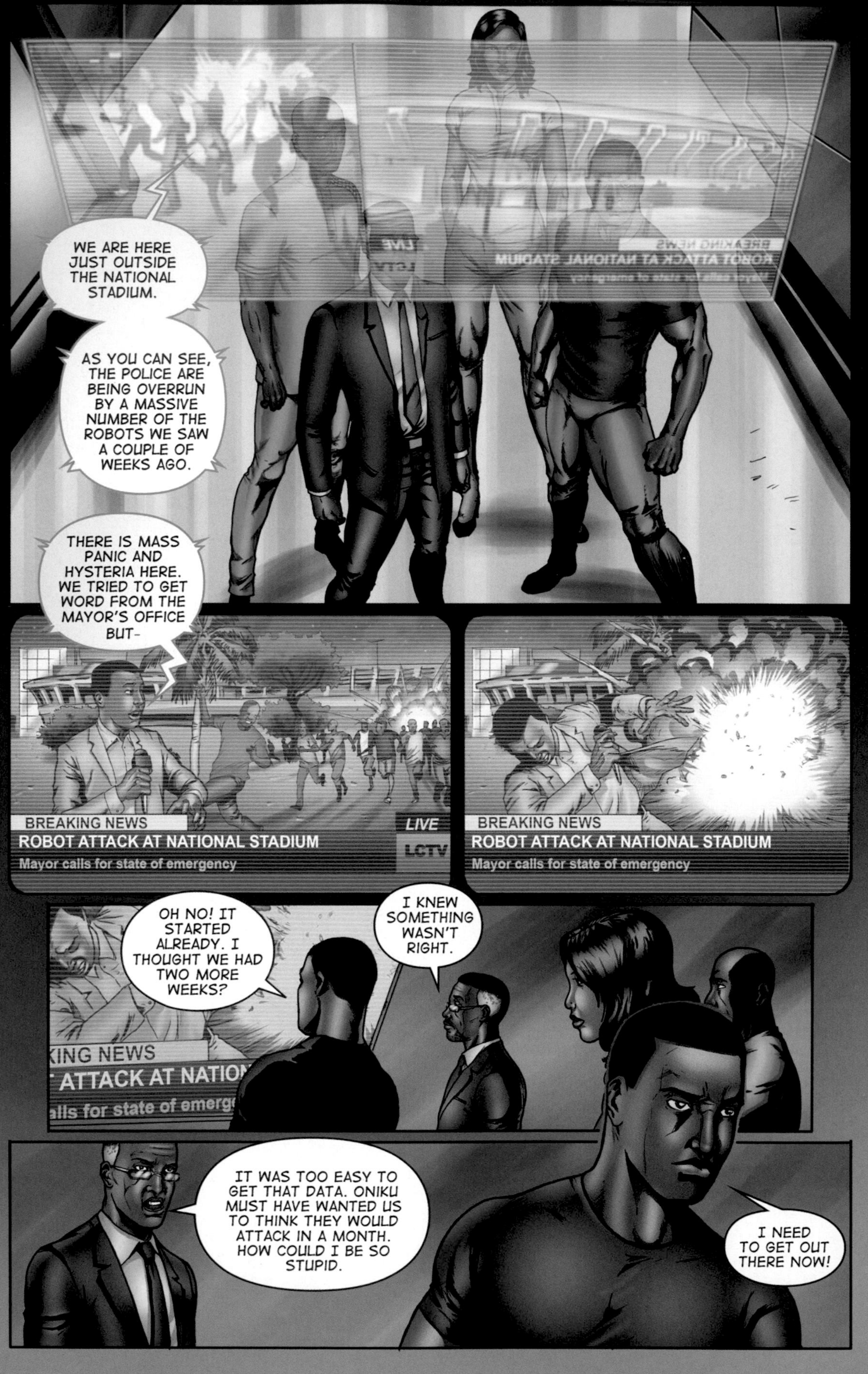
BREAKING NEWS
ROBOT ATTACK AT NATIONAL STADIUM
WE ARE HERE JUST OUTSIDE THE NATIONAL STADIUM.
AS YOU CAN SEE, THE POLICE ARE BEING OVERRUN BY A MASSIVE NUMBER OF THE ROBOTS WE SAW A COUPLE OF WEEKS AGO.
THERE IS MASS PANIC AND HYSTERIA HERE. WE TRIED TO GET WORD FROM THE MAYOR'S OFFICE BUT-
BREAKING NEWS
LIVE
ROBOT ATTACK AT NATIONAL STADIUM
LCTV
Mayor calls for state of emergency
BREAKING NEWS
ROBOT ATTACK AT NATIONAL STADIUM
Mayor calls for state of emergency
OH NO! IT STARTED ALREADY. I THOUGHT WE HAD TWO MORE WEEKS?
I KNEW SOMETHING WASN'T RIGHT.
KING NEWS
T ATTACK AT NATION
alls for state of emerg
IT WAS TOO EASY TO GET THAT DATA. ONIKU MUST HAVE WANTED US TO THINK THEY WOULD ATTACK IN A MONTH. HOW COULD I BE SO STUPID.
I NEED TO GET OUT THERE NOW!

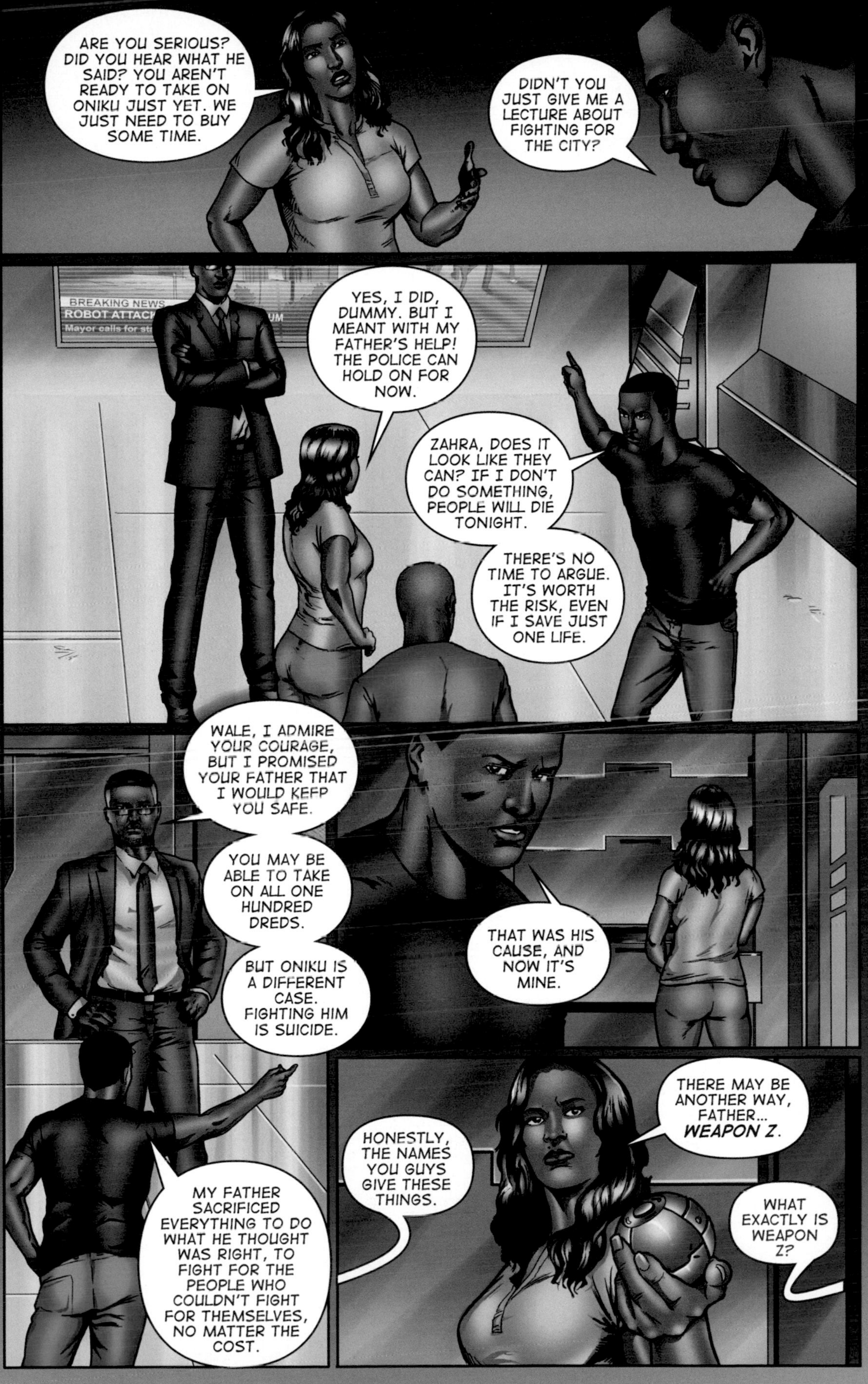
ARE YOU SERIOUS? DID YOU HEAR WHAT HE SAID? YOU AREN'T READY TO TAKE ON ONIKU JUST YET. WE JUST NEED TO BUY SOME TIME.
DIDN'T YOU JUST GIVE ME A LECTURE ABOUT FIGHTING FOR THE CITY?
BREAKING NEWS
ROBOT ATTACK
Mayor calls for sta
YES, I DID, DUMMY. BUT I MEANT WITH MY FATHER'S HELP! THE POLICE CAN HOLD ON FOR NOW.
ZAHRA, DOES IT LOOK LIKE THEY CAN? IF I DON'T DO SOMETHING, PEOPLE WILL DIE TONIGHT.
THERE'S NO TIME TO ARGUE. IT'S WORTH THE RISK, EVEN IF I SAVE JUST ONE LIFE.
WALE, I ADMIRE YOUR COURAGE, BUT I PROMISED YOUR FATHER THAT I WOULD KEEP YOU SAFE.
YOU MAY BE ABLE TO TAKE ON ALL ONE HUNDRED DREDS.
BUT ONIKU IS A DIFFERENT CASE. FIGHTING HIM IS SUICIDE.
THAT WAS HIS CAUSE, AND NOW IT'S MINE.
MY FATHER SACRIFICED EVERYTHING TO DO WHAT HE THOUGHT WAS RIGHT, TO FIGHT FOR THE PEOPLE WHO COULDN'T FIGHT FOR THEMSELVES, NO MATTER THE COST.
HONESTLY, THE NAMES YOU GUYS GIVE THESE THINGS.
THERE MAY BE ANOTHER WAY, FATHER... WEAPON Z.
WHAT EXACTLY IS WEAPON Z?

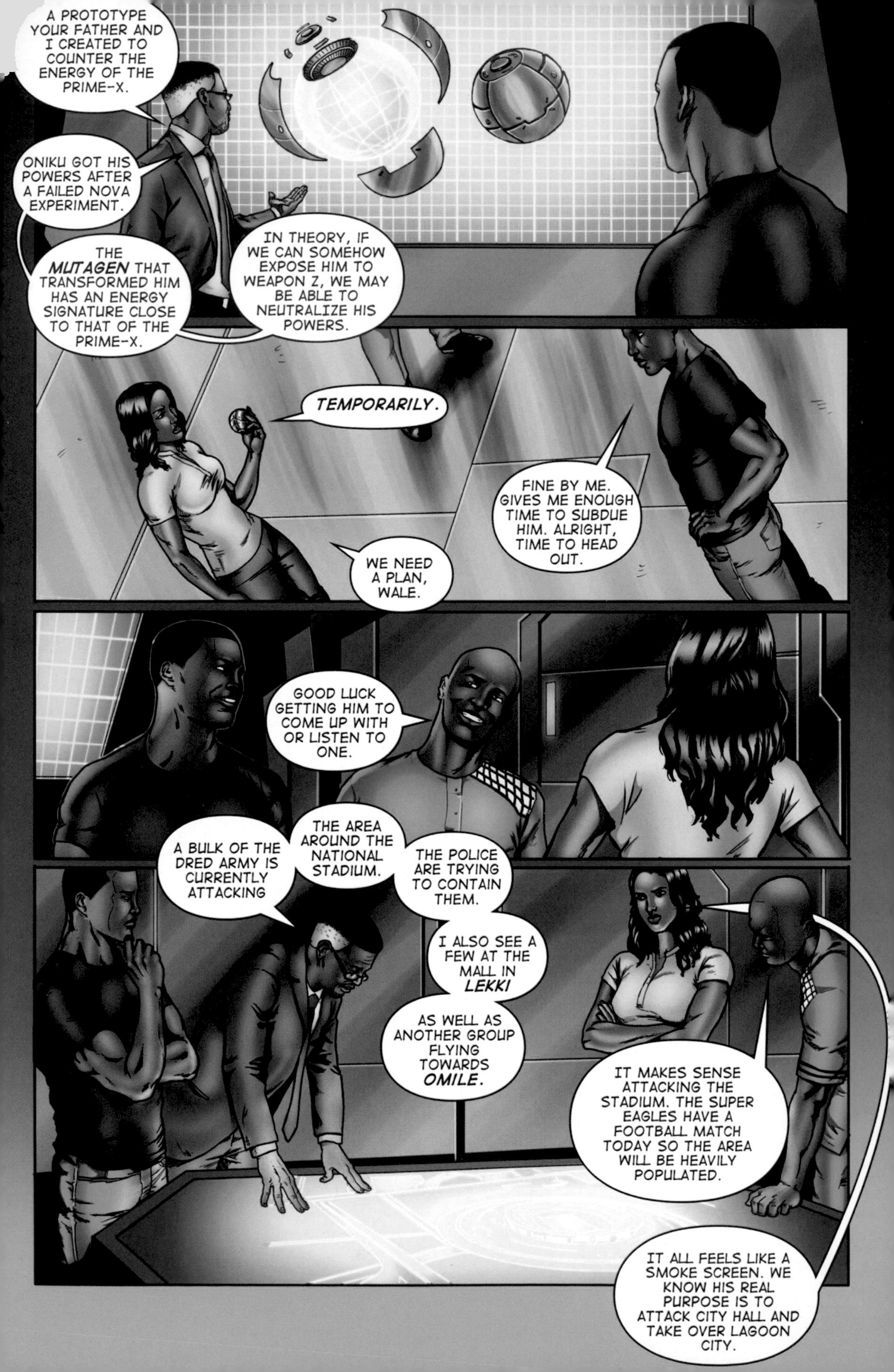
A PROTOTYPE YOUR FATHER AND I CREATED TO COUNTER THE ENERGY OF THE PRIME-X.
ONIKU GOT HIS POWERS AFTER A FAILED NOVA EXPERIMENT.
THE *MUTAGEN* THAT TRANSFORMED HIM HAS AN ENERGY SIGNATURE CLOSE TO THAT OF THE PRIME-X.
IN THEORY, IF WE CAN SOMEHOW EXPOSE HIM TO WEAPON Z, WE MAY BE ABLE TO NEUTRALIZE HIS POWERS.
TEMPORARILY.
FINE BY ME. GIVES ME ENOUGH TIME TO SUBDUE HIM. ALRIGHT, TIME TO HEAD OUT.
WE NEED A PLAN, WALE.
GOOD LUCK GETTING HIM TO COME UP WITH OR LISTEN TO ONE.
A BULK OF THE DRED ARMY IS CURRENTLY ATTACKING
THE AREA AROUND THE NATIONAL STADIUM.
THE POLICE ARE TRYING TO CONTAIN THEM.
I ALSO SEE A FEW AT THE MALL IN *LEKKI*
AS WELL AS ANOTHER GROUP FLYING TOWARDS *OMILE*.
IT MAKES SENSE ATTACKING THE STADIUM. THE SUPER EAGLES HAVE A FOOTBALL MATCH TODAY SO THE AREA WILL BE HEAVILY POPULATED.
IT ALL FEELS LIKE A SMOKE SCREEN. WE KNOW HIS REAL PURPOSE IS TO ATTACK CITY HALL AND TAKE OVER LAGOON CITY.

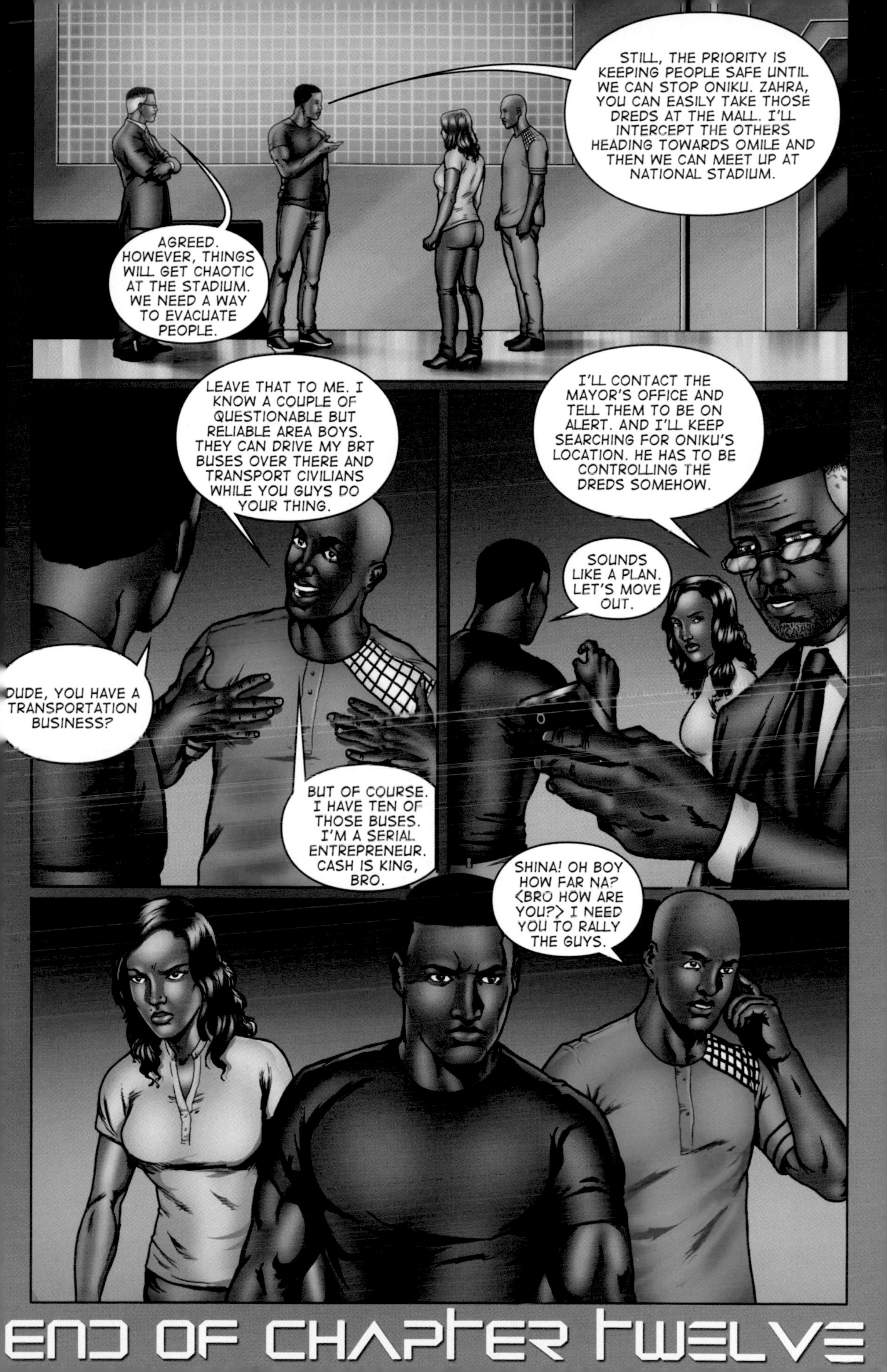
STILL, THE PRIORITY IS KEEPING PEOPLE SAFE UNTIL WE CAN STOP ONIKU. ZAHRA, YOU CAN EASILY TAKE THOSE DREDS AT THE MALL. I'LL INTERCEPT THE OTHERS HEADING TOWARDS OMILE AND THEN WE CAN MEET UP AT NATIONAL STADIUM.
AGREED. HOWEVER, THINGS WILL GET CHAOTIC AT THE STADIUM. WE NEED A WAY TO EVACUATE PEOPLE.
LEAVE THAT TO ME. I KNOW A COUPLE OF QUESTIONABLE BUT RELIABLE AREA BOYS. THEY CAN DRIVE MY BRT BUSES OVER THERE AND TRANSPORT CIVILIANS WHILE YOU GUYS DO YOUR THING.
DUDE, YOU HAVE A TRANSPORTATION BUSINESS?
BUT OF COURSE. I HAVE TEN OF THOSE BUSES. I'M A SERIAL ENTREPRENEUR. CASH IS KING, BRO.
I'LL CONTACT THE MAYOR'S OFFICE AND TELL THEM TO BE ON ALERT. AND I'LL KEEP SEARCHING FOR ONIKU'S LOCATION. HE HAS TO BE CONTROLLING THE DREDS SOMEHOW.
SOUNDS LIKE A PLAN. LET'S MOVE OUT.
SHINA! OH BOY HOW FAR NA? <BRO HOW ARE YOU?> I NEED YOU TO RALLY THE GUYS.
END OF CHAPTER TWELVE

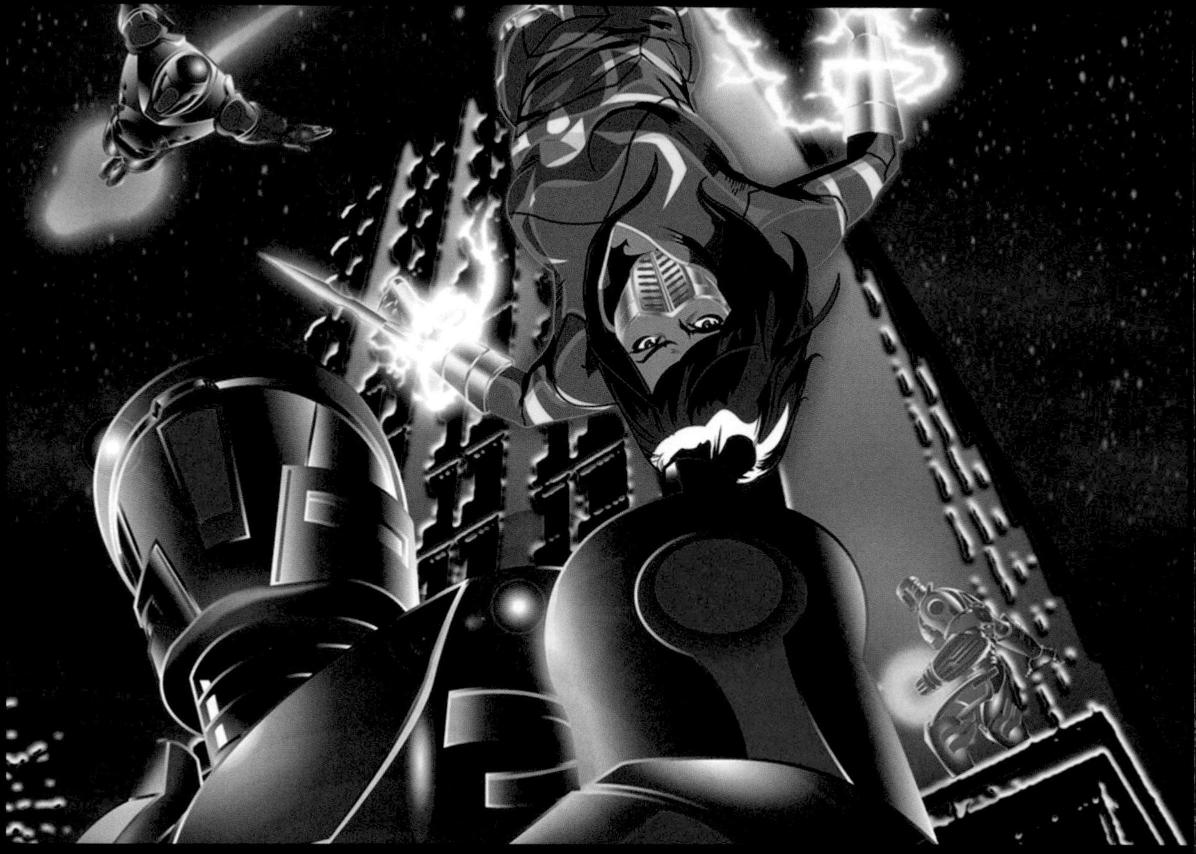

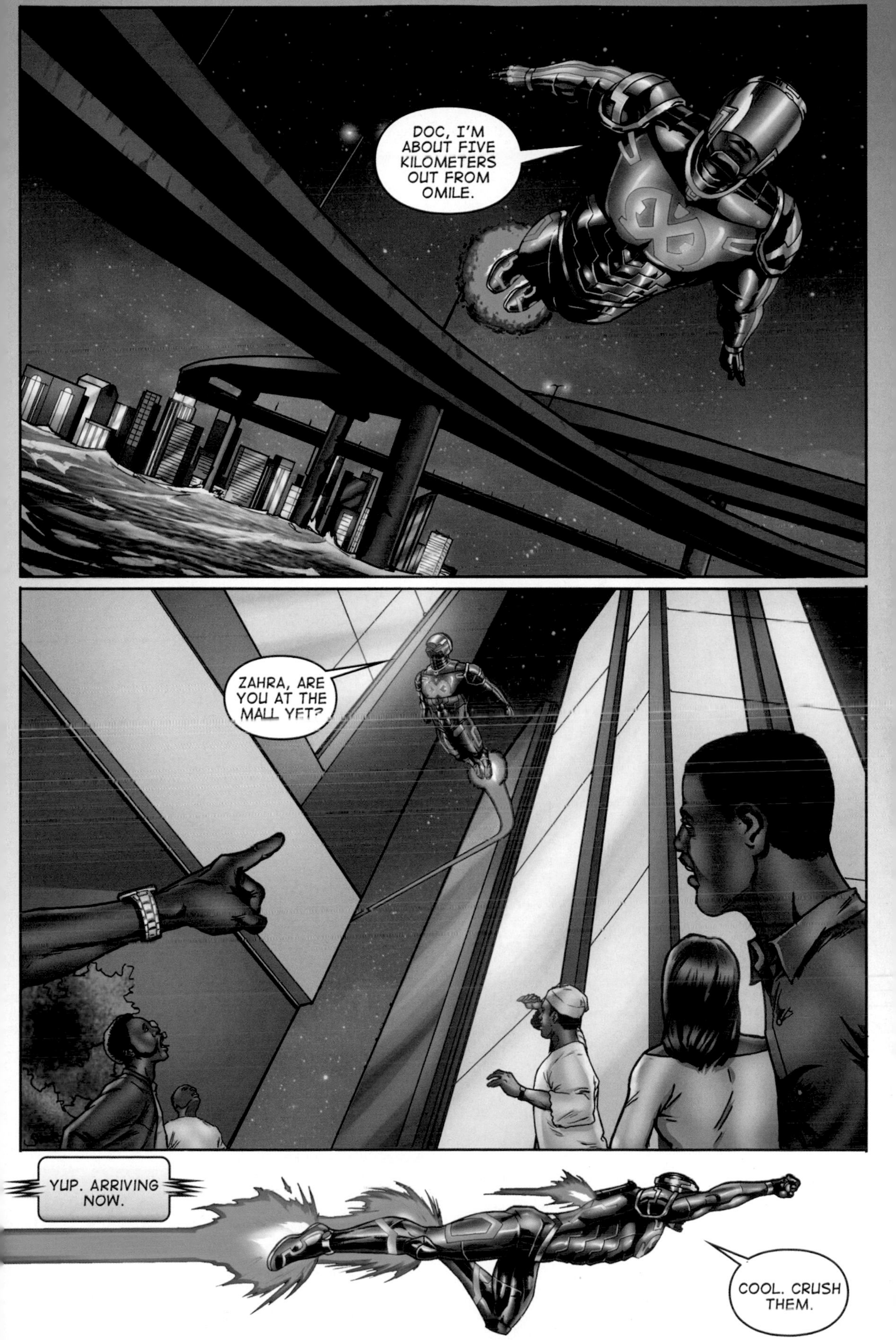
DOC, I'M ABOUT FIVE KILOMETERS OUT FROM OMILE.
ZAHRA, ARE YOU AT THE MALL YET?
YUP. ARRIVING NOW.
COOL. CRUSH THEM.

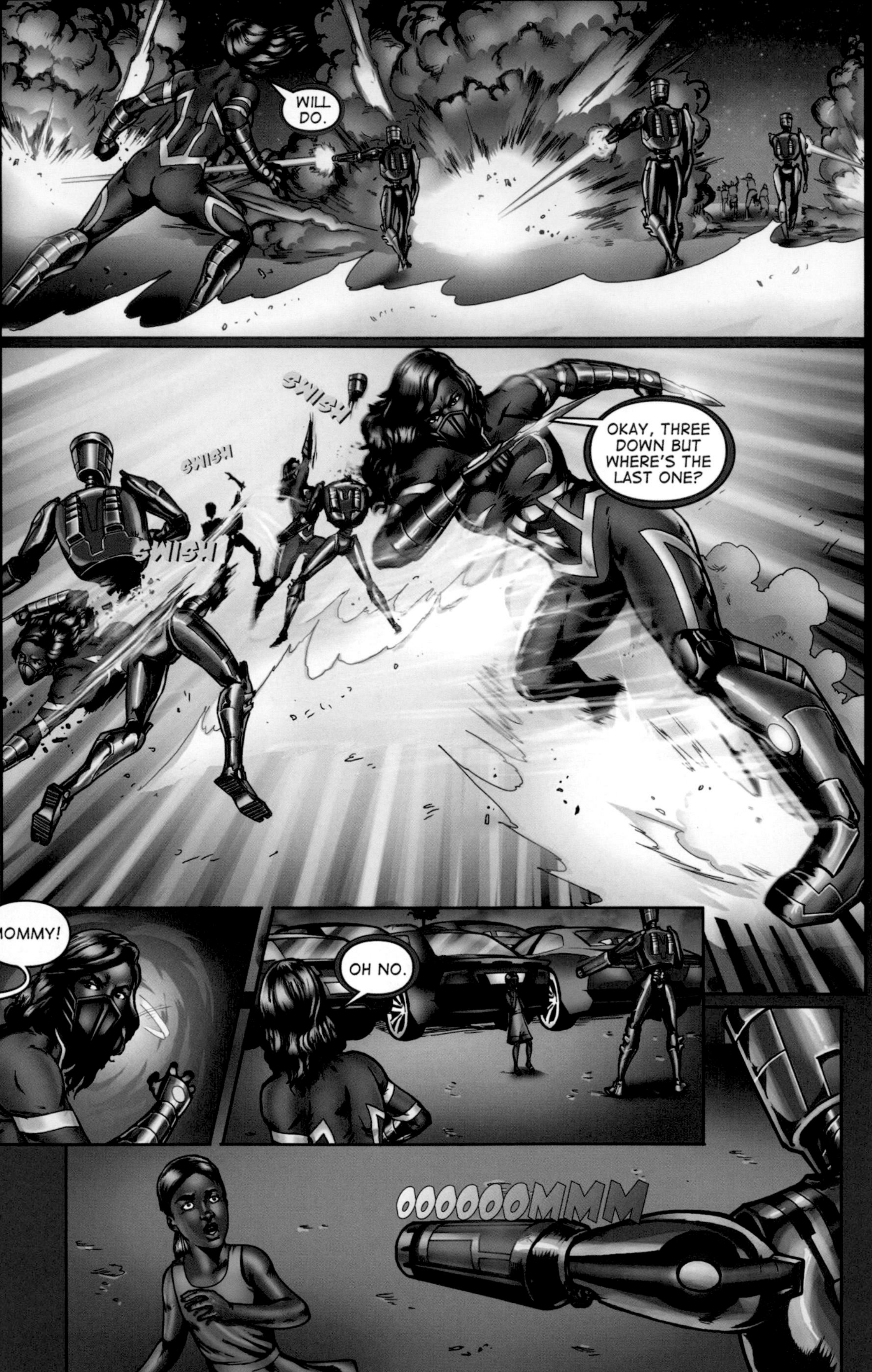

WILL DO.
SWISH
SWISH
SWISH
OKAY, THREE DOWN BUT WHERE'S THE LAST ONE?
MOMMY!
OH NO.
OOOOOOMMMM

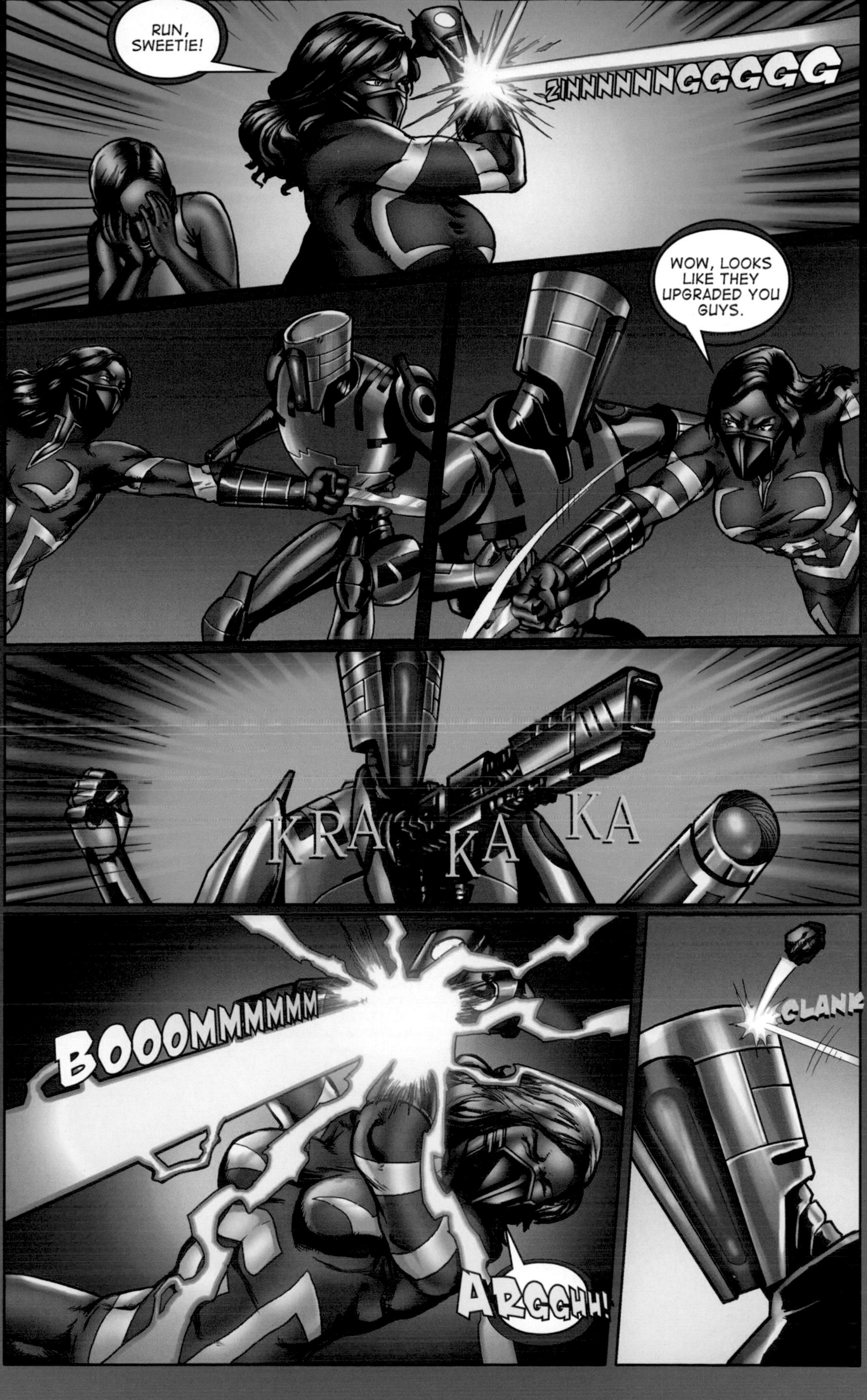
RUN, SWEETIE!
ZINNNNNNGGGGG
WOW, LOOKS LIKE THEY UPGRADED YOU GUYS.
KRA
KA
KA
BOOOMMMMMM
ARGGHH!
CLANK

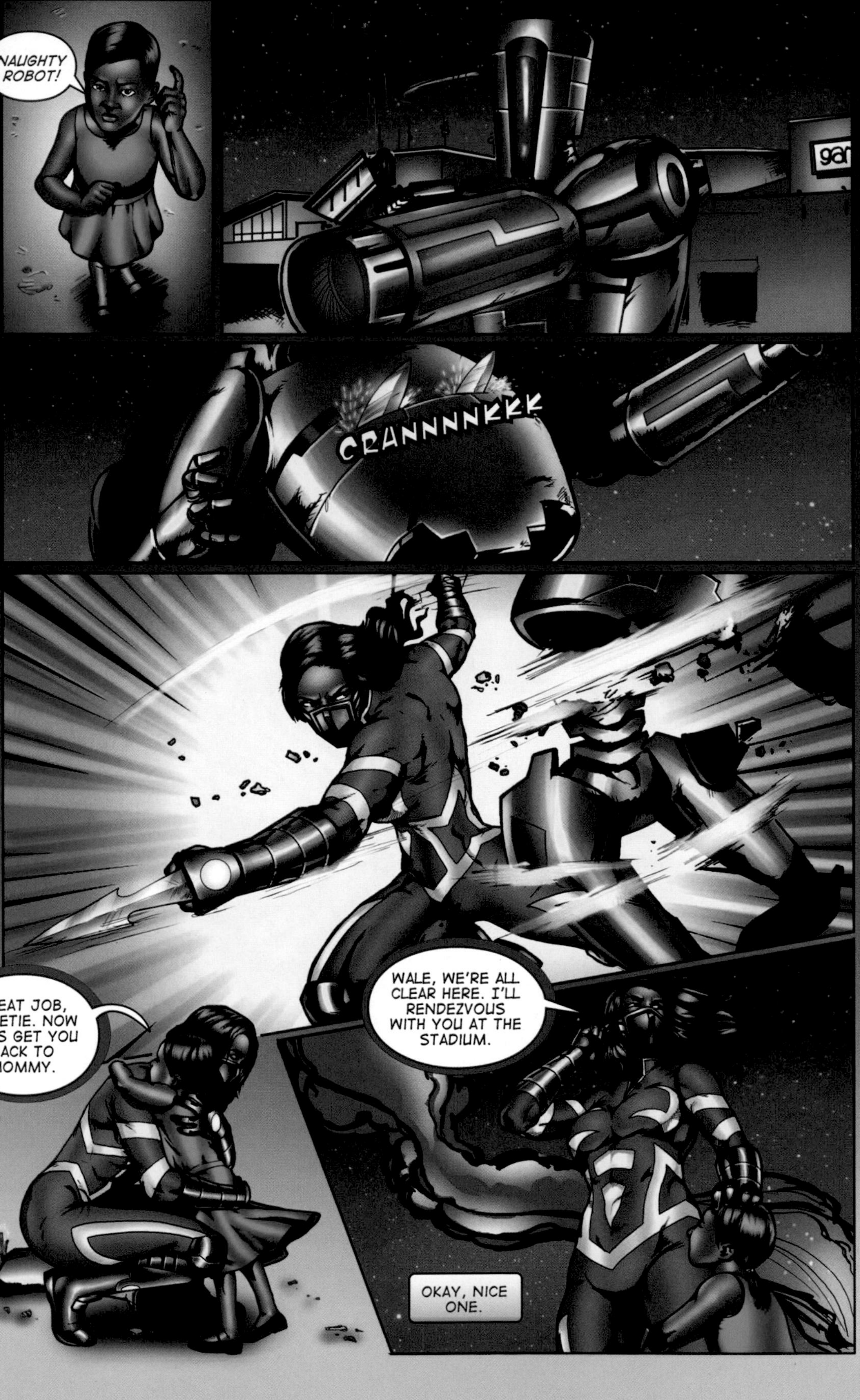
NAUGHTY ROBOT!
CRANNNNKKK
GREAT JOB, SWEETIE. NOW LET'S GET YOU BACK TO MOMMY.
WALE, WE'RE ALL CLEAR HERE. I'LL RENDEZVOUS WITH YOU AT THE STADIUM.
OKAY, NICE ONE.

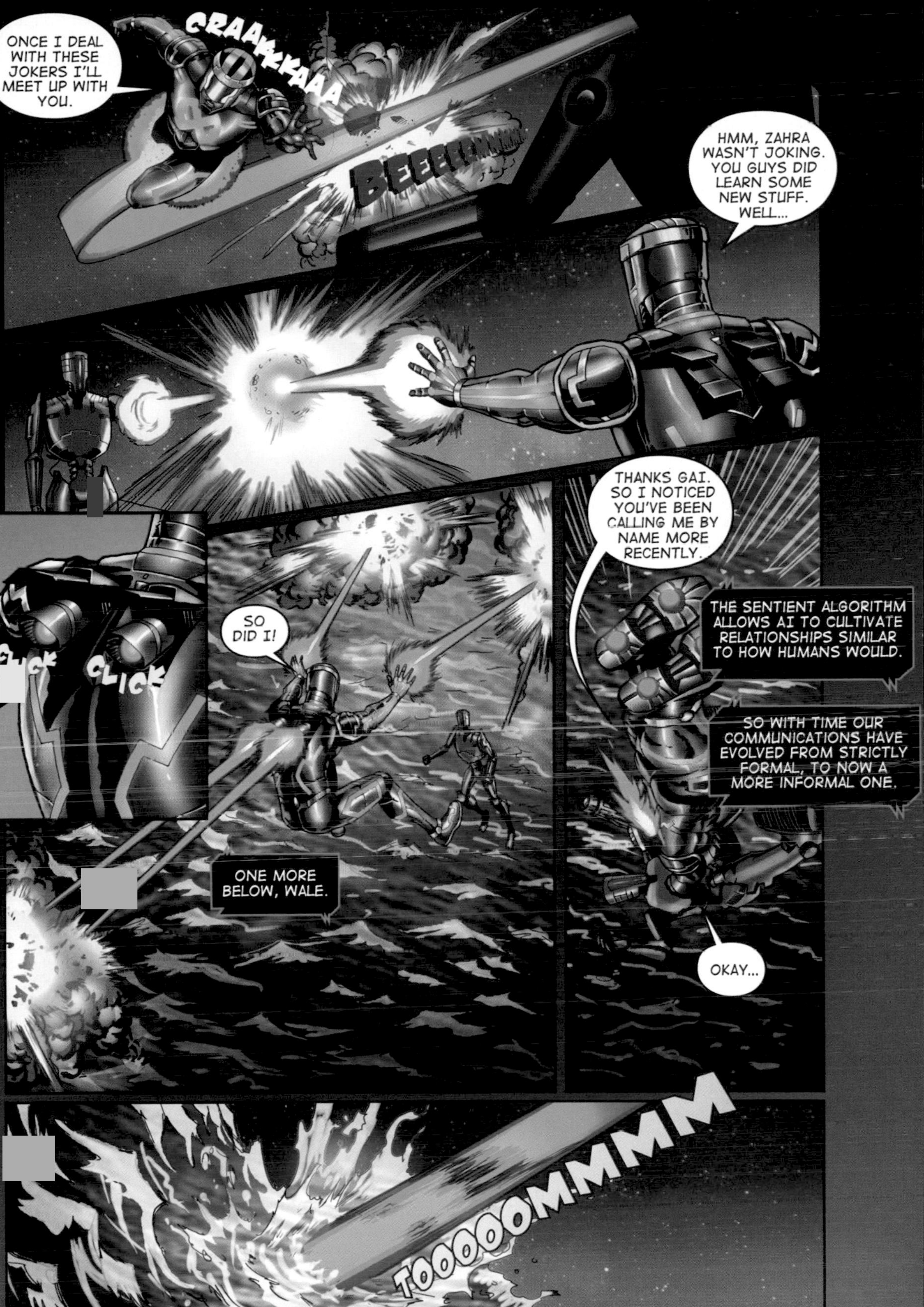
ONCE I DEAL WITH THESE JOKERS I'LL MEET UP WITH YOU.
HMM, ZAHRA WASN'T JOKING. YOU GUYS DID LEARN SOME NEW STUFF. WELL...
CLICK
SO DID I!
THANKS GAI. SO I NOTICED YOU'VE BEEN CALLING ME BY NAME MORE RECENTLY.
THE SENTIENT ALGORITHM ALLOWS AI TO CULTIVATE RELATIONSHIPS SIMILAR TO HOW HUMANS WOULD.
SO WITH TIME OUR COMMUNICATIONS HAVE EVOLVED FROM STRICTLY FORMAL, TO NOW A MORE INFORMAL ONE.
ONE MORE BELOW, WALE.
OKAY...

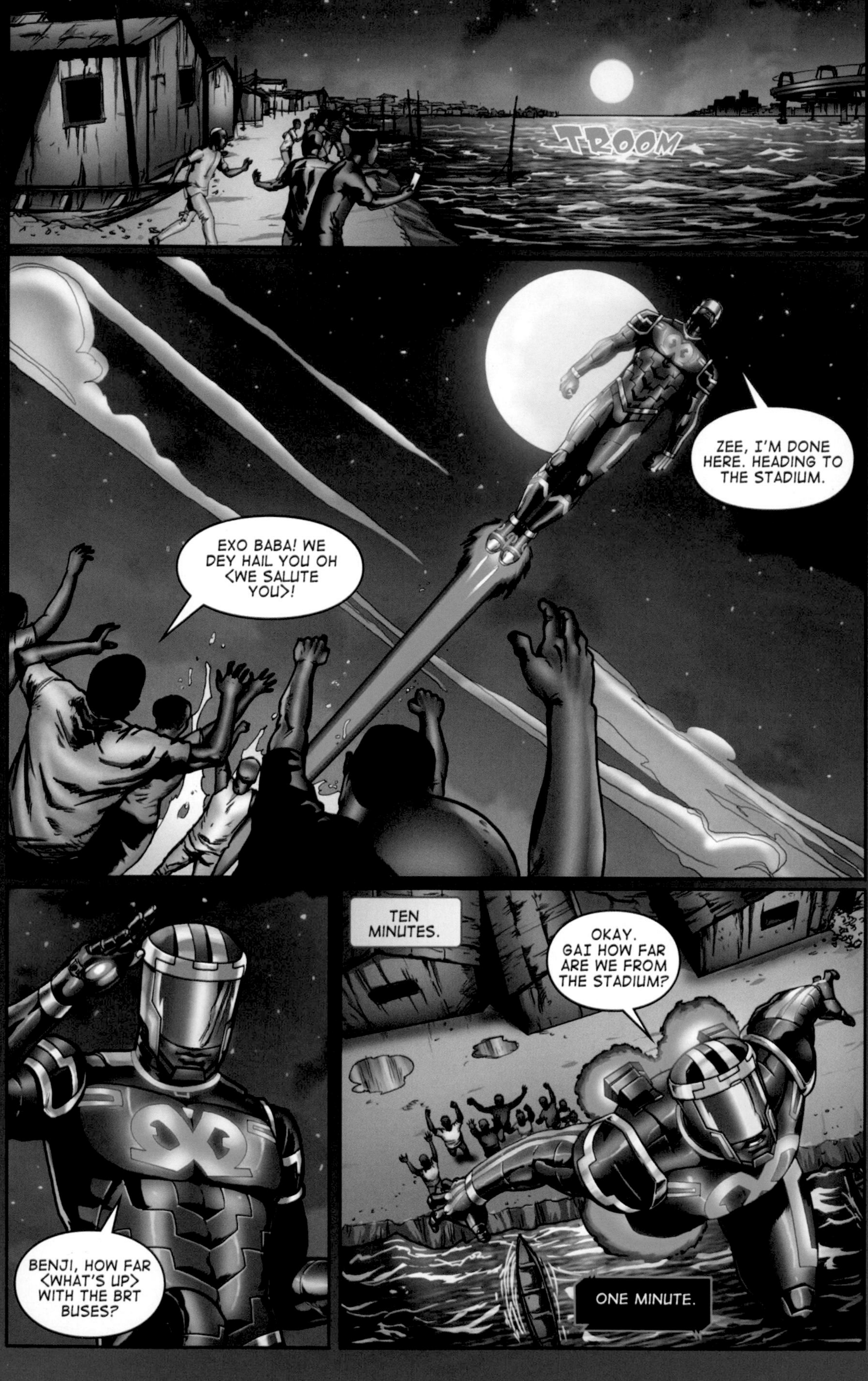
TROOM
ZEE, I'M DONE HERE. HEADING TO THE STADIUM.
EXO BABA! WE DEY HAIL YOU OH <WE SALUTE YOU>!
BENJI, HOW FAR <WHAT'S UP> WITH THE BRT BUSES?
TEN MINUTES.
OKAY. GAI HOW FAR ARE WE FROM THE STADIUM?
ONE MINUTE.

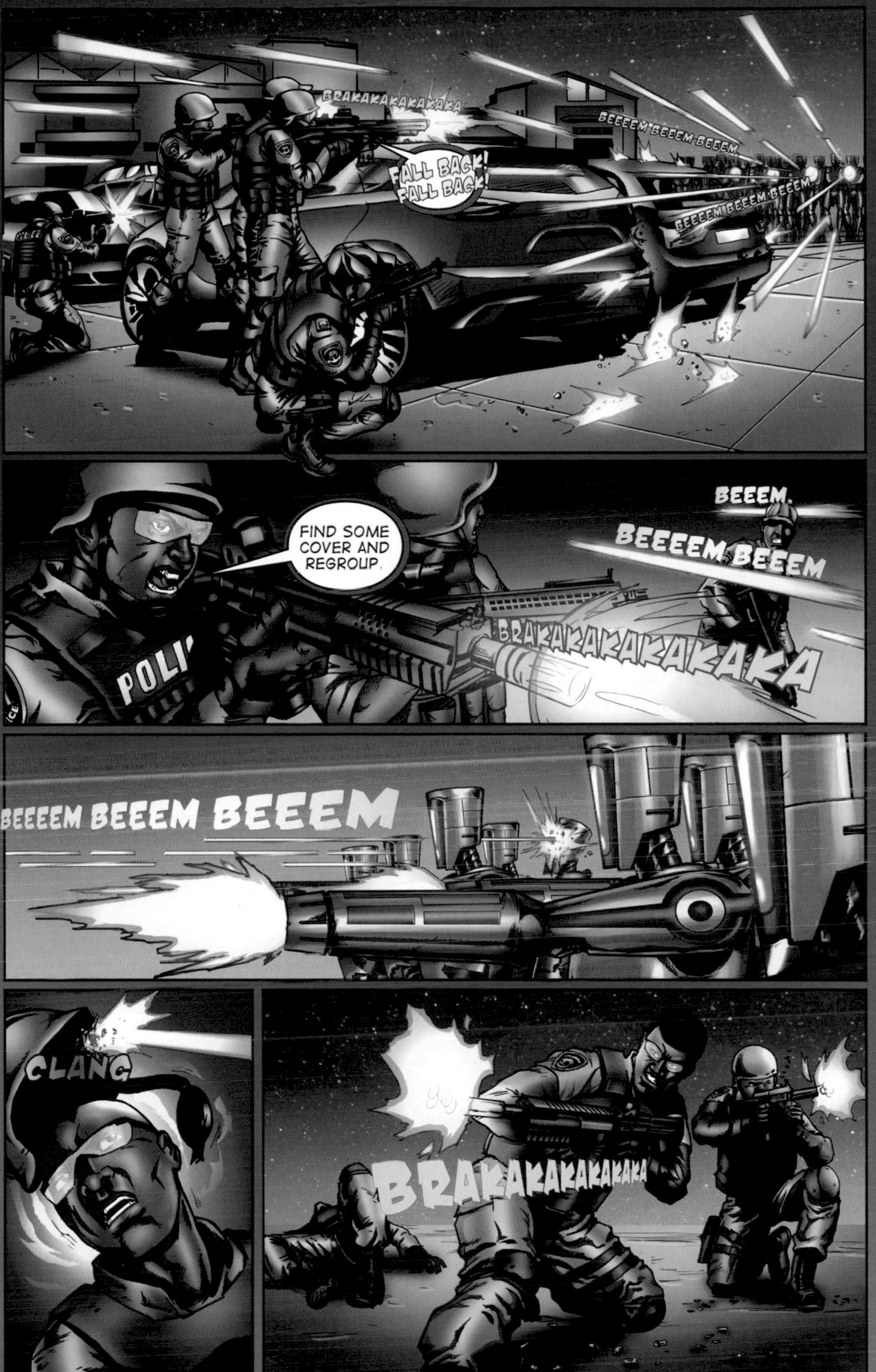
BRAKAKAKAKAKAKA
BEEEEM BEEEM BEEEM.
FALL BACK! FALL BACK!
BEEEEM BEEEM BEEEM
POLICE
BEEEM.
FIND SOME COVER AND REGROUP.
BEEEEM BEEEM
POLI
BRAKAKAKAKAKAKA
BEEEEM BEEEM BEEEM
CLANG
BRAKAKAKAKAKAKA

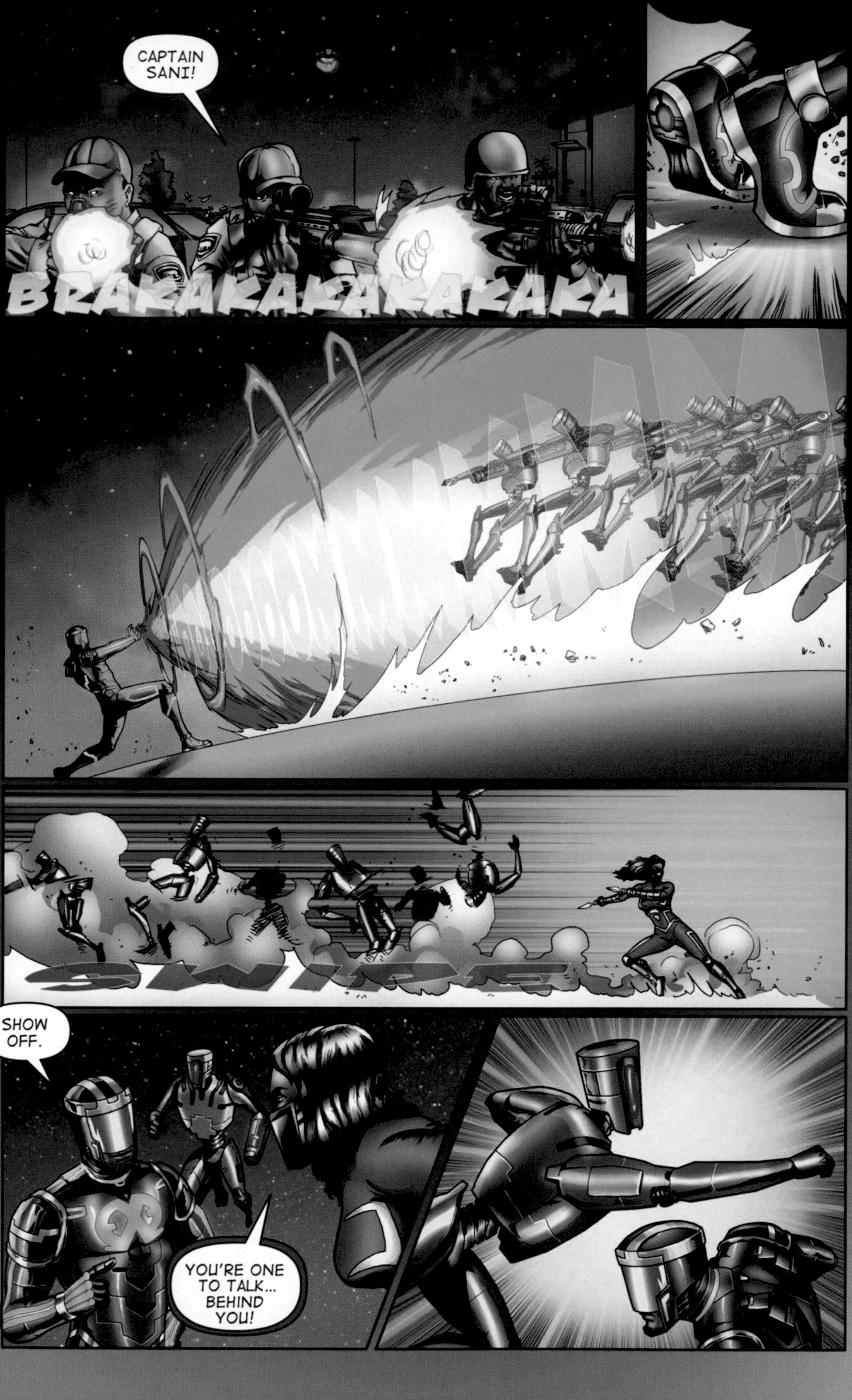
CAPTAIN SANI!
BRAKAKAKAKAKAKA
SHOW OFF.
YOU'RE ONE TO TALK... BEHIND YOU!

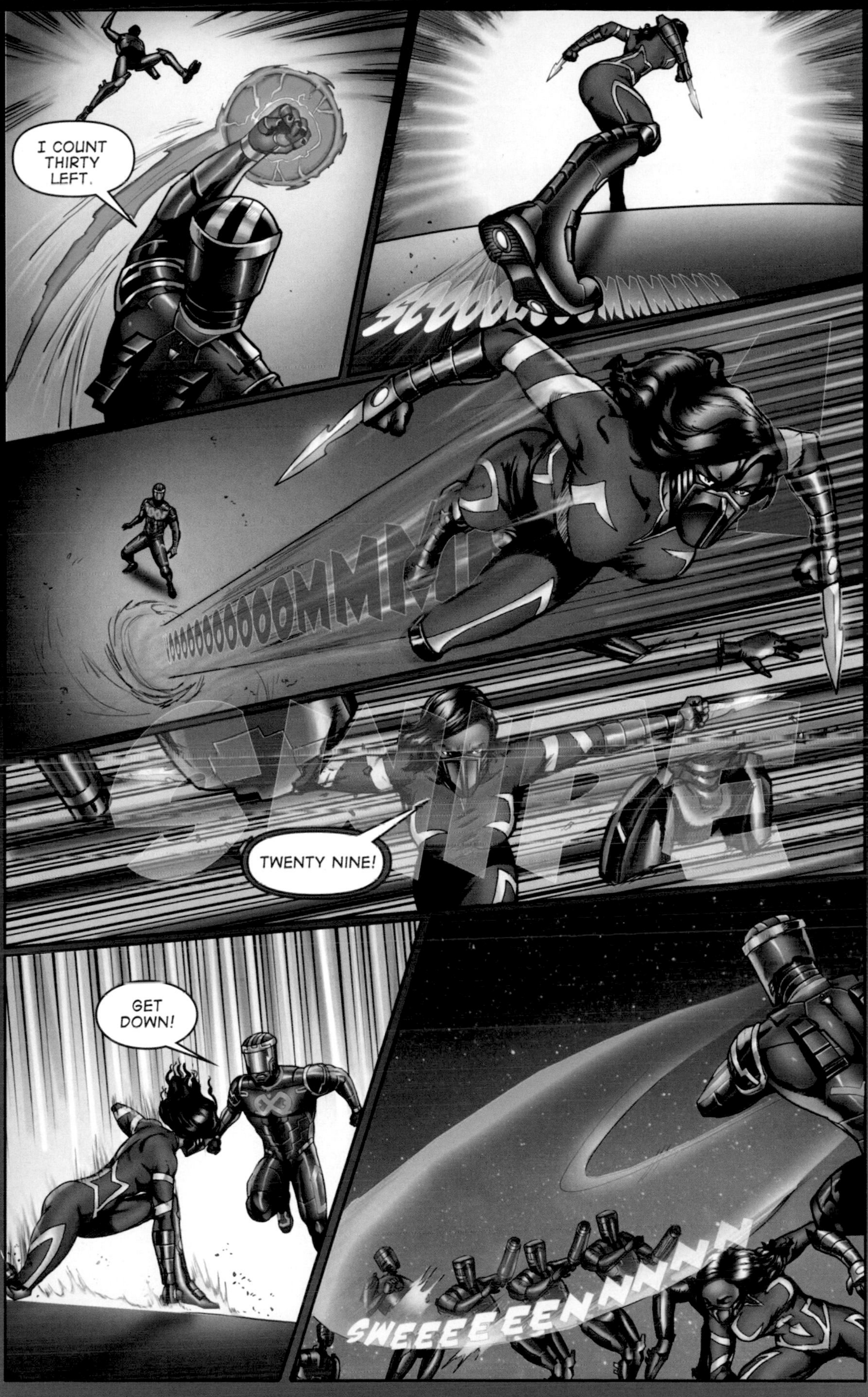
I COUNT THIRTY LEFT.
TWENTY NINE!
GET DOWN!

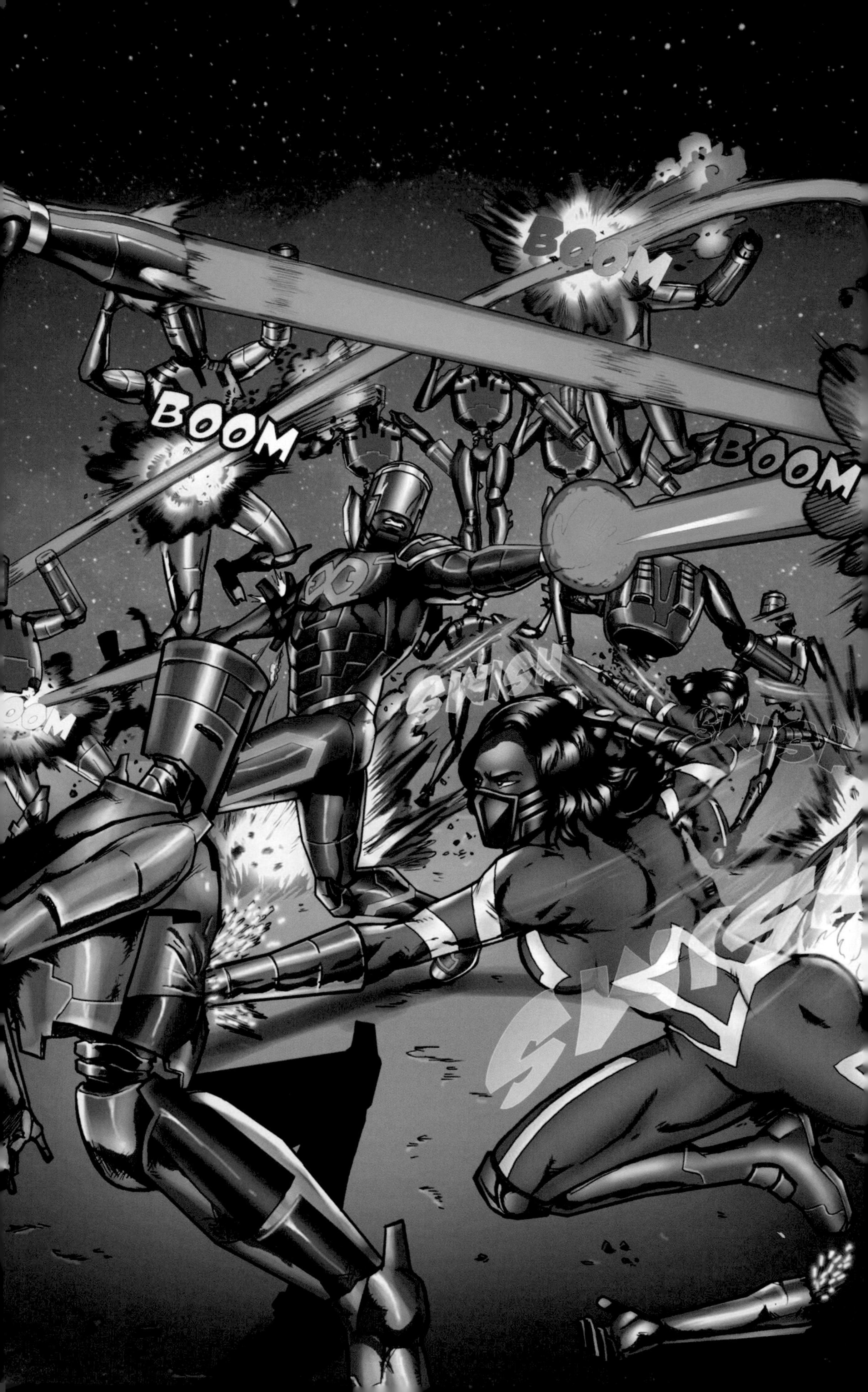
BOOM
BOOM
BOOM
SWISH

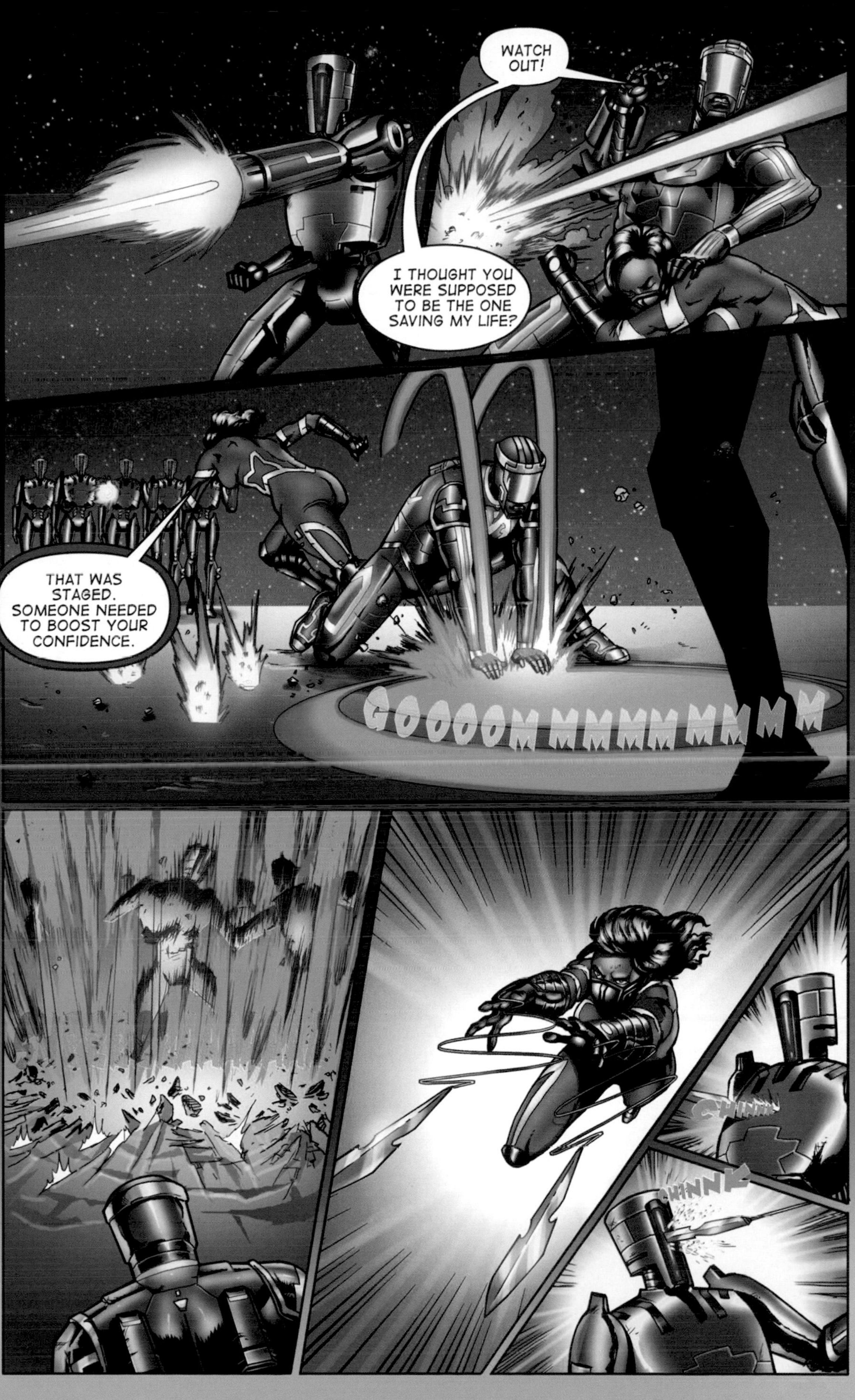
WATCH OUT!
I THOUGHT YOU WERE SUPPOSED TO BE THE ONE SAVING MY LIFE?
THAT WAS STAGED. SOMEONE NEEDED TO BOOST YOUR CONFIDENCE.
GOOOOMMMMMMMMM
CHINNK
CHINNK

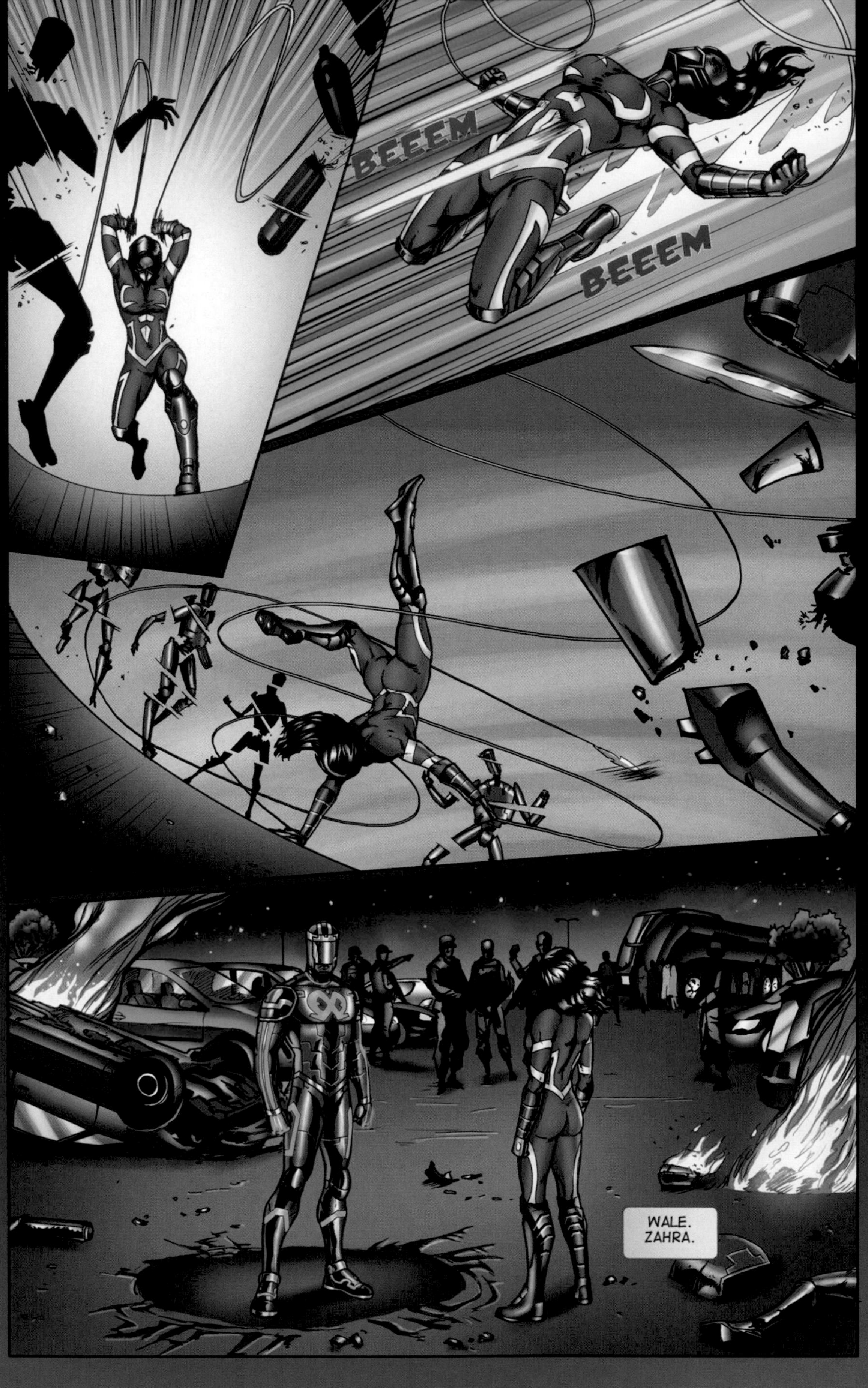
BEEEM
BEEEM
WALE. ZAHRA.

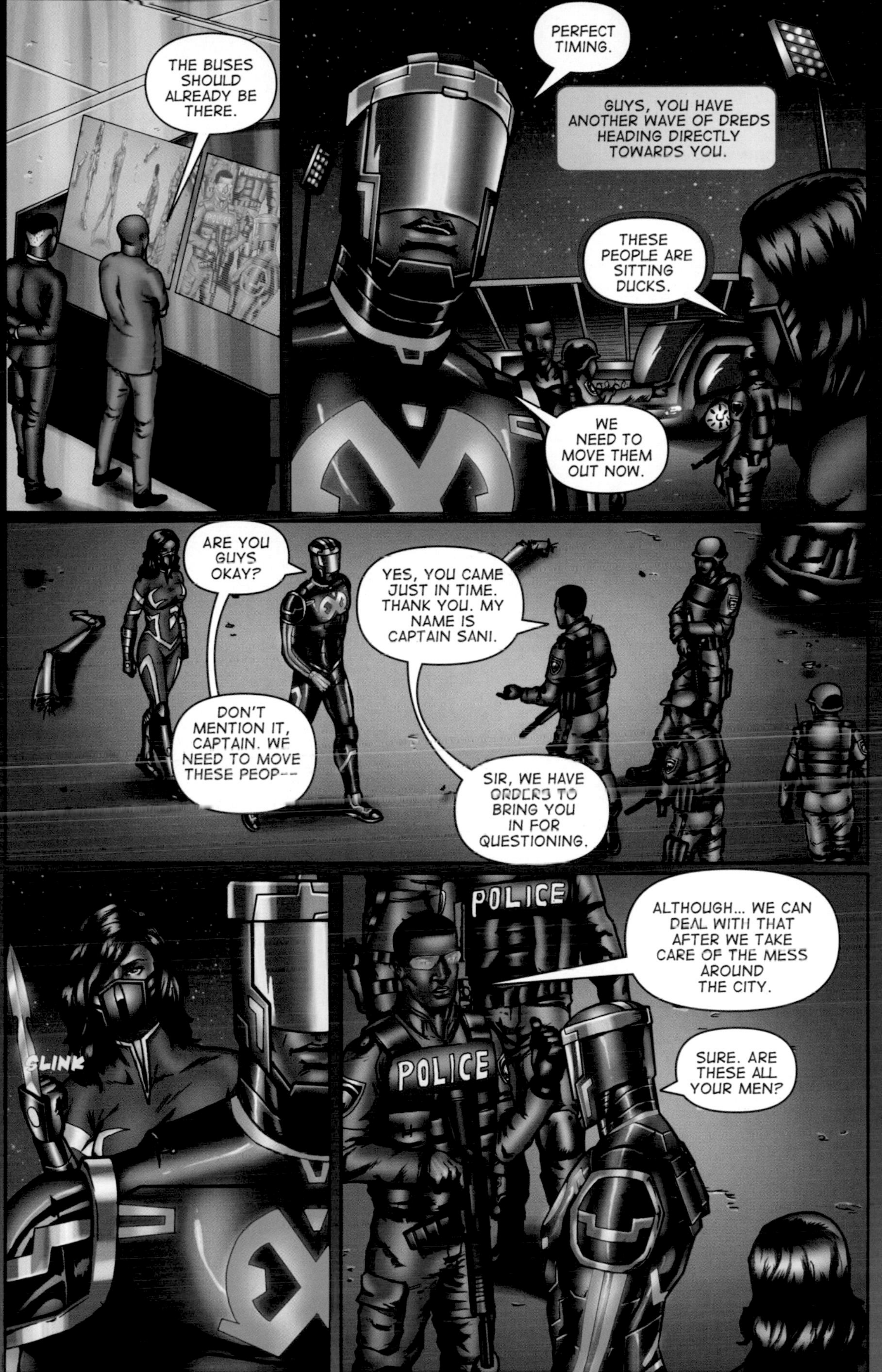

THE BUSES SHOULD ALREADY BE THERE.
PERFECT TIMING.
GUYS, YOU HAVE ANOTHER WAVE OF DREDS HEADING DIRECTLY TOWARDS YOU.
THESE PEOPLE ARE SITTING DUCKS.
WE NEED TO MOVE THEM OUT NOW.
POLICE
ARE YOU GUYS OKAY?
YES, YOU CAME JUST IN TIME. THANK YOU. MY NAME IS CAPTAIN SANI.
DON'T MENTION IT, CAPTAIN. WE NEED TO MOVE THESE PEOP--
SIR, WE HAVE ORDERS TO BRING YOU IN FOR QUESTIONING.
GLINK
POLICE
POLICE
ALTHOUGH... WE CAN DEAL WITH THAT AFTER WE TAKE CARE OF THE MESS AROUND THE CITY.
SURE. ARE THESE ALL YOUR MEN?

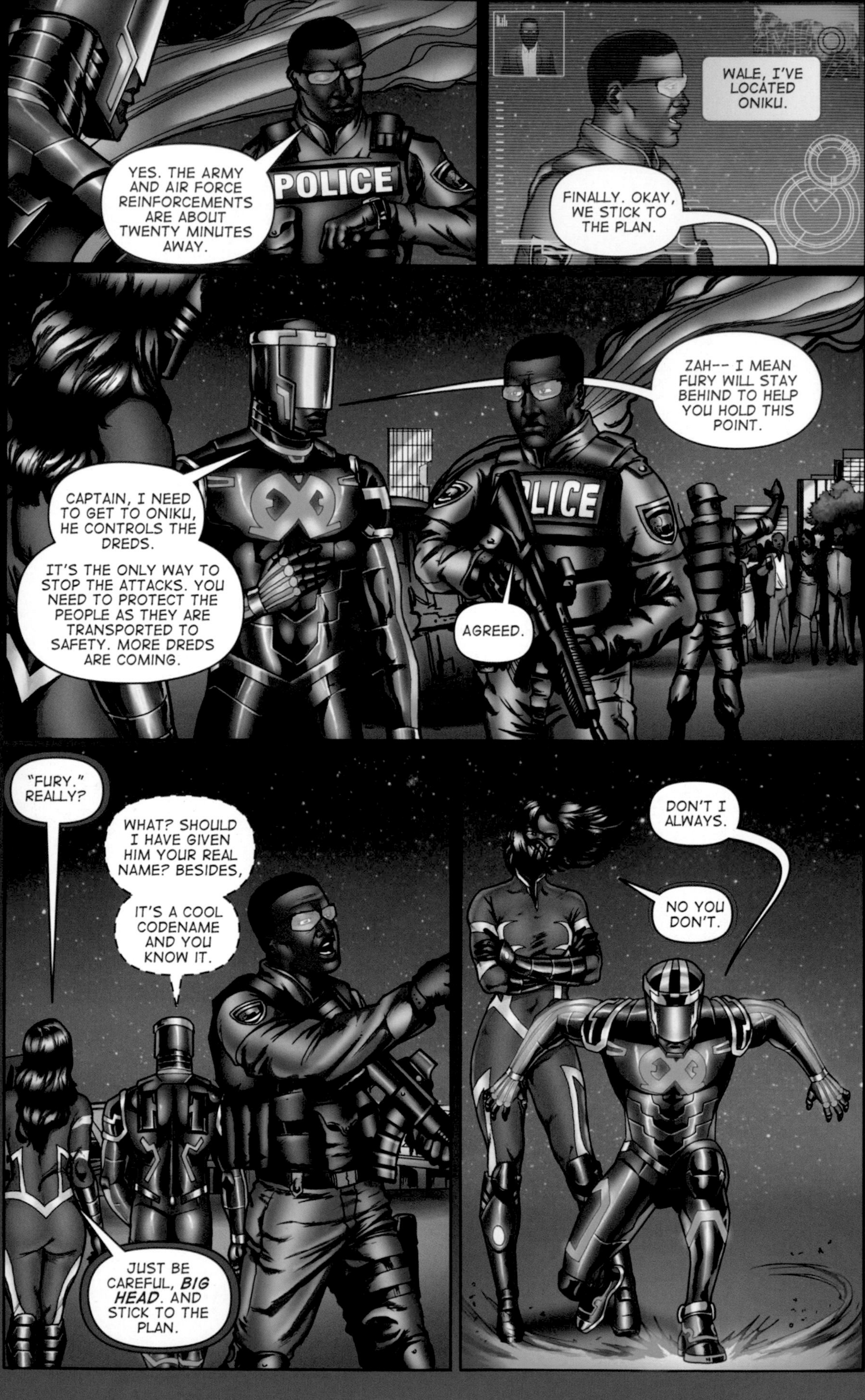
YES. THE ARMY AND AIR FORCE REINFORCEMENTS ARE ABOUT TWENTY MINUTES AWAY.
POLICE
WALE, I'VE LOCATED ONIKU.
FINALLY. OKAY, WE STICK TO THE PLAN.
ZAH-- I MEAN FURY WILL STAY BEHIND TO HELP YOU HOLD THIS POINT.
CAPTAIN, I NEED TO GET TO ONIKU, HE CONTROLS THE DREDS.
IT'S THE ONLY WAY TO STOP THE ATTACKS. YOU NEED TO PROTECT THE PEOPLE AS THEY ARE TRANSPORTED TO SAFETY. MORE DREDS ARE COMING.
POLICE
AGREED.
"FURY." REALLY?
WHAT? SHOULD I HAVE GIVEN HIM YOUR REAL NAME? BESIDES,
IT'S A COOL CODENAME AND YOU KNOW IT.
JUST BE CAREFUL, ***BIG HEAD***. AND STICK TO THE PLAN.
DON'T I ALWAYS.
NO YOU DON'T.

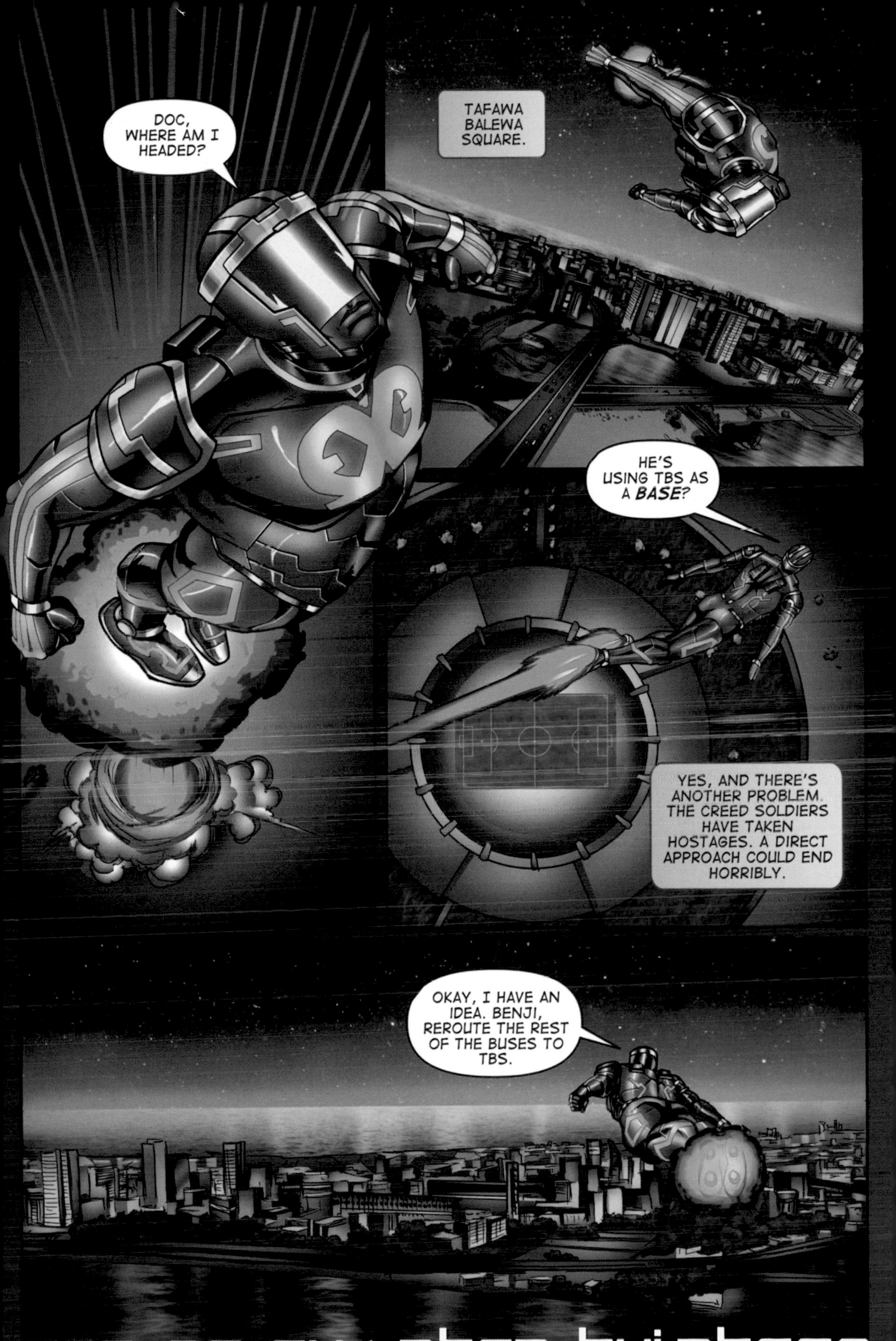
DOC, WHERE AM I HEADED?
TAFAWA BALEWA SQUARE.
HE'S USING TBS AS A BASE?
YES, AND THERE'S ANOTHER PROBLEM. THE CREED SOLDIERS HAVE TAKEN HOSTAGES. A DIRECT APPROACH COULD END HORRIBLY.
OKAY, I HAVE AN IDEA. BENJI, REROUTE THE REST OF THE BUSES TO TBS.

END OF CHAPTER THIRTEEN

– Fan Art by Everard McBain

Fun Fact: E.X.O. is an ongoing series of books broken into several sagas. The Legend of Wale Williams (Part One & Two) is the first saga. The next will be titled...

CHAPTER
FOURTEEN

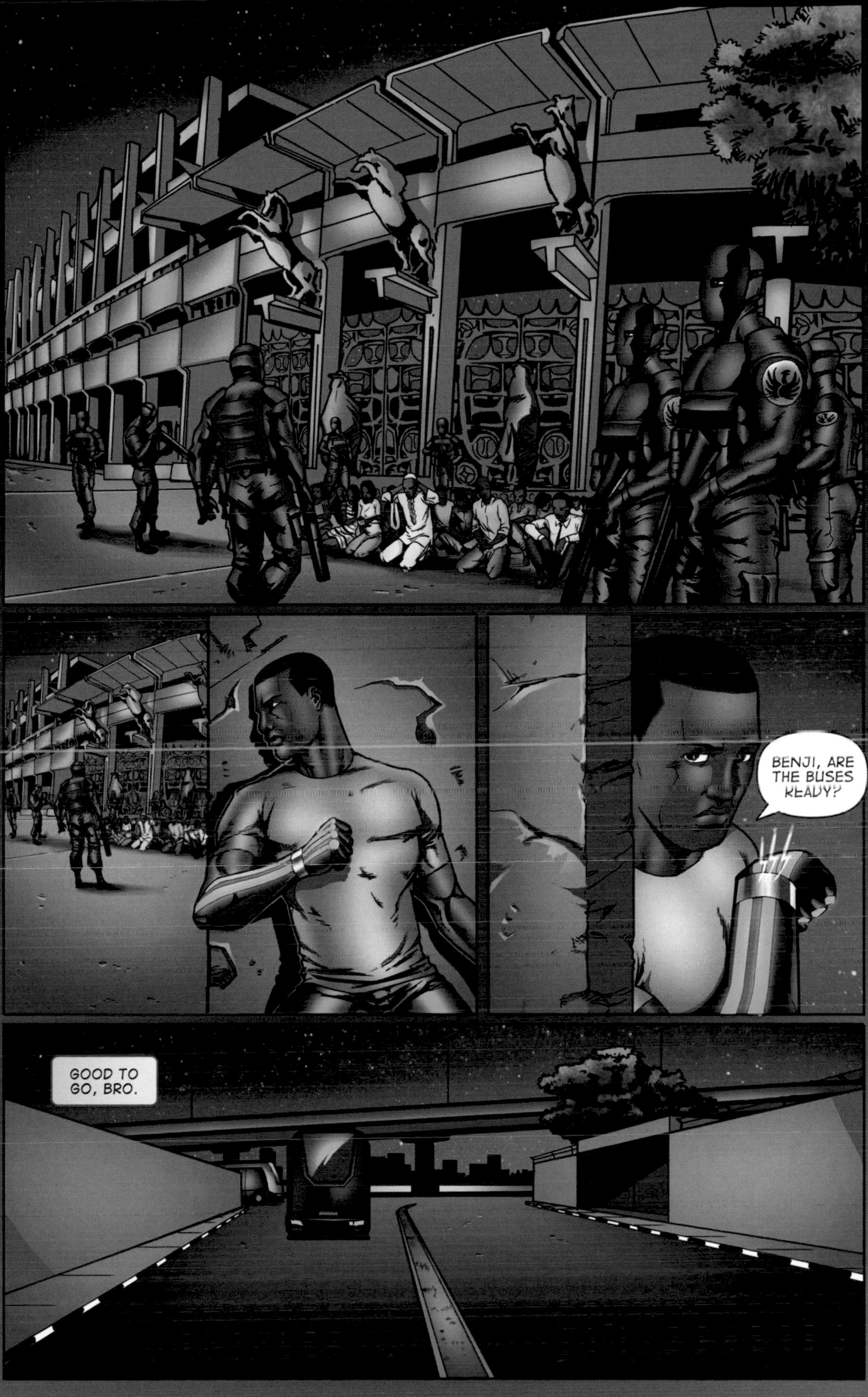
BENJI, ARE THE BUSES READY?
GOOD TO GO, BRO.

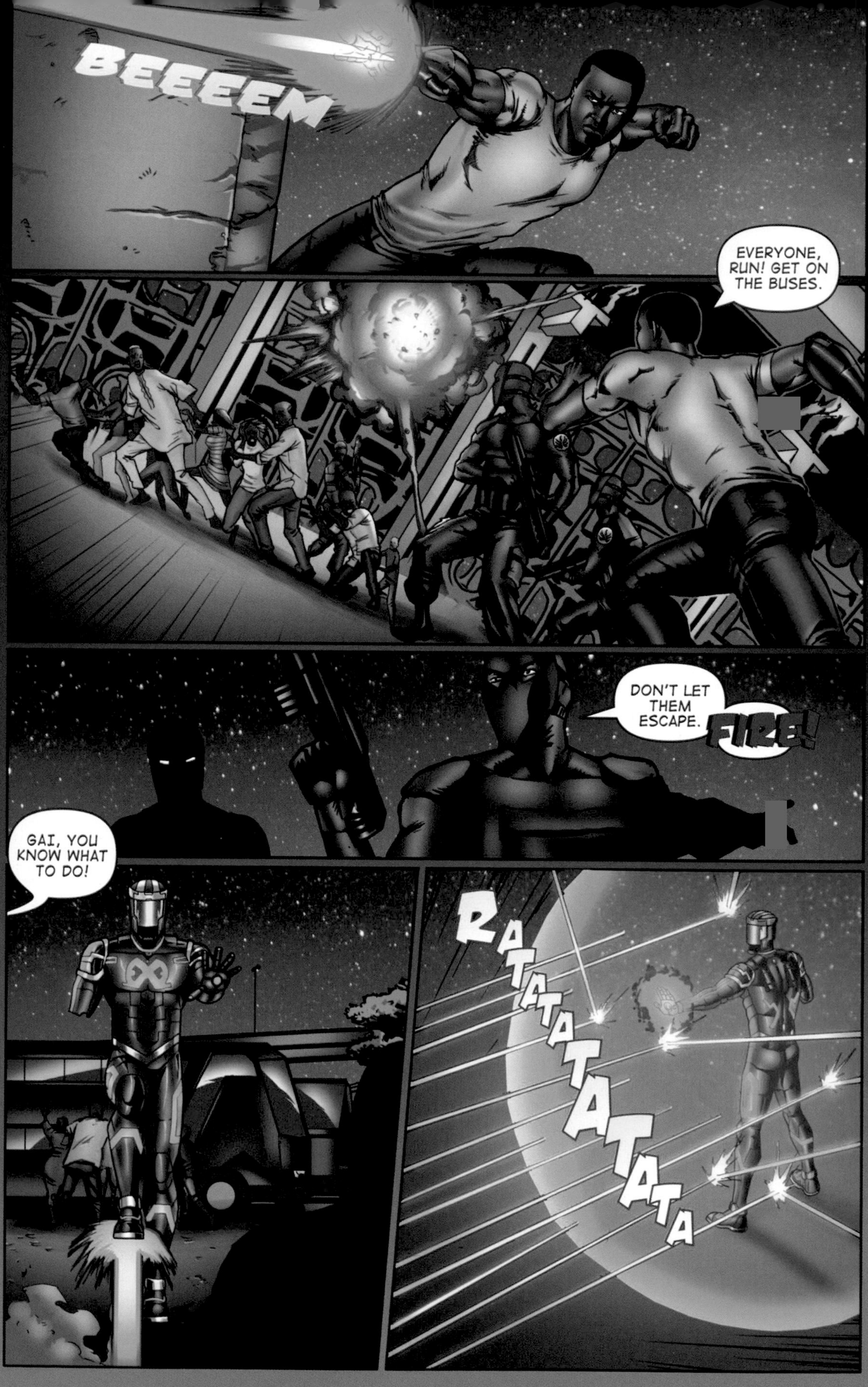
BEEEEEM
EVERYONE, RUN! GET ON THE BUSES.
DON'T LET THEM ESCAPE. FIRE!
GAI, YOU KNOW WHAT TO DO!
RATATATATATATATA

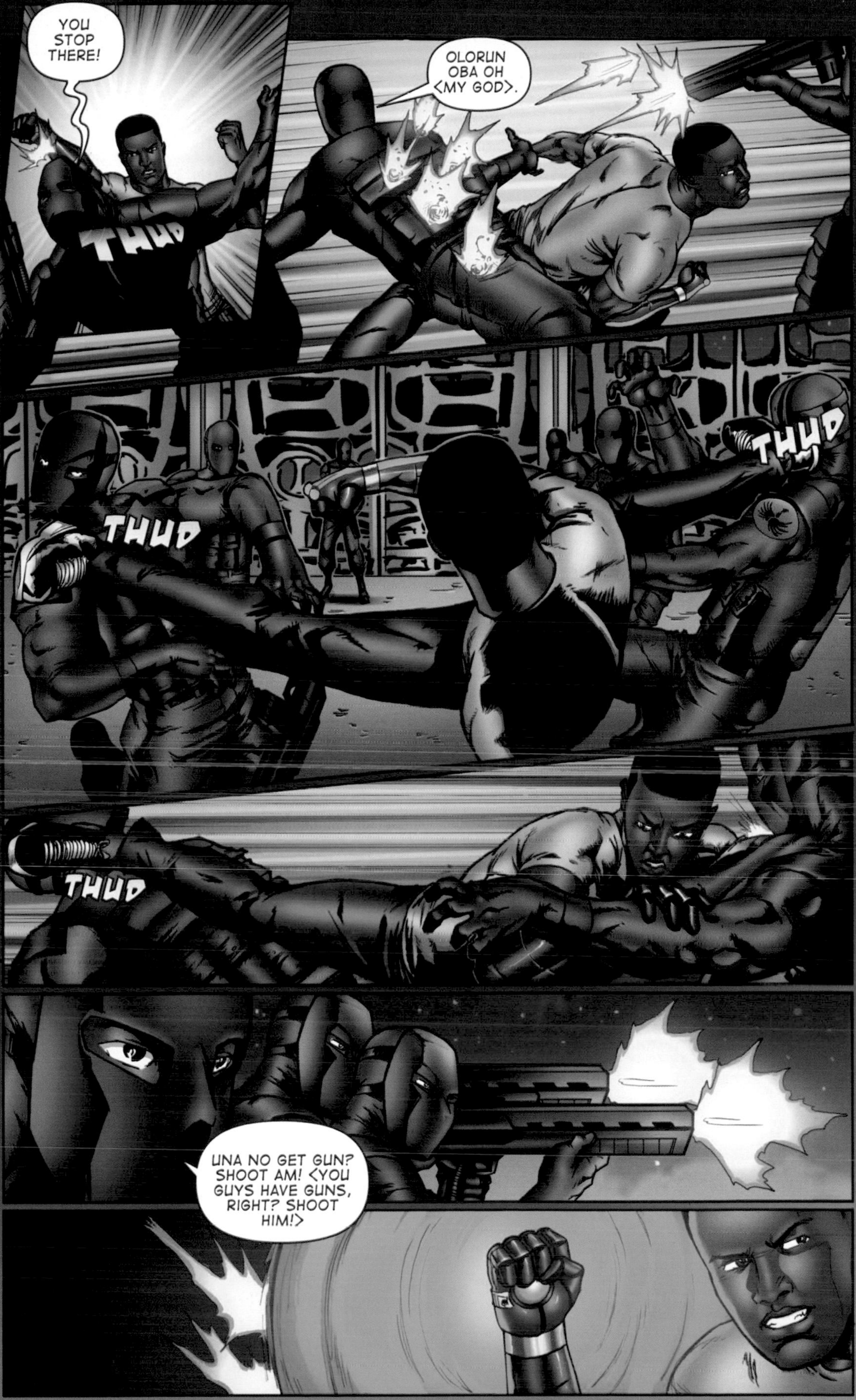
YOU STOP THERE!
THUD
OLORUN OBA OH <MY GOD>.
THUD
THUD
THUD
UNA NO GET GUN? SHOOT AM! <YOU GUYS HAVE GUNS, RIGHT? SHOOT HIM!>

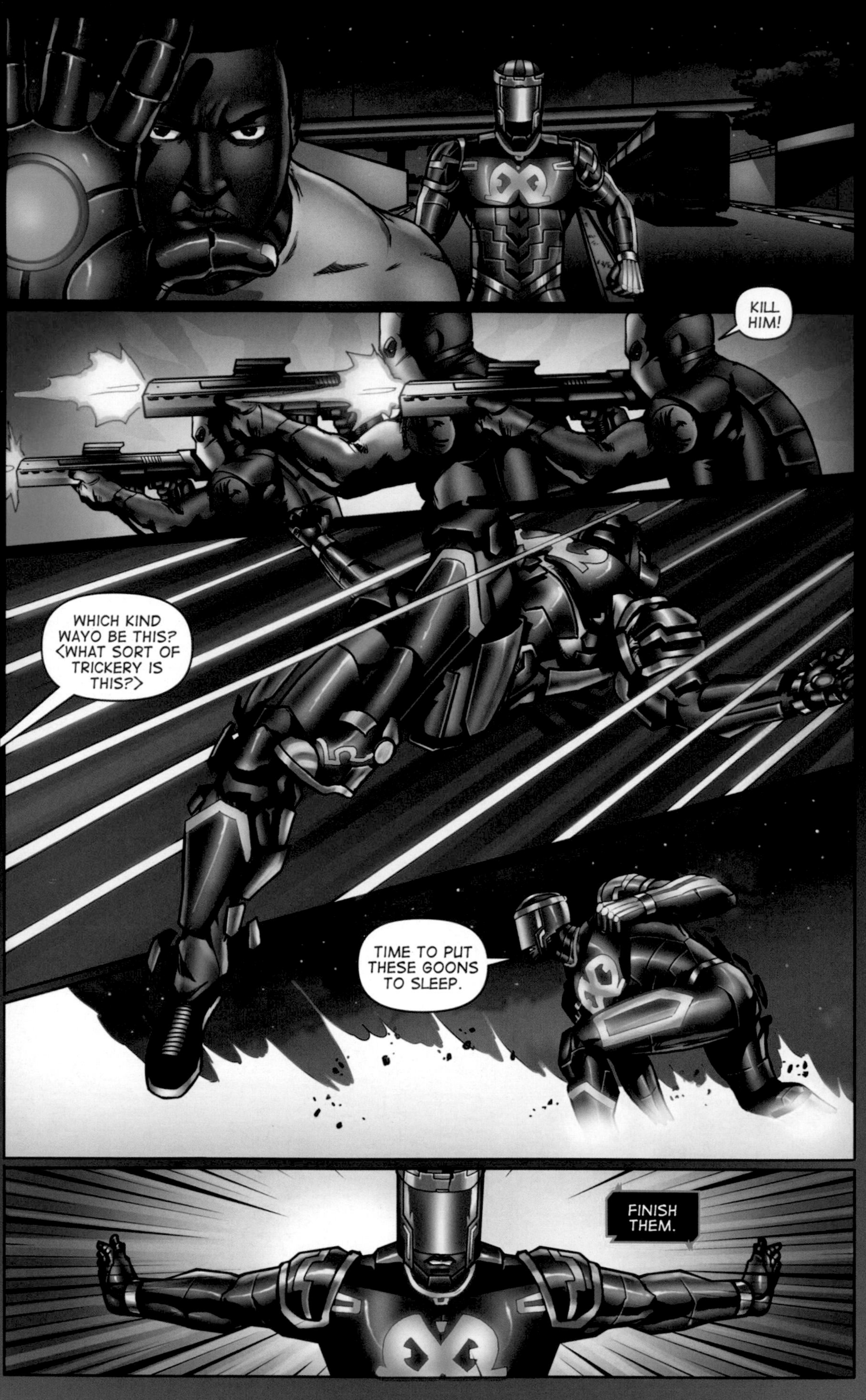
KILL HIM!
WHICH KIND WAYO BE THIS? <WHAT SORT OF TRICKERY IS THIS?>
TIME TO PUT THESE GOONS TO SLEEP.
FINISH THEM.

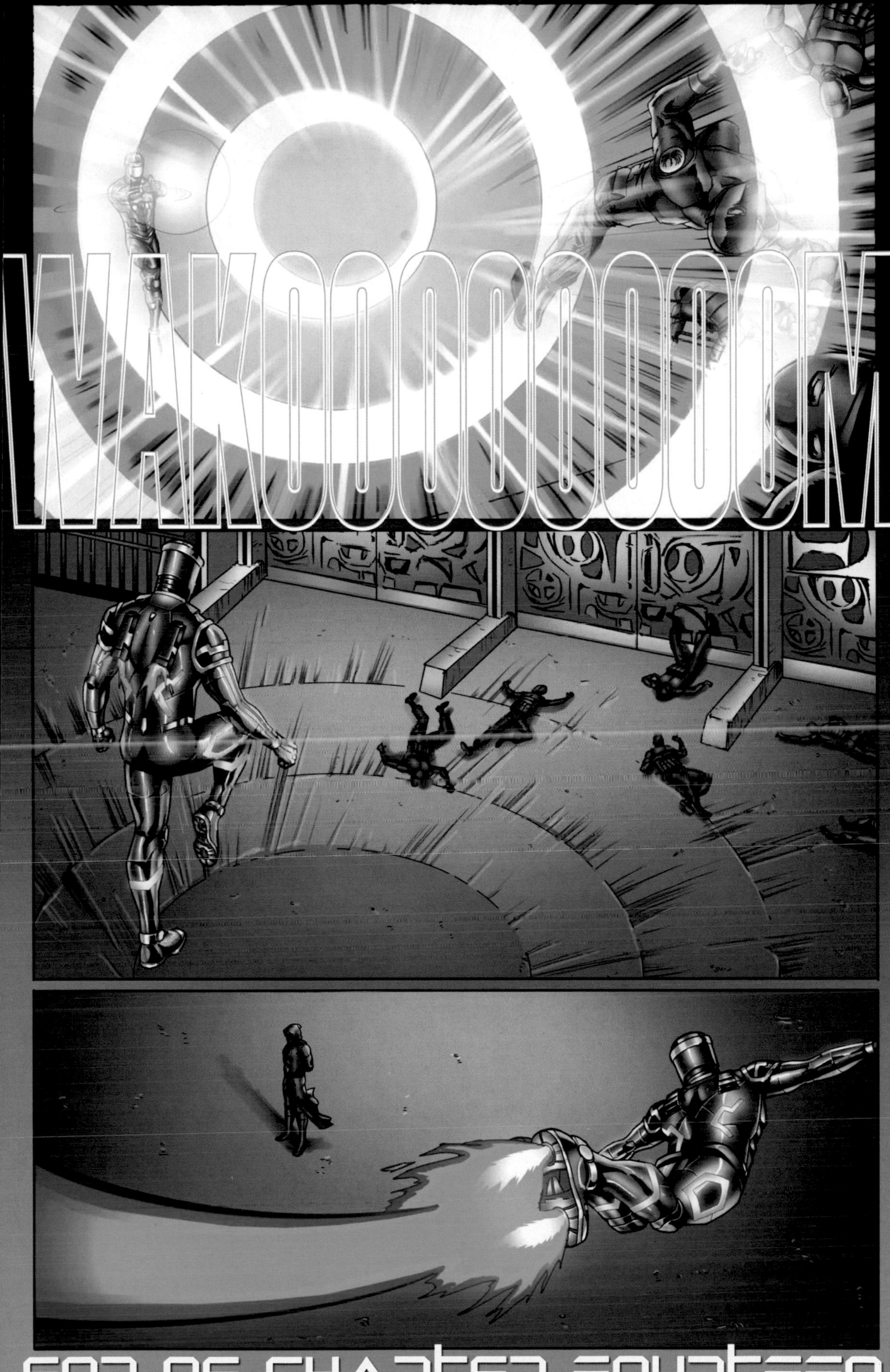
WAKOOOOOOOOM

END OF CHAPTER FOURTEEN

- Art by Godwin Akpan

Fun Fact: E.X.O. is the first superhero graphic novel published by YouNeek Studios. It (as well as all of it's heroes, villains and characters) exist within what is called the "YouNeek YouNiverse." The YouNeek YouNiverse was created by Roye Okupe to house a diverse list of awesome heroes, villains and locations with endless crossover possibilities from book to book. The next entry in the YouNeek YouNiverse will be Malika: Warrior Queen! A superhero fantasy story set in sixteenth century West Africa.

CHAPTER
FIFTEEN

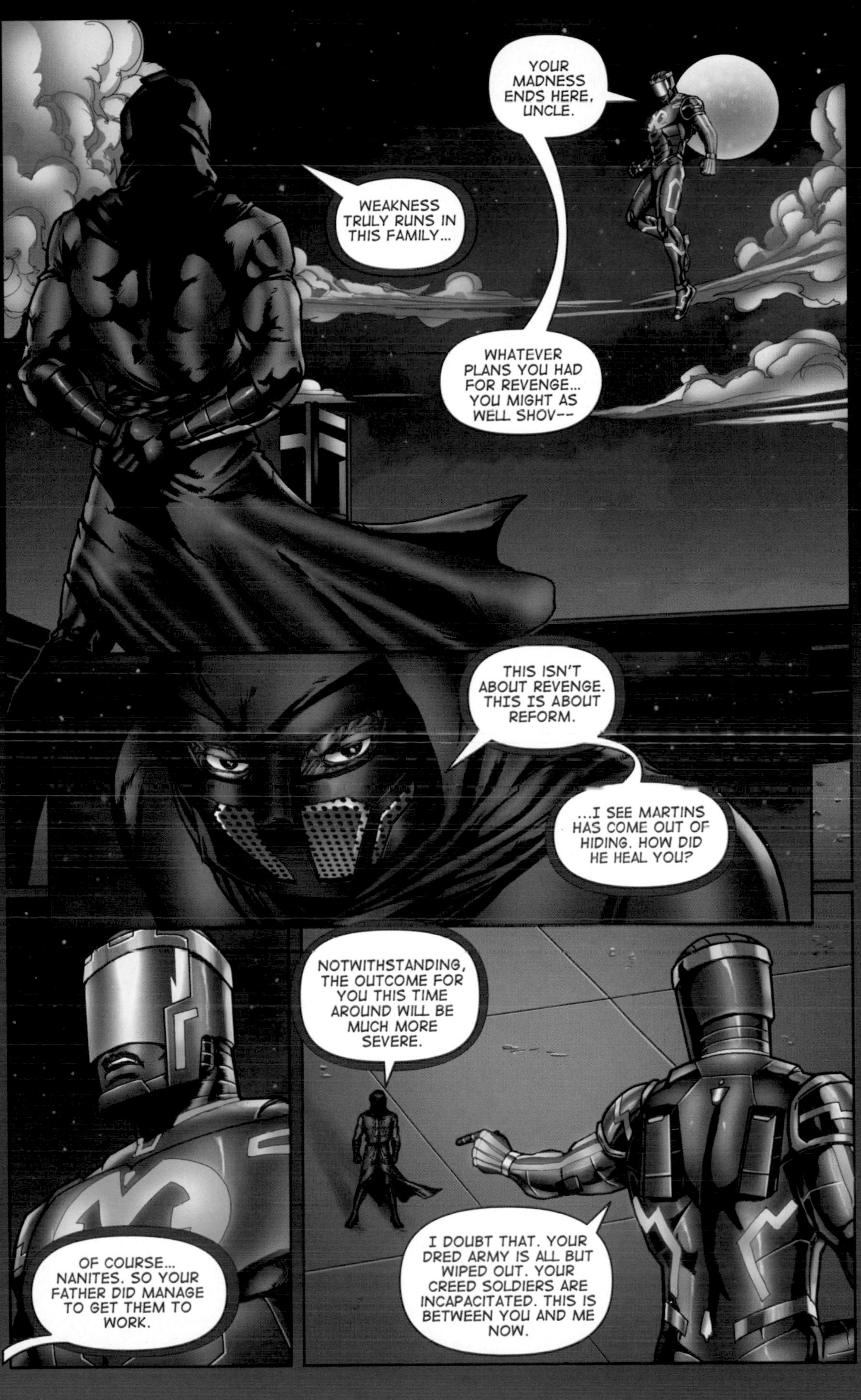

YOUR MADNESS ENDS HERE, UNCLE.
WEAKNESS TRULY RUNS IN THIS FAMILY...
WHATEVER PLANS YOU HAD FOR REVENGE... YOU MIGHT AS WELL SHOV--
THIS ISN'T ABOUT REVENGE. THIS IS ABOUT REFORM.
...I SEE MARTINS HAS COME OUT OF HIDING. HOW DID HE HEAL YOU?
OF COURSE... NANITES. SO YOUR FATHER DID MANAGE TO GET THEM TO WORK.
NOTWITHSTANDING, THE OUTCOME FOR YOU THIS TIME AROUND WILL BE MUCH MORE SEVERE.
I DOUBT THAT. YOUR DRED ARMY IS ALL BUT WIPED OUT. YOUR CREED SOLDIERS ARE INCAPACITATED. THIS IS BETWEEN YOU AND ME NOW.

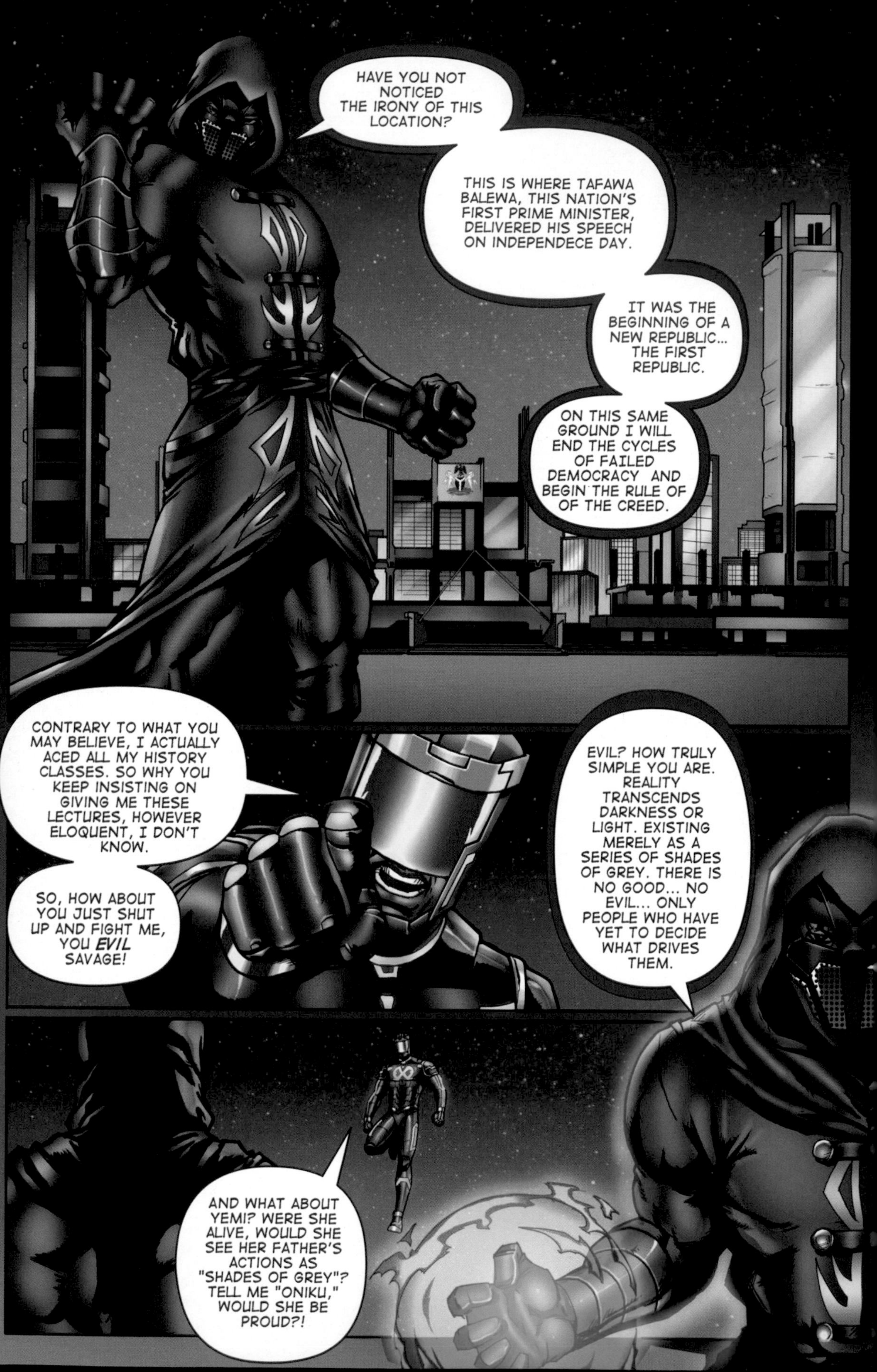
HAVE YOU NOT NOTICED THE IRONY OF THIS LOCATION?
THIS IS WHERE TAFAWA BALEWA, THIS NATION'S FIRST PRIME MINISTER, DELIVERED HIS SPEECH ON INDEPENDECE DAY.
IT WAS THE BEGINNING OF A NEW REPUBLIC... THE FIRST REPUBLIC.
ON THIS SAME GROUND I WILL END THE CYCLES OF FAILED DEMOCRACY AND BEGIN THE RULE OF OF THE CREED.
CONTRARY TO WHAT YOU MAY BELIEVE, I ACTUALLY ACED ALL MY HISTORY CLASSES. SO WHY YOU KEEP INSISTING ON GIVING ME THESE LECTURES, HOWEVER ELOQUENT, I DON'T KNOW.
SO, HOW ABOUT YOU JUST SHUT UP AND FIGHT ME, YOU *EVIL* SAVAGE!
EVIL? HOW TRULY SIMPLE YOU ARE. REALITY TRANSCENDS DARKNESS OR LIGHT. EXISTING MERELY AS A SERIES OF SHADES OF GREY. THERE IS NO GOOD... NO EVIL... ONLY PEOPLE WHO HAVE YET TO DECIDE WHAT DRIVES THEM.
AND WHAT ABOUT YEMI? WERE SHE ALIVE, WOULD SHE SEE HER FATHER'S ACTIONS AS "SHADES OF GREY"? TELL ME "ONIKU," WOULD SHE BE PROUD?!

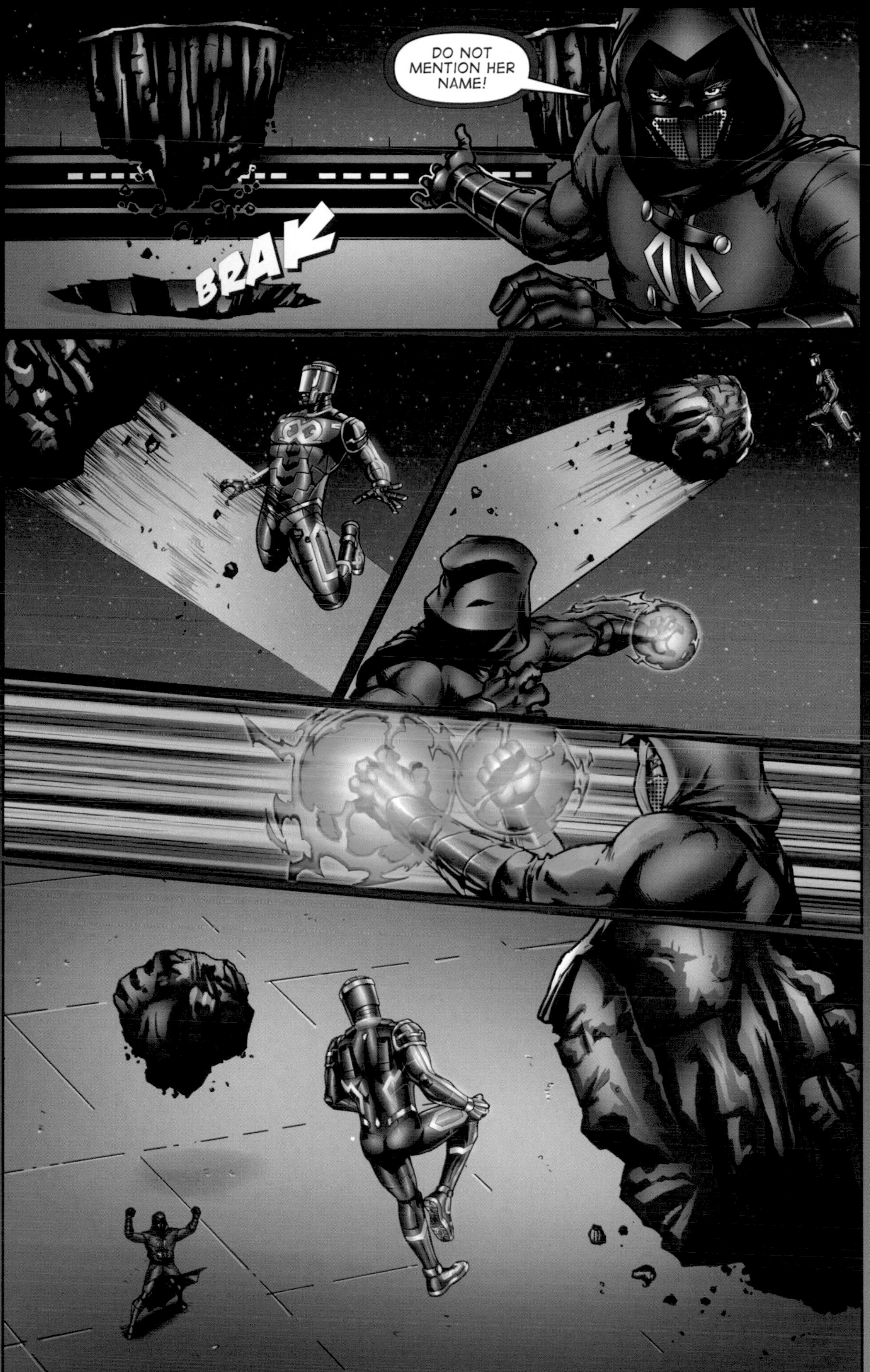
DO NOT MENTION HER NAME!
BRAK

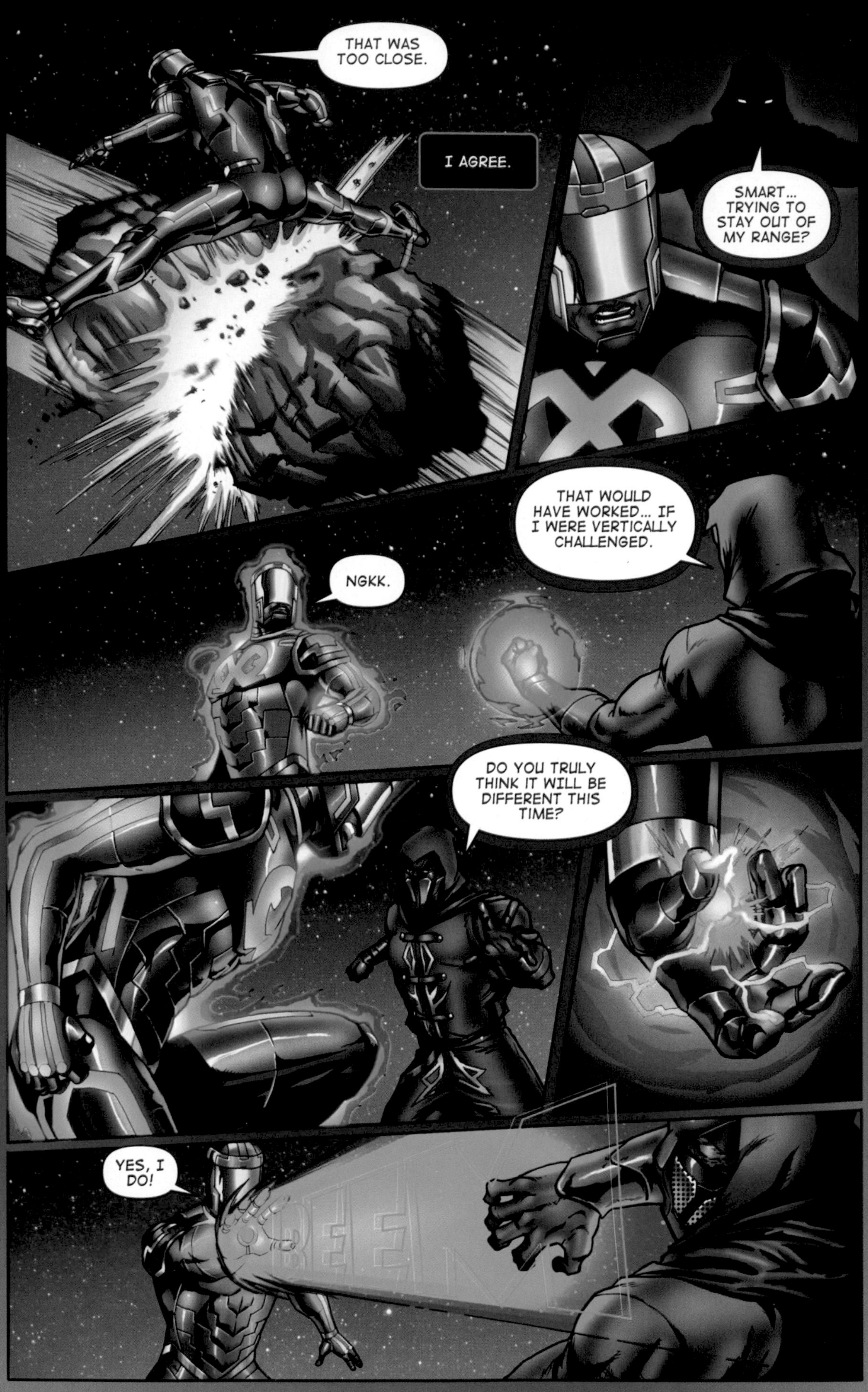
THAT WAS TOO CLOSE.
I AGREE.
SMART... TRYING TO STAY OUT OF MY RANGE?
THAT WOULD HAVE WORKED... IF I WERE VERTICALLY CHALLENGED.
NGKK.
DO YOU TRULY THINK IT WILL BE DIFFERENT THIS TIME?
YES, I DO!

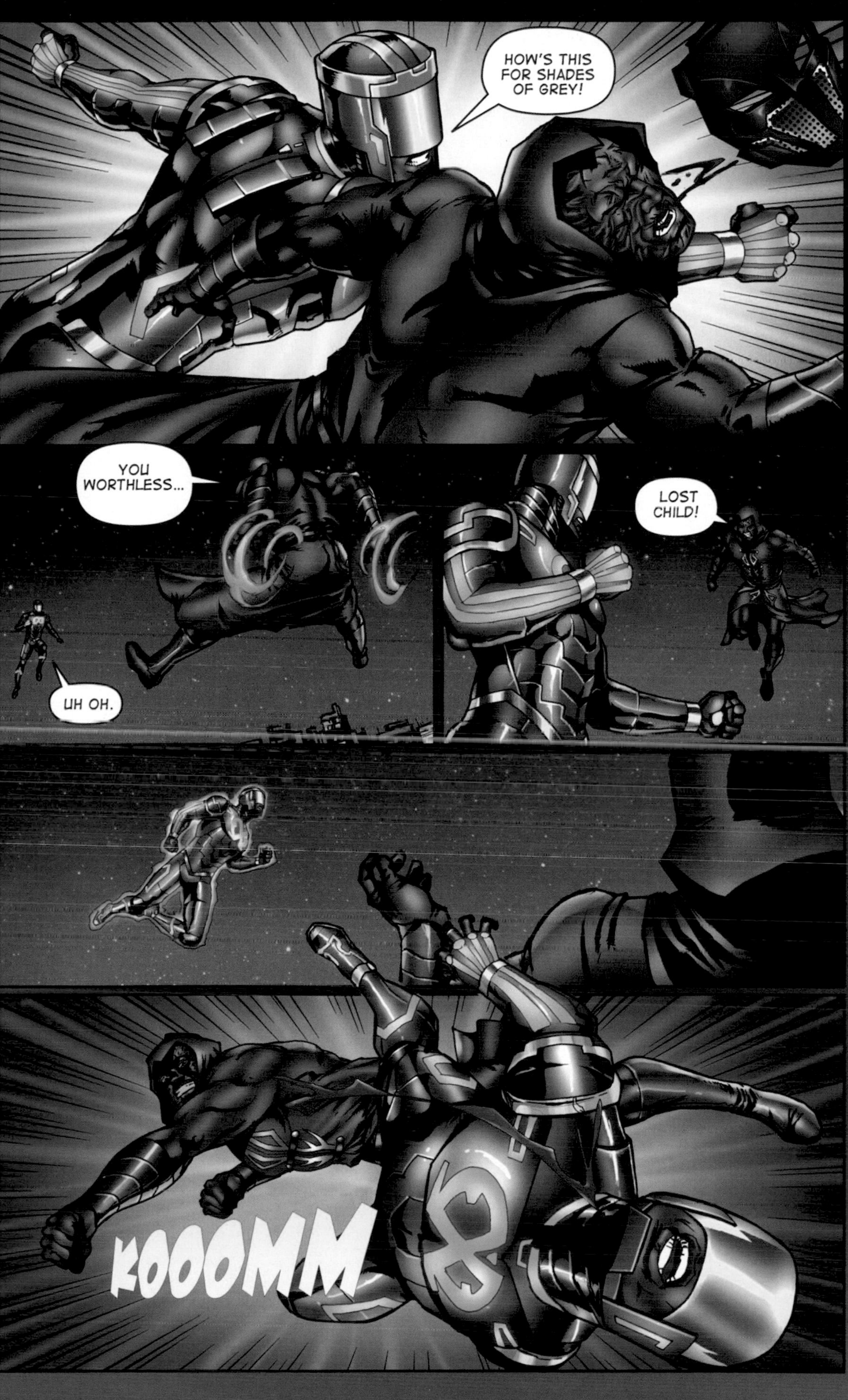
HOW'S THIS FOR SHADES OF GREY!
YOU WORTHLESS...
UH OH.
LOST CHILD!
KOOOMM

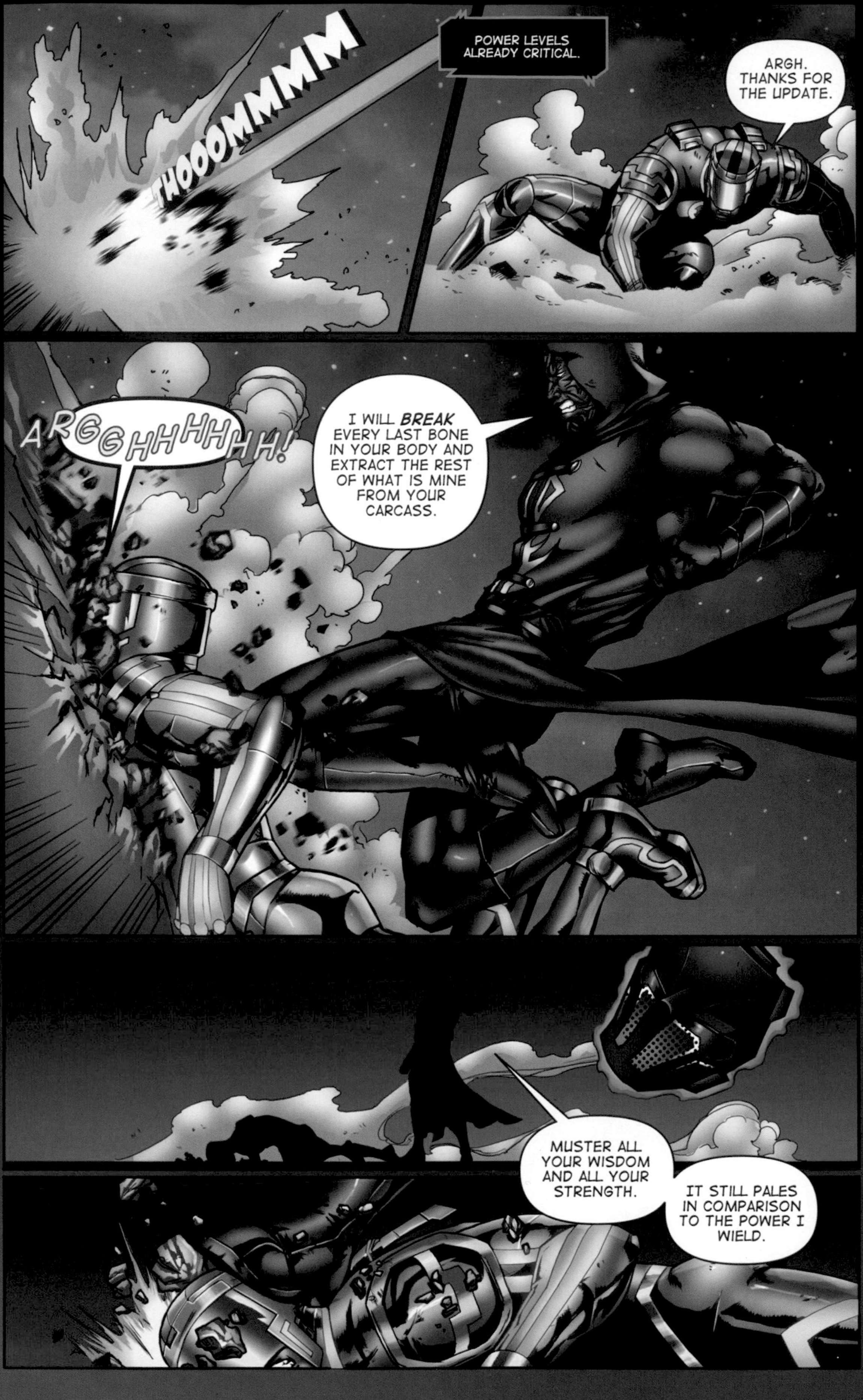
THOOOMMMM
POWER LEVELS ALREADY CRITICAL.
ARGH. THANKS FOR THE UPDATE.
ARGGHHHHHH!
I WILL BREAK EVERY LAST BONE IN YOUR BODY AND EXTRACT THE REST OF WHAT IS MINE FROM YOUR CARCASS.
MUSTER ALL YOUR WISDOM AND ALL YOUR STRENGTH.
IT STILL PALES IN COMPARISON TO THE POWER I WIELD.

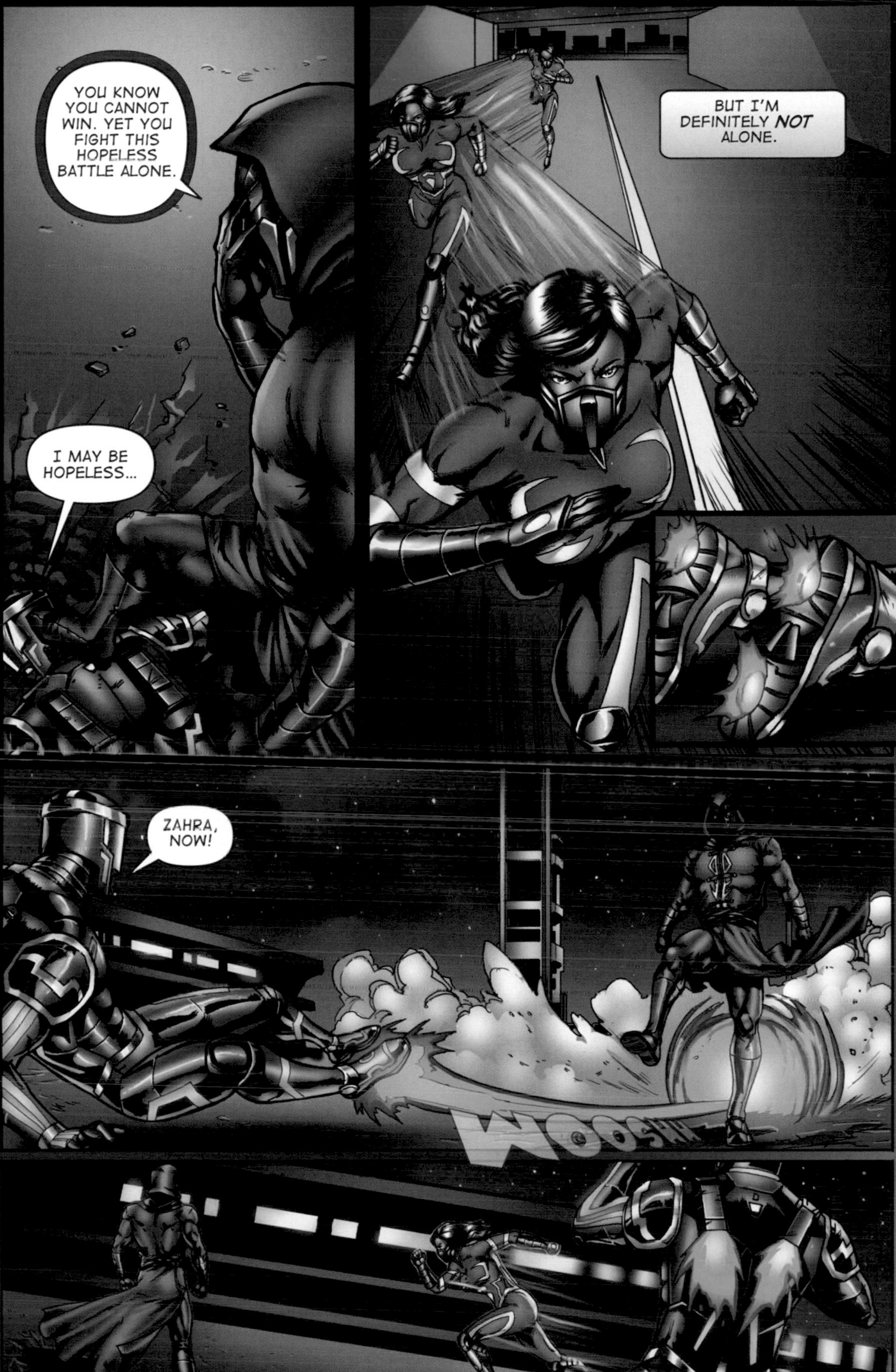
YOU KNOW YOU CANNOT WIN. YET YOU FIGHT THIS HOPELESS BATTLE ALONE.
I MAY BE HOPELESS...
BUT I'M DEFINITELY *NOT* ALONE.
ZAHRA, NOW!
WOOSH

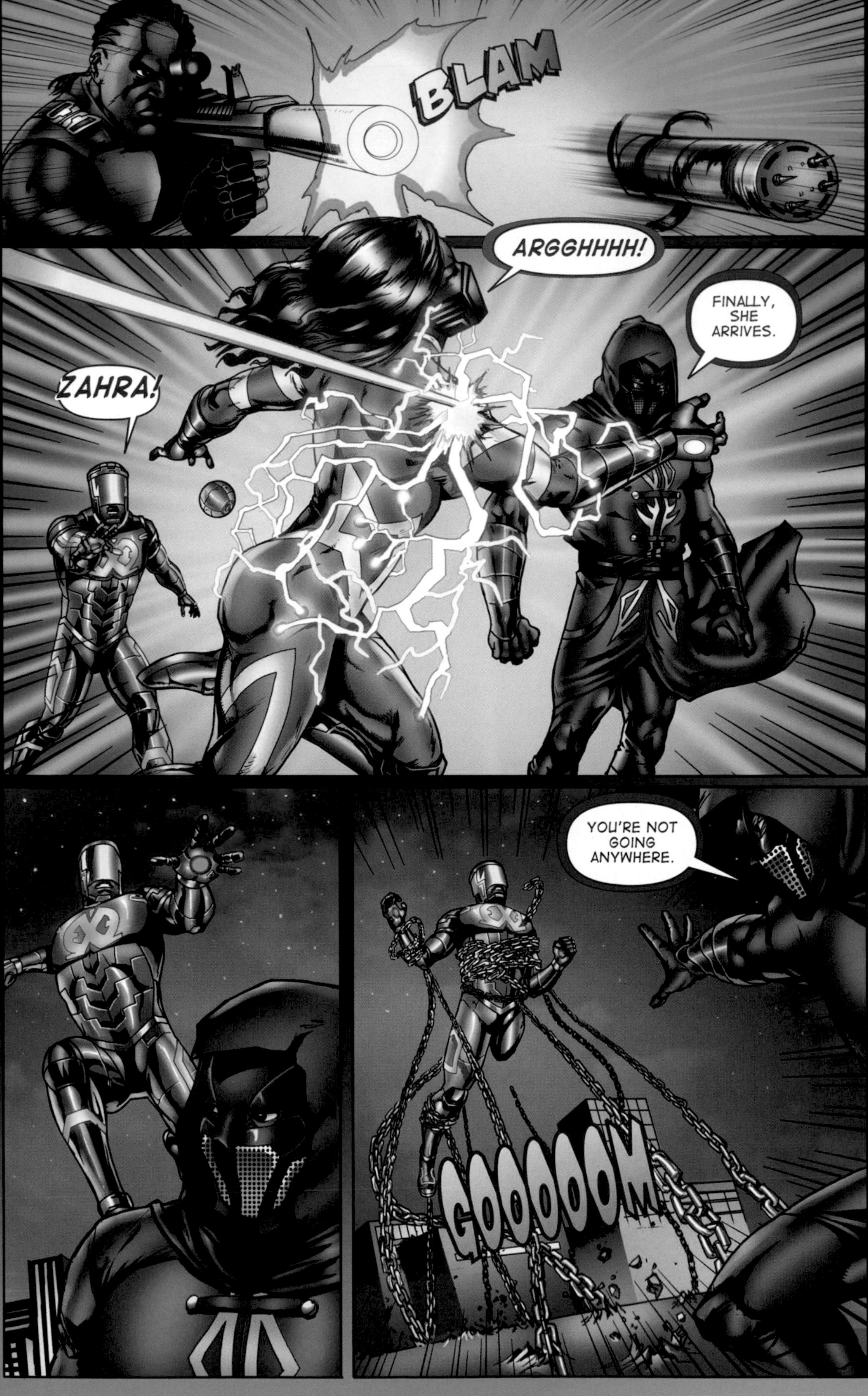
BLAM
ARGGHHHH!
FINALLY, SHE ARRIVES.
ZAHRA!
YOU'RE NOT GOING ANYWHERE.
GOOOOOM

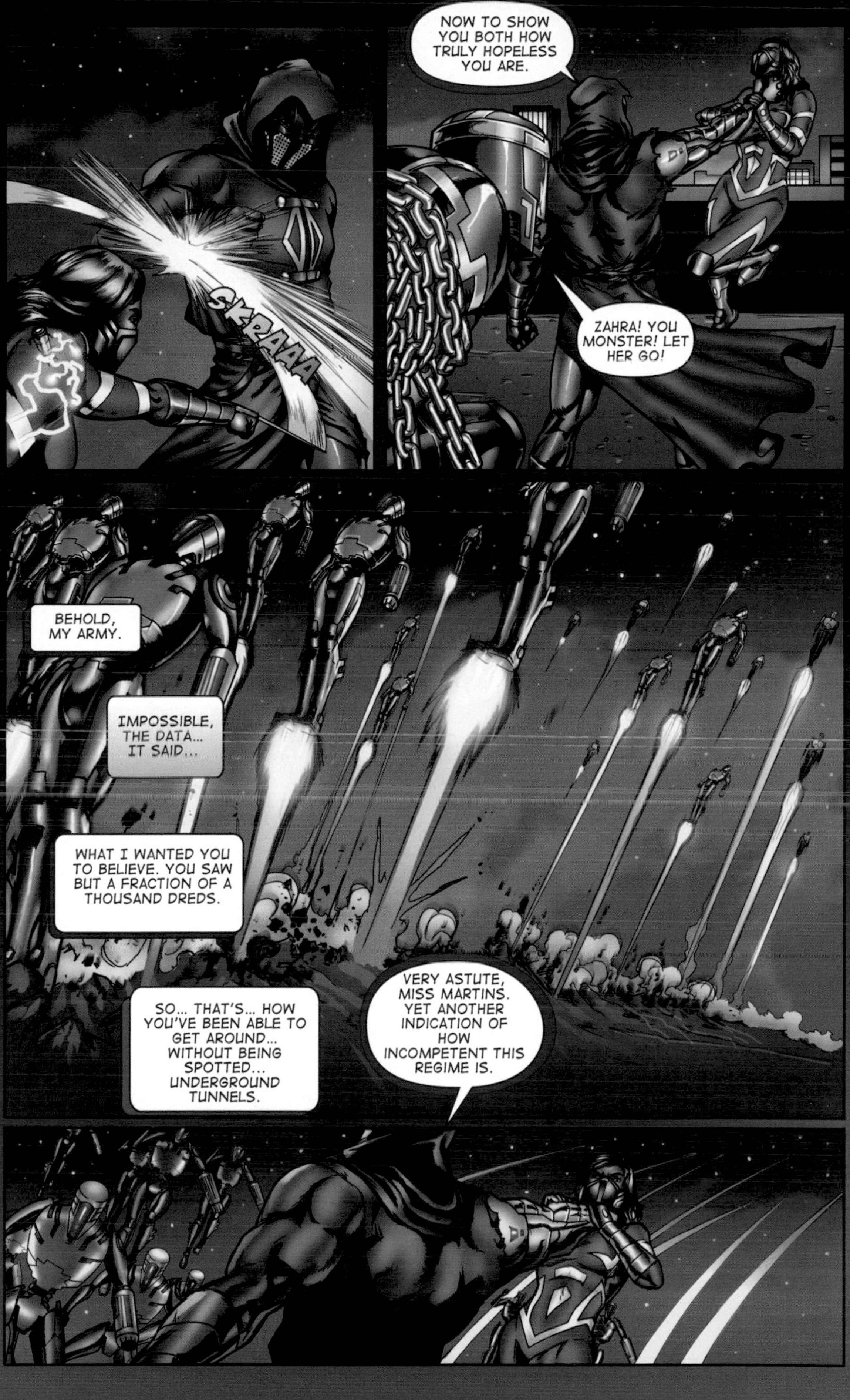
SKRAAA
NOW TO SHOW YOU BOTH HOW TRULY HOPELESS YOU ARE.
ZAHRA! YOU MONSTER! LET HER GO!
BEHOLD, MY ARMY.
IMPOSSIBLE, THE DATA... IT SAID...
WHAT I WANTED YOU TO BELIEVE. YOU SAW BUT A FRACTION OF A THOUSAND DREDS.
SO... THAT'S... HOW YOU'VE BEEN ABLE TO GET AROUND... WITHOUT BEING SPOTTED... UNDERGROUND TUNNELS.
VERY ASTUTE, MISS MARTINS. YET ANOTHER INDICATION OF HOW INCOMPETENT THIS REGIME IS.

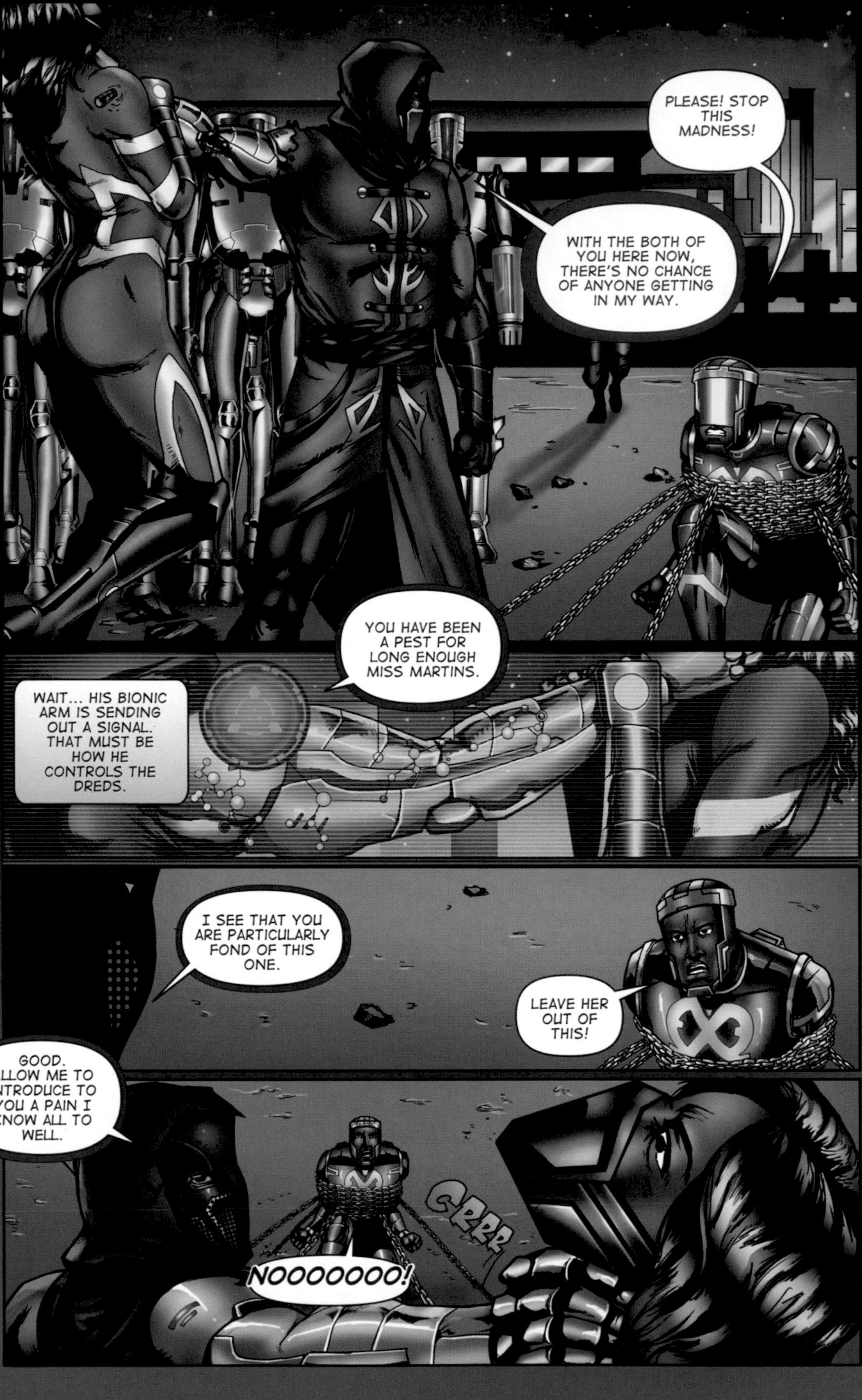
PLEASE! STOP THIS MADNESS!
WITH THE BOTH OF YOU HERE NOW, THERE'S NO CHANCE OF ANYONE GETTING IN MY WAY.
YOU HAVE BEEN A PEST FOR LONG ENOUGH MISS MARTINS.
WAIT... HIS BIONIC ARM IS SENDING OUT A SIGNAL. THAT MUST BE HOW HE CONTROLS THE DREDS.
I SEE THAT YOU ARE PARTICULARLY FOND OF THIS ONE.
LEAVE HER OUT OF THIS!
GOOD. ALLOW ME TO INTRODUCE TO YOU A PAIN I KNOW ALL TO WELL.
GRRR
NOOOOOOO!

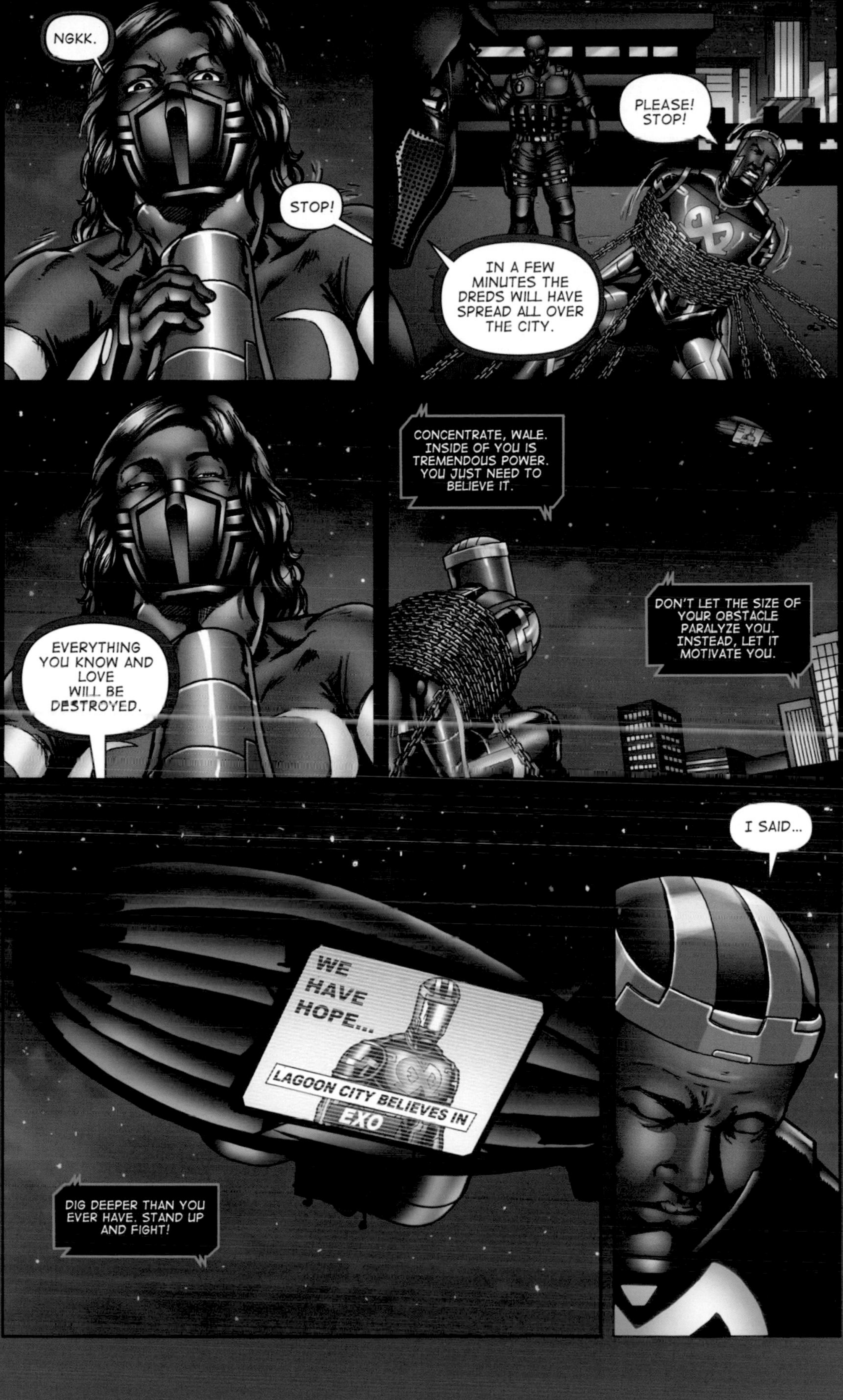
NGKK.
STOP!
PLEASE! STOP!
IN A FEW MINUTES THE DREDS WILL HAVE SPREAD ALL OVER THE CITY.
EVERYTHING YOU KNOW AND LOVE WILL BE DESTROYED.
CONCENTRATE, WALE. INSIDE OF YOU IS TREMENDOUS POWER. YOU JUST NEED TO BELIEVE IT.
DON'T LET THE SIZE OF YOUR OBSTACLE PARALYZE YOU. INSTEAD, LET IT MOTIVATE YOU.
I SAID...
WE HAVE HOPE...
LAGOON CITY BELIEVES IN EXO
DIG DEEPER THAN YOU EVER HAVE. STAND UP AND FIGHT!

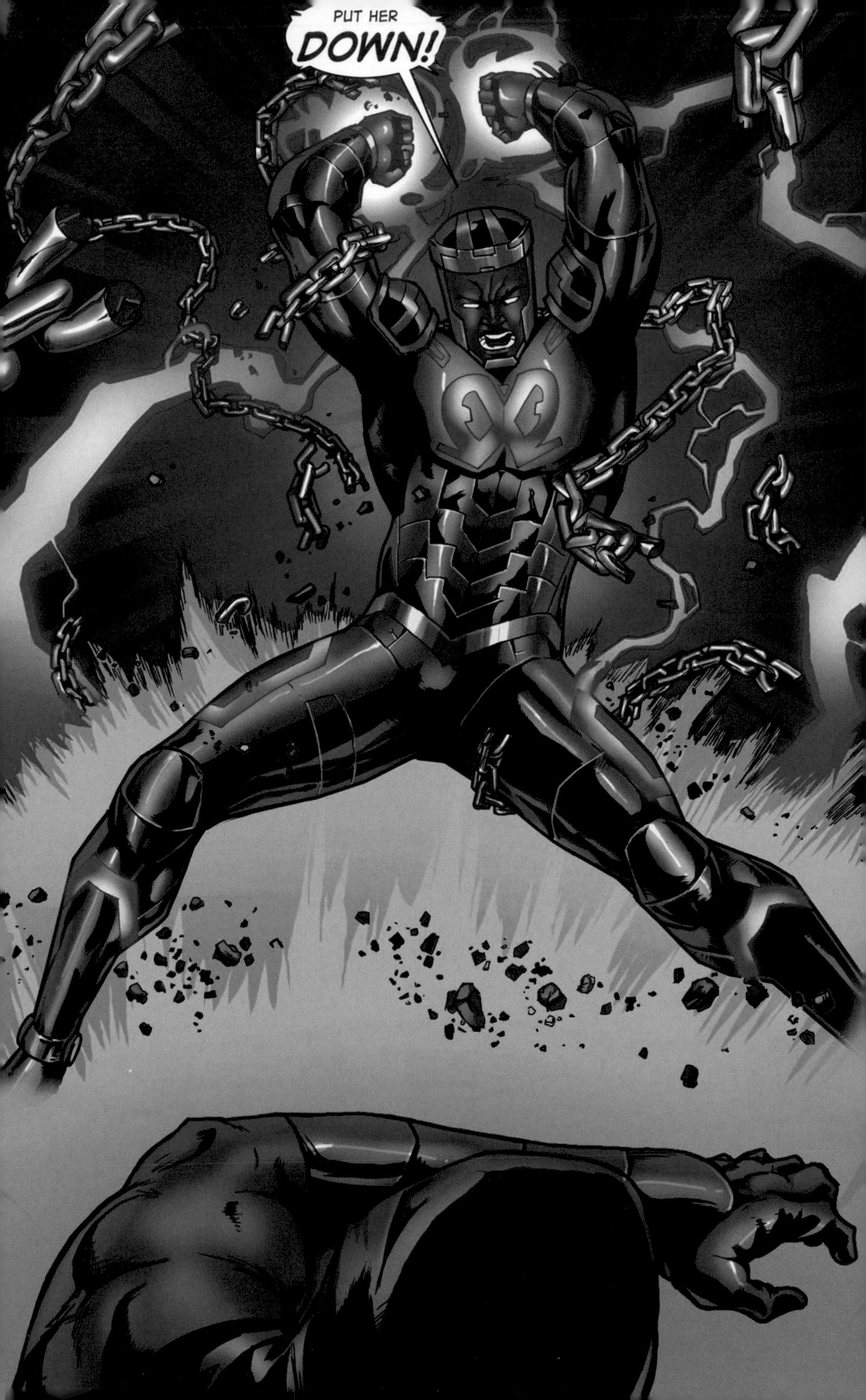
PUT HER
DOWN!

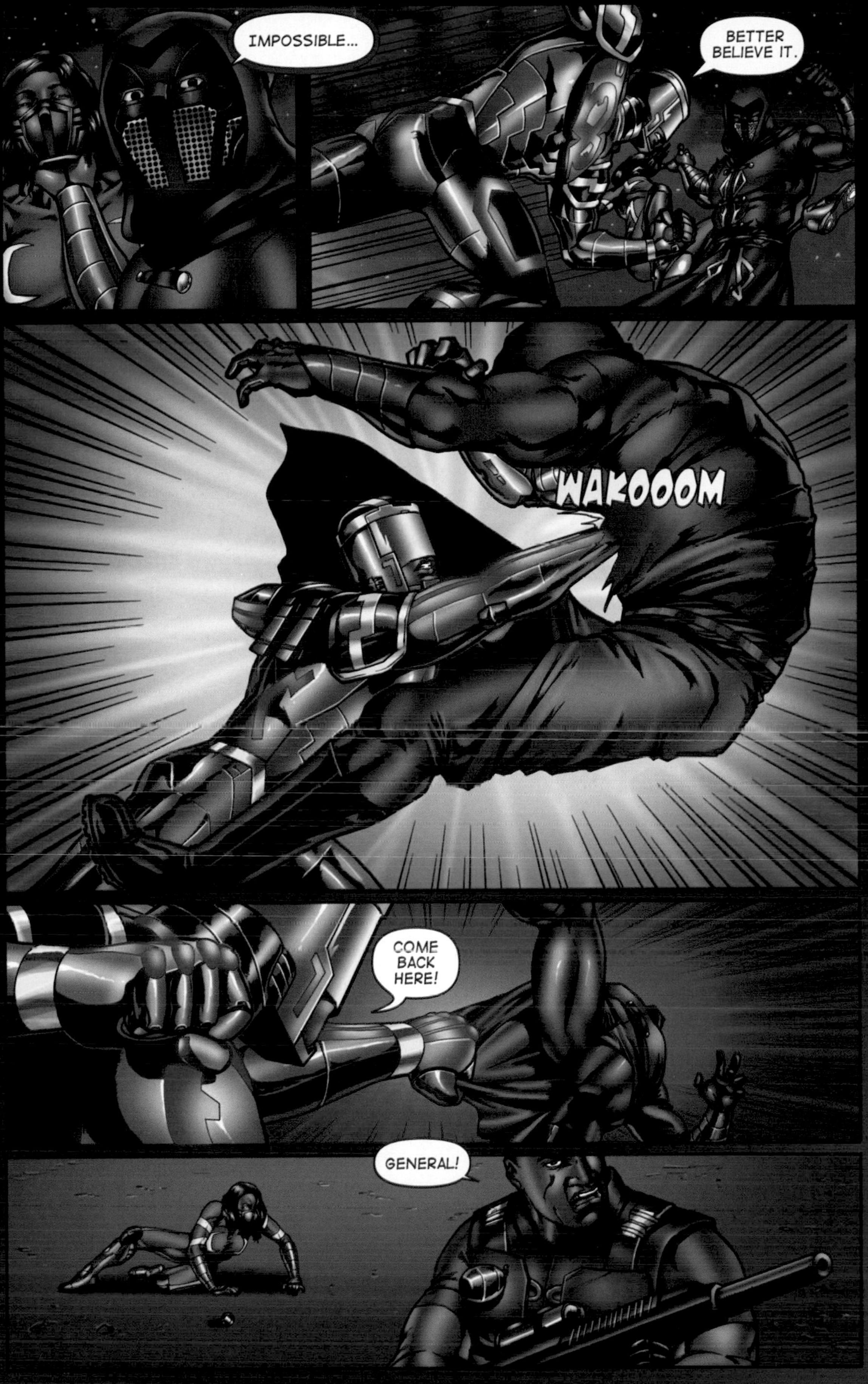
IMPOSSIBLE...
BETTER BELIEVE IT.
WAKOOOM
COME BACK HERE!
GENERAL!

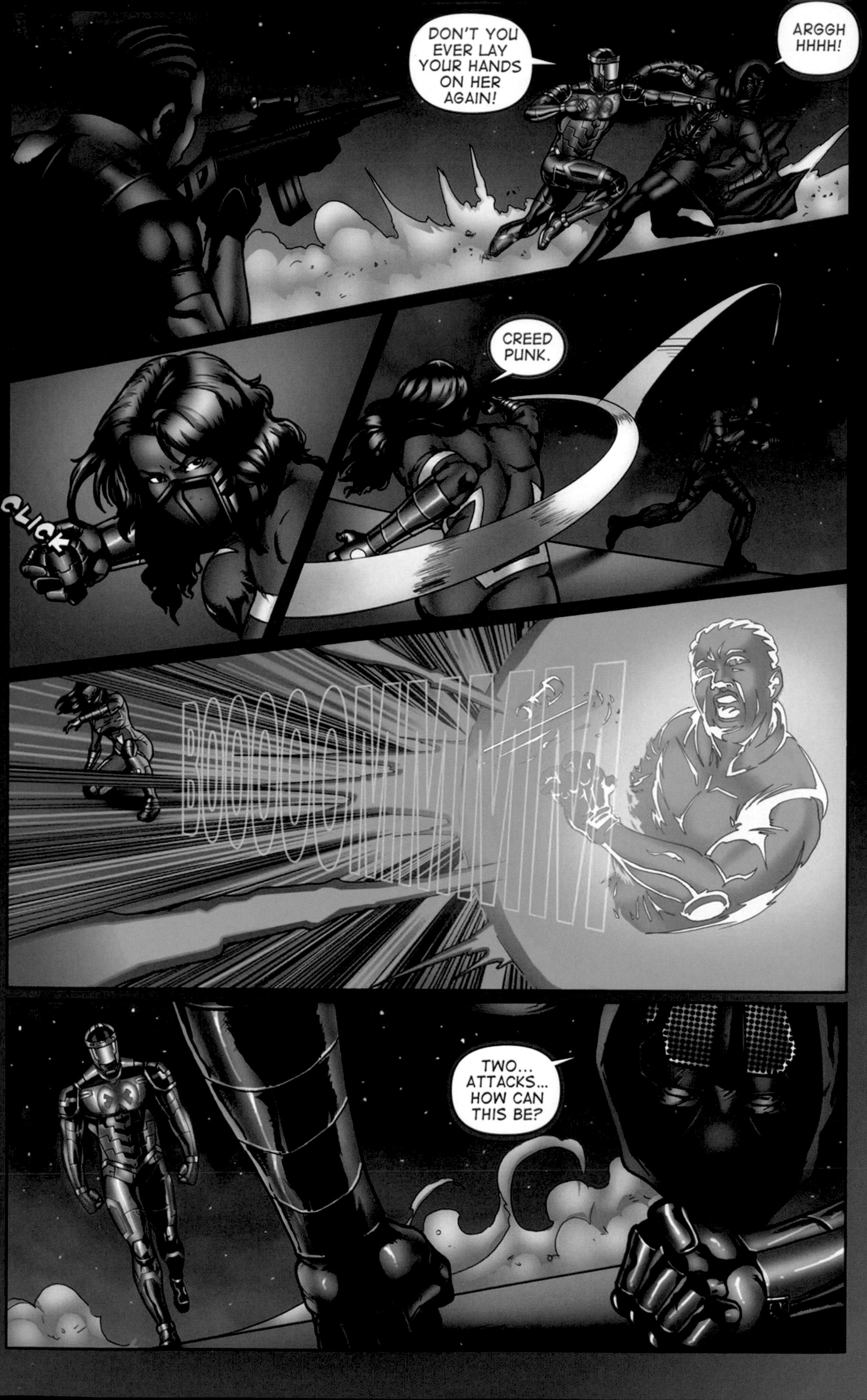
DON'T YOU EVER LAY YOUR HANDS ON HER AGAIN!
ARGGH HHHH!
CLICK
CREED PUNK.
BOOOOOMMMMMM
TWO... ATTACKS... HOW CAN THIS BE?

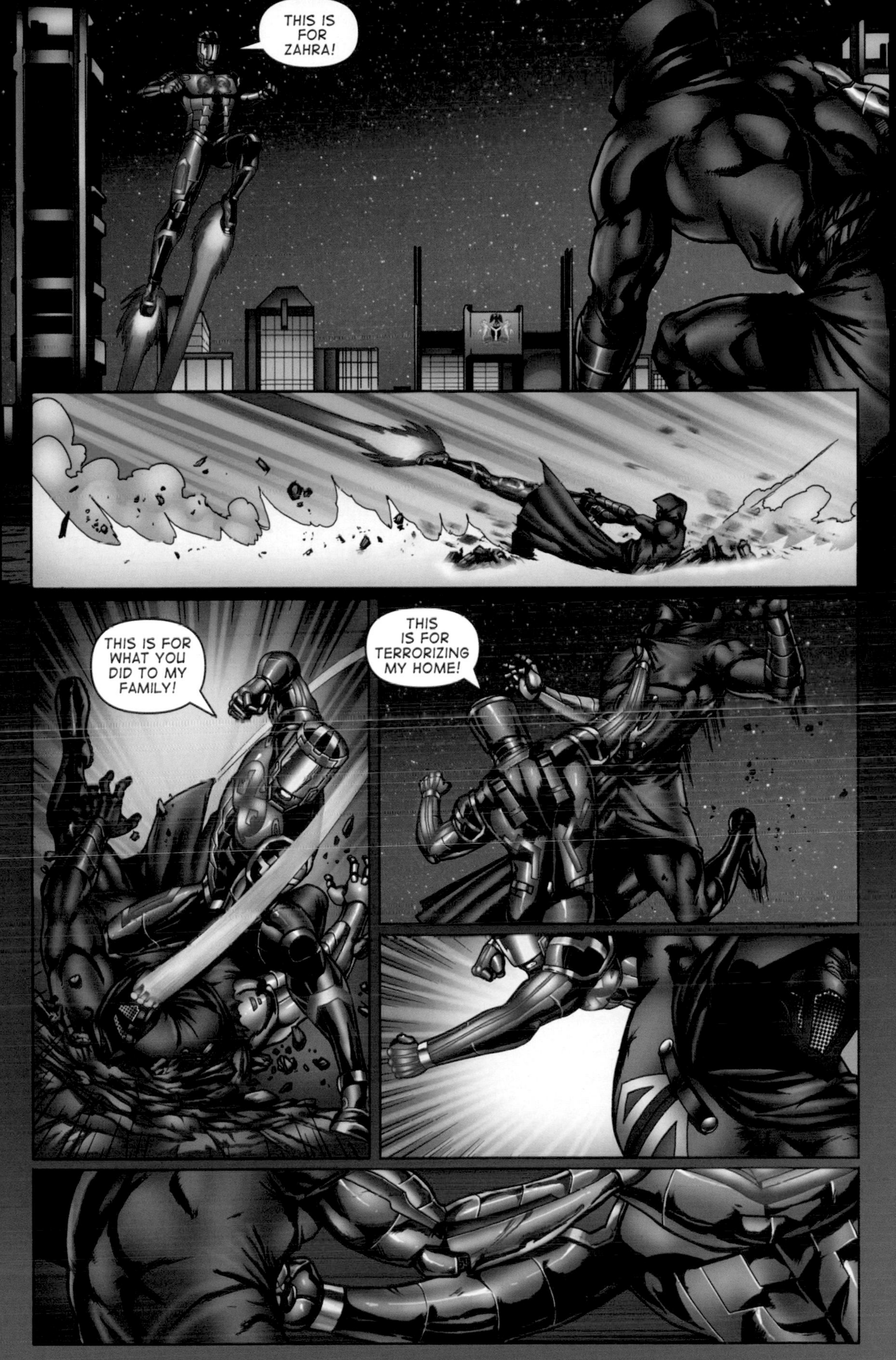
THIS IS FOR ZAHRA!
THIS IS FOR WHAT YOU DID TO MY FAMILY!
THIS IS FOR TERRORIZING MY HOME!

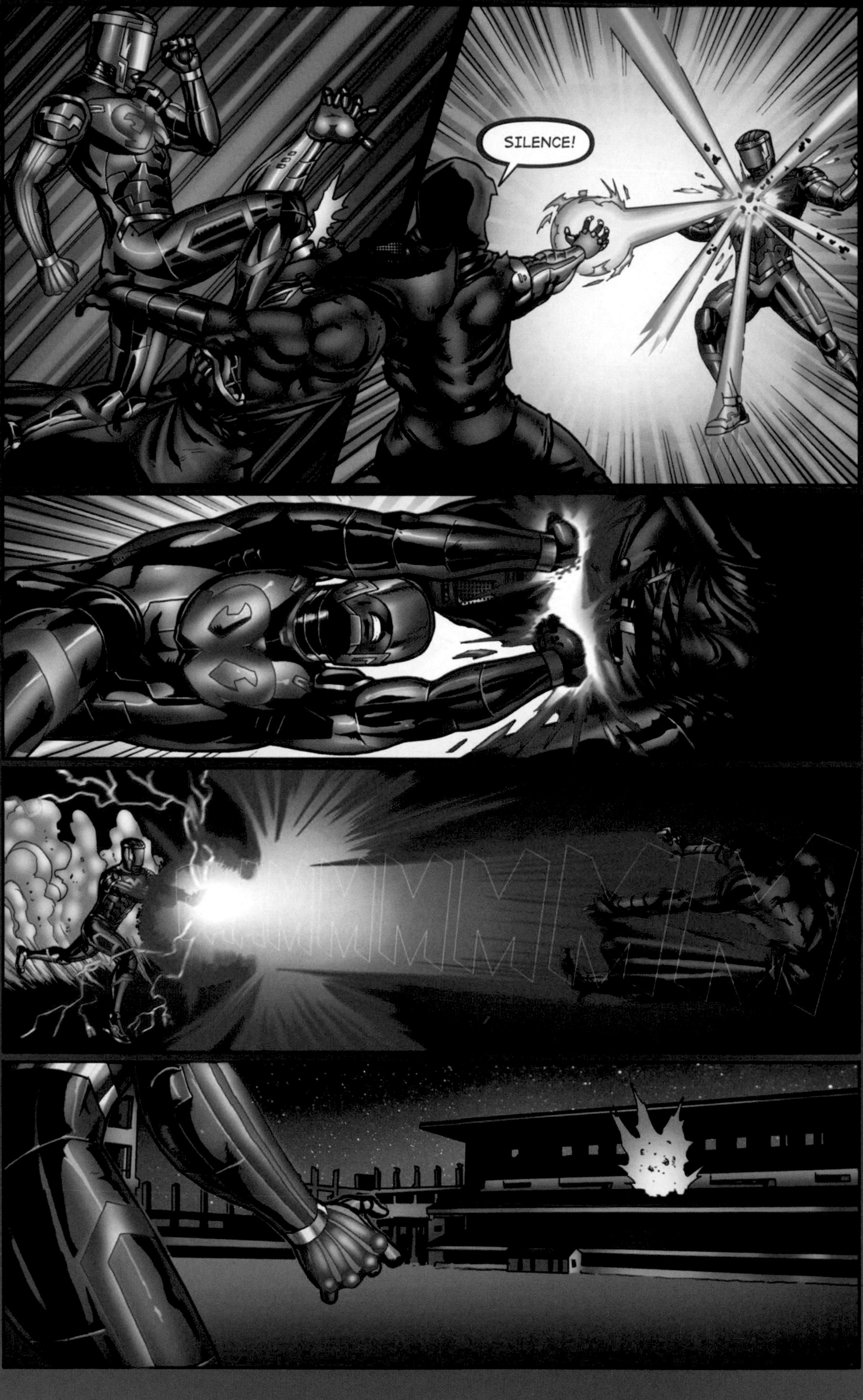
SILENCE!

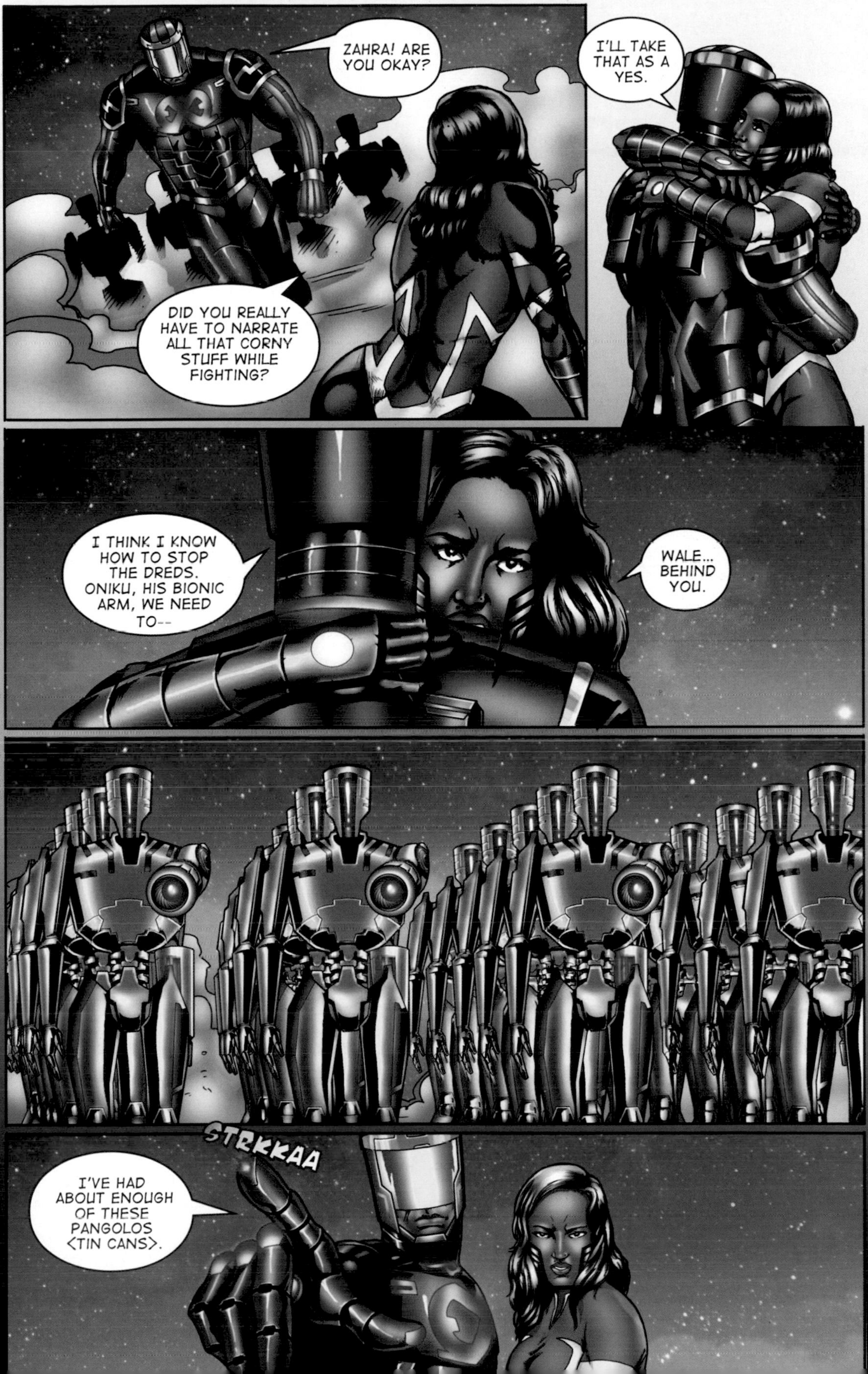
ZAHRA! ARE YOU OKAY?
DID YOU REALLY HAVE TO NARRATE ALL THAT CORNY STUFF WHILE FIGHTING?
I'LL TAKE THAT AS A YES.
I THINK I KNOW HOW TO STOP THE DREDS. ONIKU, HIS BIONIC ARM, WE NEED TO--
WALE... BEHIND YOU.
STRKKAA
I'VE HAD ABOUT ENOUGH OF THESE PANGOLOS <TIN CANS>.

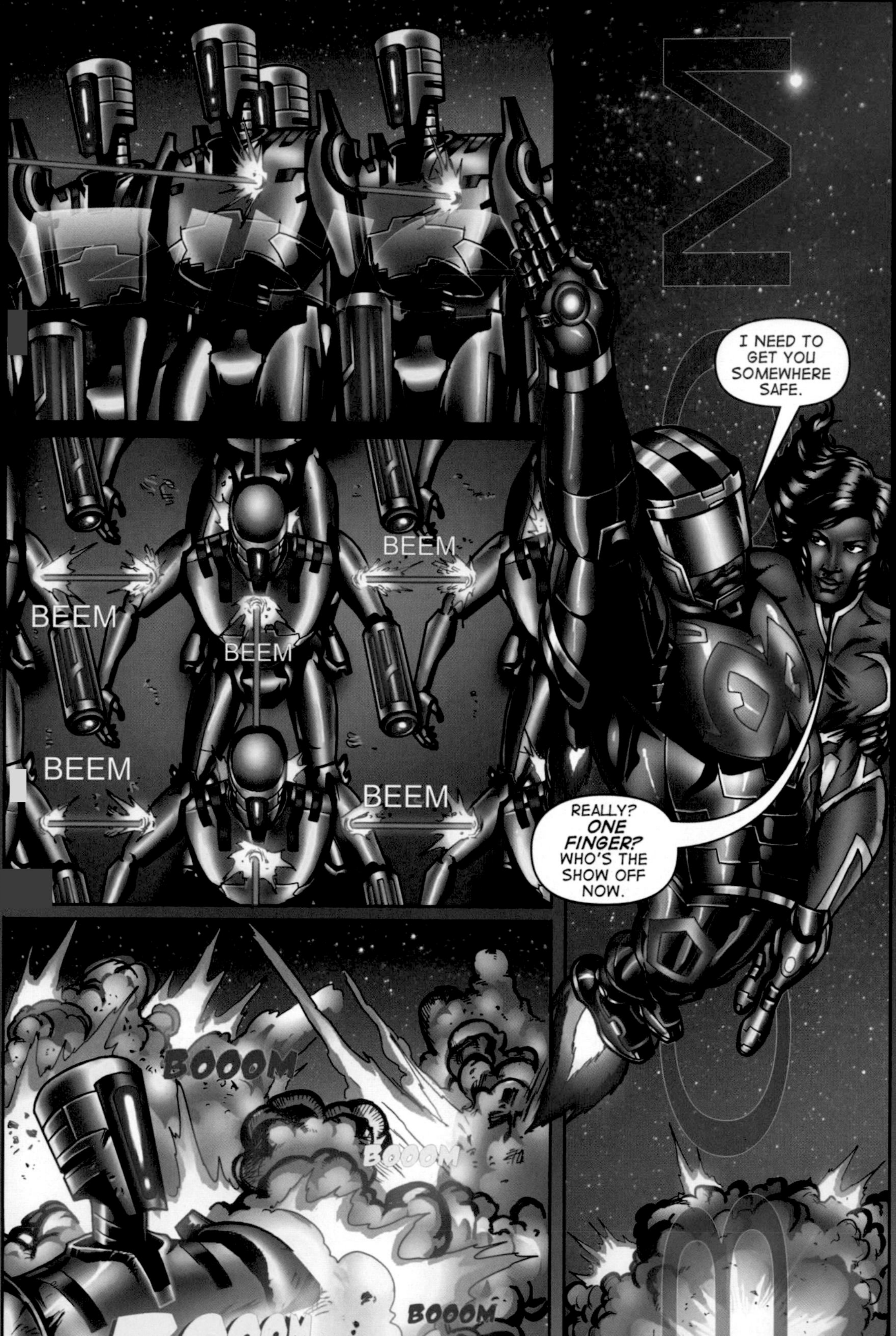
BEEM
BEEM
BEEM
BEEM
BEEM
BOOOM
BOOOM
BOOOM
BOOOM
I NEED TO GET YOU SOMEWHERE SAFE.
REALLY? *ONE FINGER?* WHO'S THE SHOW OFF NOW.

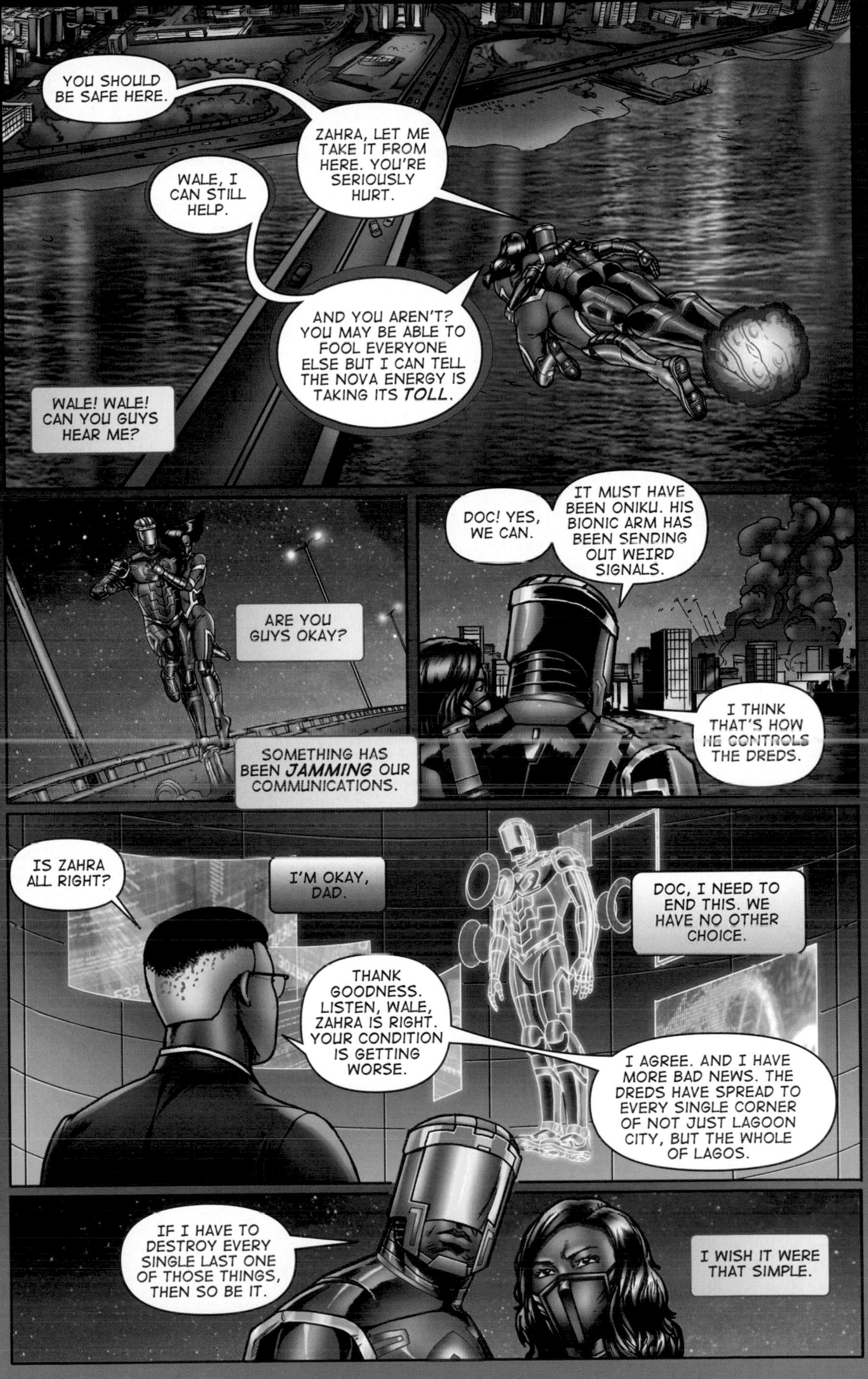
YOU SHOULD BE SAFE HERE.
WALE, I CAN STILL HELP.
ZAHRA, LET ME TAKE IT FROM HERE. YOU'RE SERIOUSLY HURT.
AND YOU AREN'T? YOU MAY BE ABLE TO FOOL EVERYONE ELSE BUT I CAN TELL THE NOVA ENERGY IS TAKING ITS TOLL.
WALE! WALE! CAN YOU GUYS HEAR ME?
ARE YOU GUYS OKAY?
SOMETHING HAS BEEN JAMMING OUR COMMUNICATIONS.
DOC! YES, WE CAN.
IT MUST HAVE BEEN ONIKU. HIS BIONIC ARM HAS BEEN SENDING OUT WEIRD SIGNALS.
I THINK THAT'S HOW HE CONTROLS THE DREDS.
IS ZAHRA ALL RIGHT?
I'M OKAY, DAD.
THANK GOODNESS. LISTEN, WALE, ZAHRA IS RIGHT. YOUR CONDITION IS GETTING WORSE.
DOC, I NEED TO END THIS. WE HAVE NO OTHER CHOICE.
I AGREE. AND I HAVE MORE BAD NEWS. THE DREDS HAVE SPREAD TO EVERY SINGLE CORNER OF NOT JUST LAGOON CITY, BUT THE WHOLE OF LAGOS.
IF I HAVE TO DESTROY EVERY SINGLE LAST ONE OF THOSE THINGS, THEN SO BE IT.
I WISH IT WERE THAT SIMPLE.

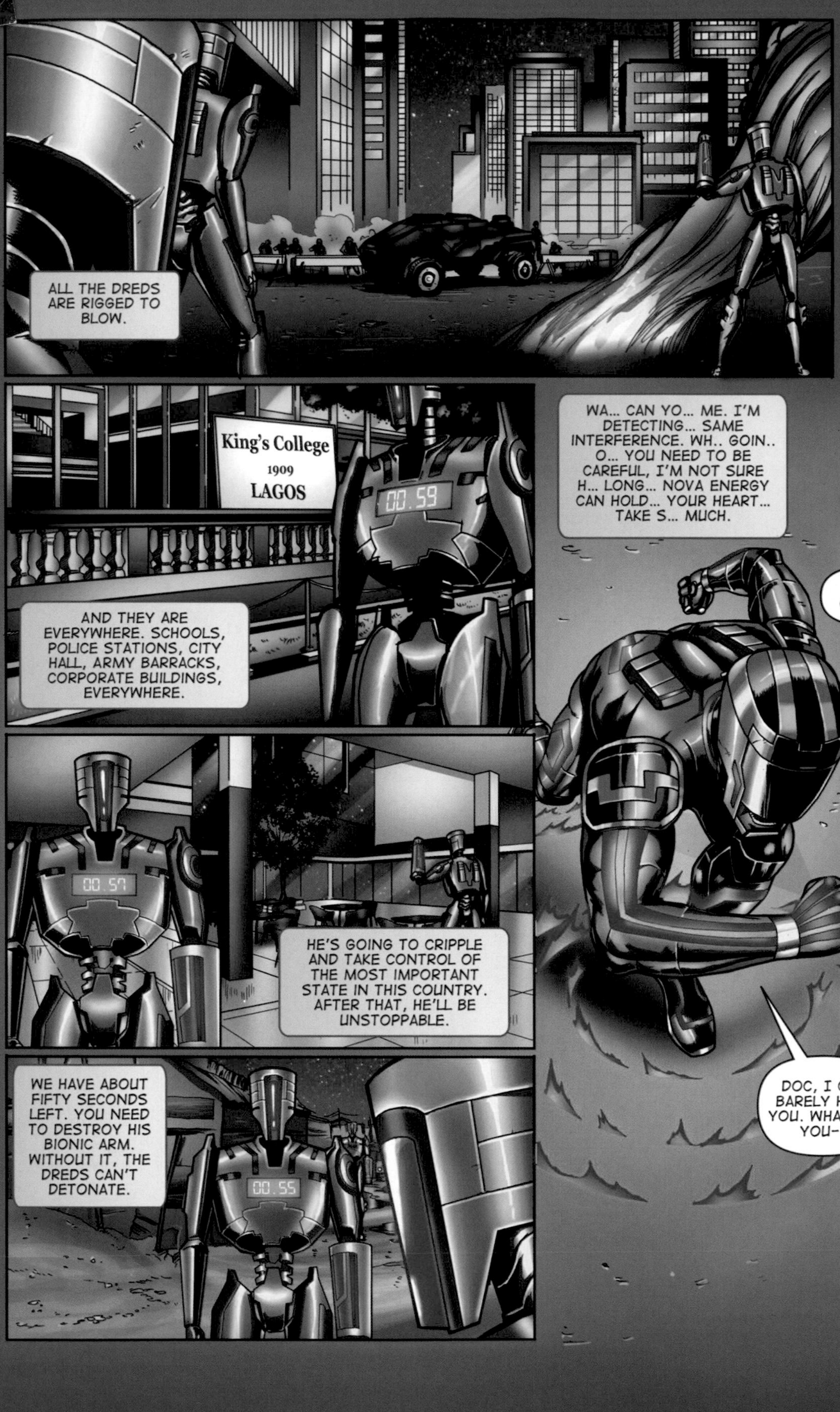

ALL THE DREDS ARE RIGGED TO BLOW.
King's College 1909 LAGOS
00.59
AND THEY ARE EVERYWHERE. SCHOOLS, POLICE STATIONS, CITY HALL, ARMY BARRACKS, CORPORATE BUILDINGS, EVERYWHERE.
00.57
HE'S GOING TO CRIPPLE AND TAKE CONTROL OF THE MOST IMPORTANT STATE IN THIS COUNTRY. AFTER THAT, HE'LL BE UNSTOPPABLE.
WE HAVE ABOUT FIFTY SECONDS LEFT. YOU NEED TO DESTROY HIS BIONIC ARM. WITHOUT IT, THE DREDS CAN'T DETONATE.
00.55
WA... CAN YO... ME. I'M DETECTING... SAME INTERFERENCE. WH.. GOIN.. O... YOU NEED TO BE CAREFUL, I'M NOT SURE H... LONG... NOVA ENERGY CAN HOLD... YOUR HEART... TAKE S... MUCH.
THAT COWARD!
DOC, I CAN BARELY HEAR YOU. WHAT DID YOU--

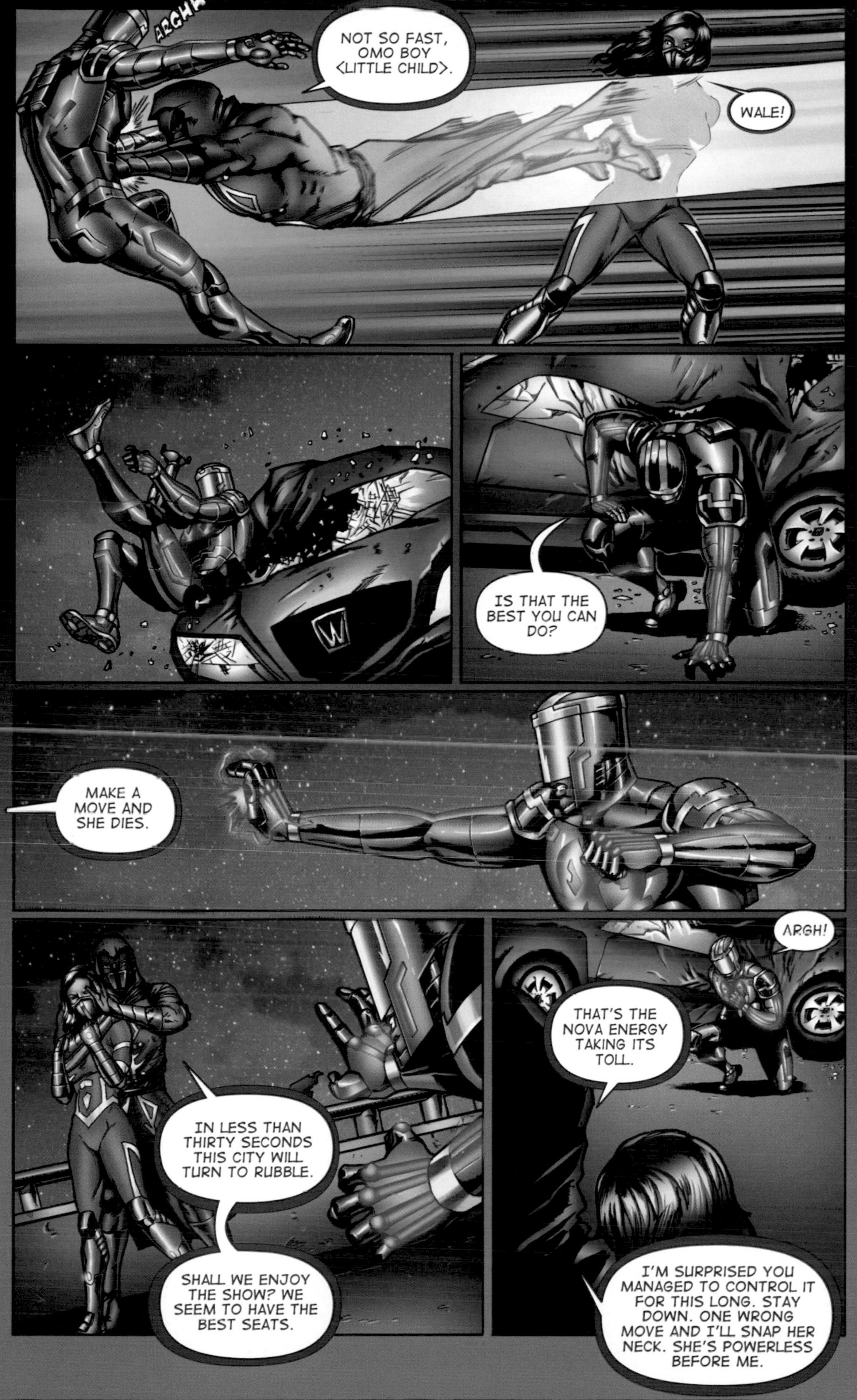
ARGH
NOT SO FAST, OMO BOY <LITTLE CHILD>.
WALE!
IS THAT THE BEST YOU CAN DO?
MAKE A MOVE AND SHE DIES.
IN LESS THAN THIRTY SECONDS THIS CITY WILL TURN TO RUBBLE.
SHALL WE ENJOY THE SHOW? WE SEEM TO HAVE THE BEST SEATS.
ARGH!
THAT'S THE NOVA ENERGY TAKING ITS TOLL.
I'M SURPRISED YOU MANAGED TO CONTROL IT FOR THIS LONG. STAY DOWN. ONE WRONG MOVE AND I'LL SNAP HER NECK. SHE'S POWERLESS BEFORE ME.

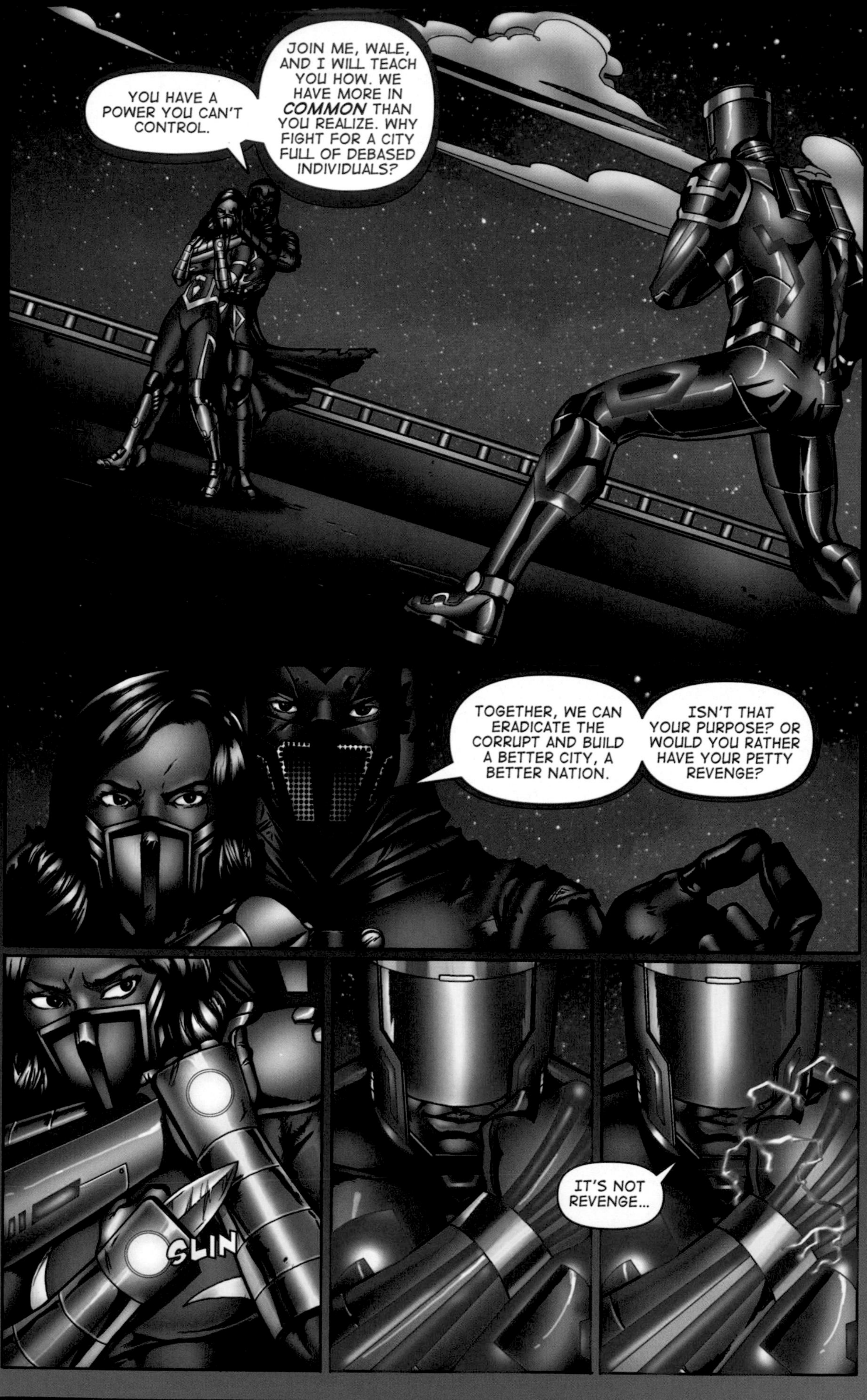
YOU HAVE A POWER YOU CAN'T CONTROL.
JOIN ME, WALE, AND I WILL TEACH YOU HOW. WE HAVE MORE IN *COMMON* THAN YOU REALIZE. WHY FIGHT FOR A CITY FULL OF DEBASED INDIVIDUALS?
TOGETHER, WE CAN ERADICATE THE CORRUPT AND BUILD A BETTER CITY, A BETTER NATION.
ISN'T THAT YOUR PURPOSE? OR WOULD YOU RATHER HAVE YOUR PETTY REVENGE?
SLIN
IT'S NOT REVENGE...

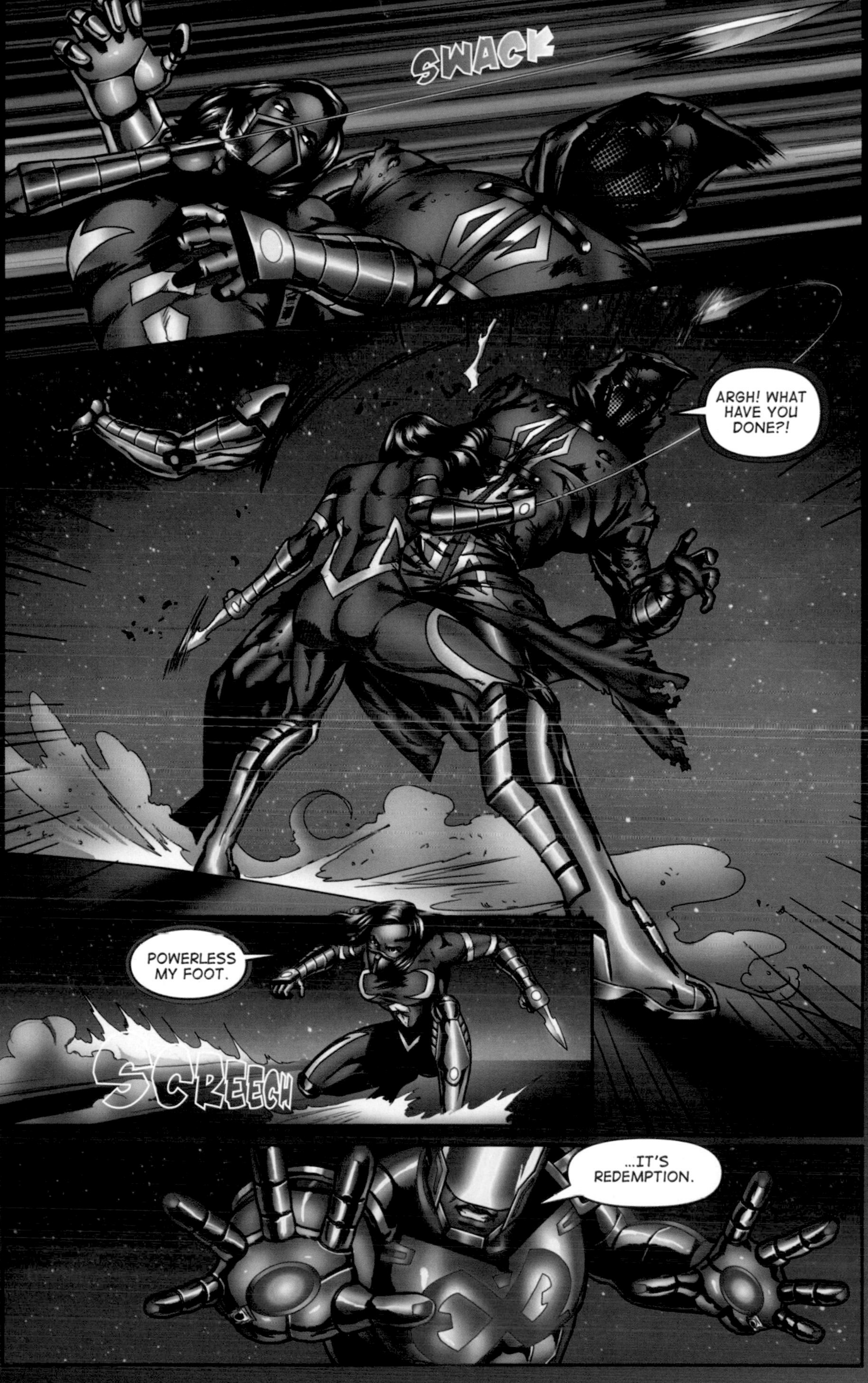
SWACK
ARGH! WHAT HAVE YOU DONE?!
POWERLESS MY FOOT.
SCREECH
...IT'S REDEMPTION.

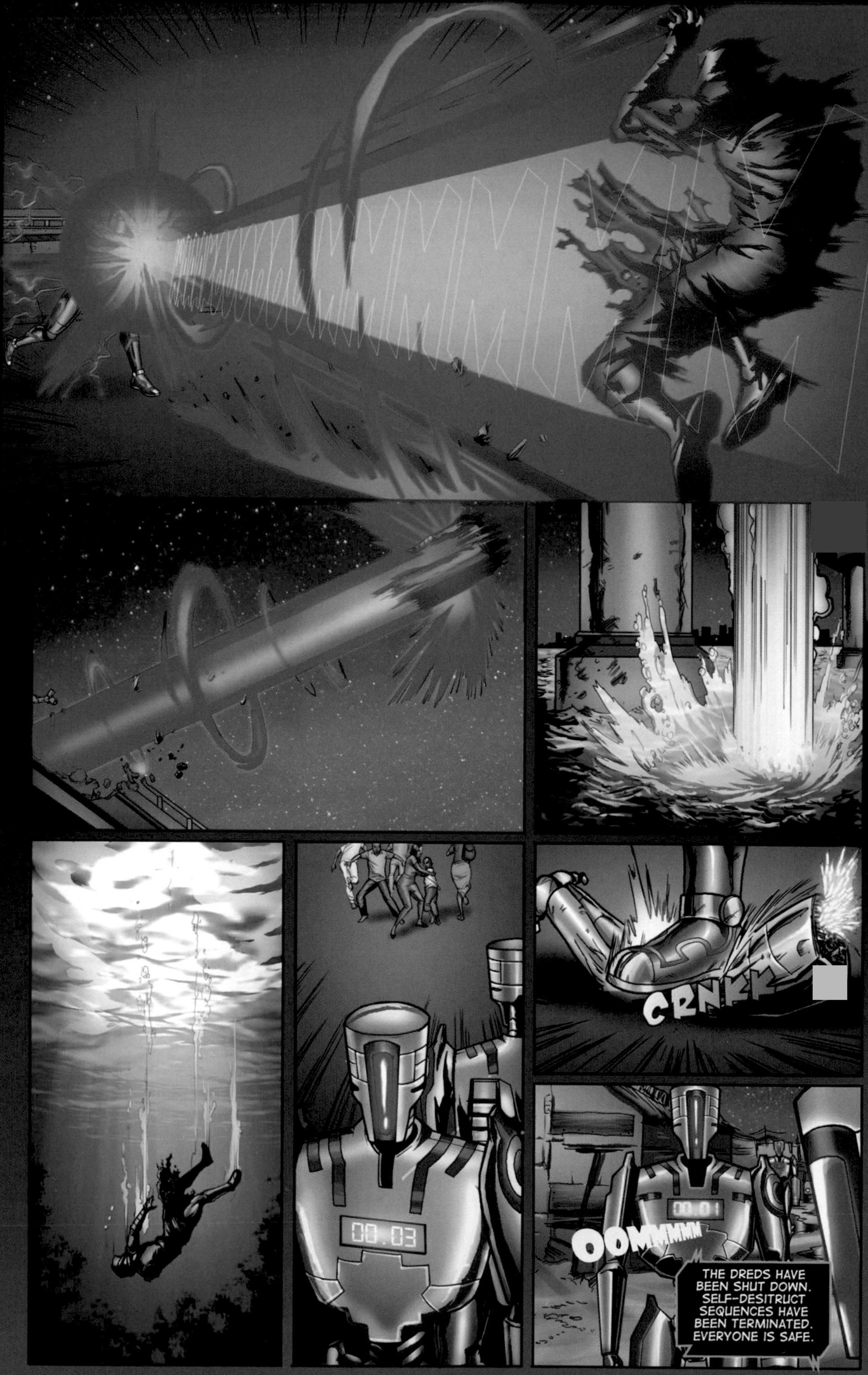
00.03
CRNKK
00.01
OOMMMMM
THE DREDS HAVE BEEN SHUT DOWN. SELF-DESITRUCT SEQUENCES HAVE BEEN TERMINATED. EVERYONE IS SAFE.

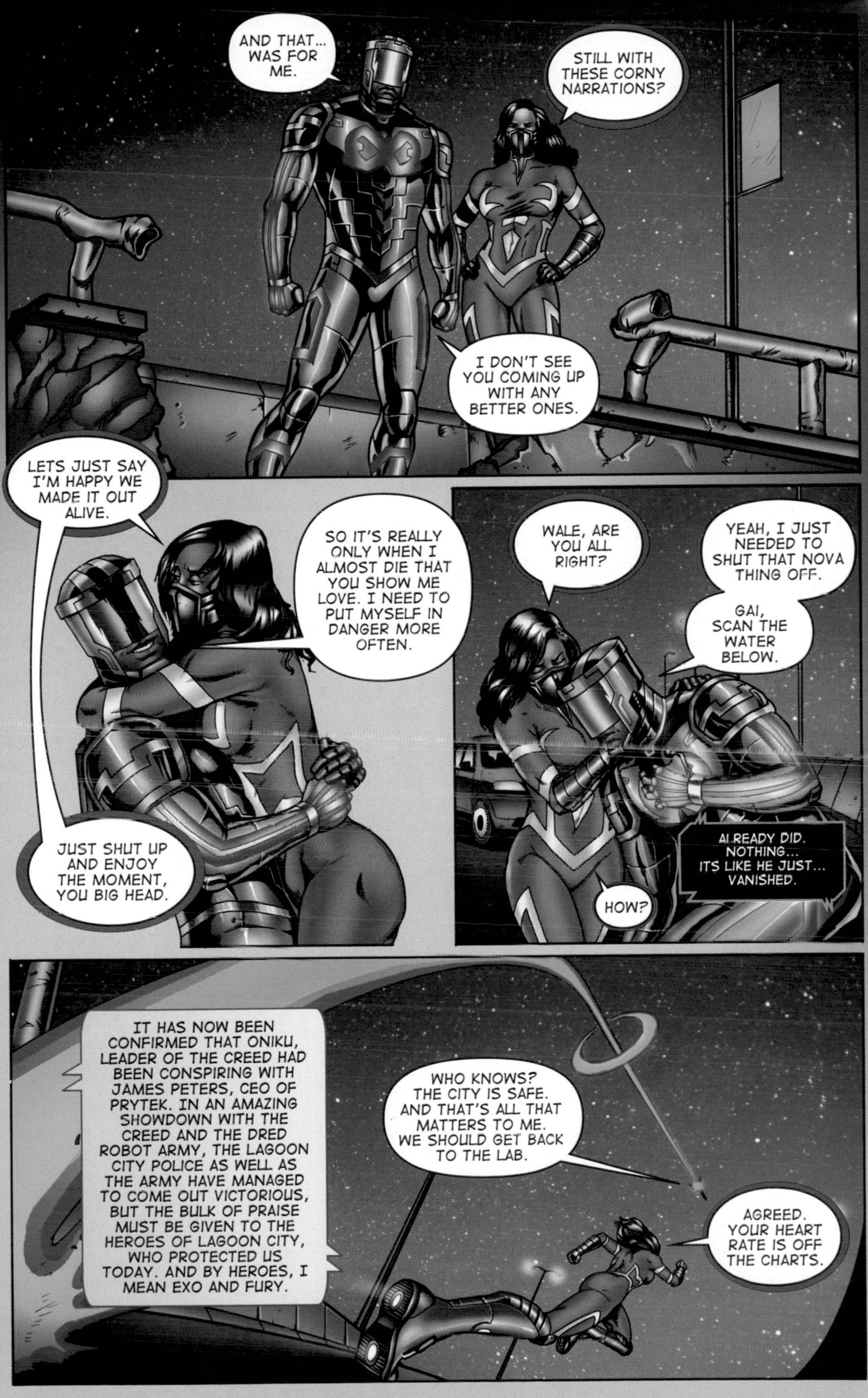
AND THAT... WAS FOR ME.
STILL WITH THESE CORNY NARRATIONS?
I DON'T SEE YOU COMING UP WITH ANY BETTER ONES.
LETS JUST SAY I'M HAPPY WE MADE IT OUT ALIVE.
SO IT'S REALLY ONLY WHEN I ALMOST DIE THAT YOU SHOW ME LOVE. I NEED TO PUT MYSELF IN DANGER MORE OFTEN.
JUST SHUT UP AND ENJOY THE MOMENT, YOU BIG HEAD.
WALE, ARE YOU ALL RIGHT?
YEAH, I JUST NEEDED TO SHUT THAT NOVA THING OFF.
GAI, SCAN THE WATER BELOW.
ALREADY DID. NOTHING... ITS LIKE HE JUST... VANISHED.
HOW?
IT HAS NOW BEEN CONFIRMED THAT ONIKU, LEADER OF THE CREED HAD BEEN CONSPIRING WITH JAMES PETERS, CEO OF PRYTEK. IN AN AMAZING SHOWDOWN WITH THE CREED AND THE DRED ROBOT ARMY, THE LAGOON CITY POLICE AS WELL AS THE ARMY HAVE MANAGED TO COME OUT VICTORIOUS, BUT THE BULK OF PRAISE MUST BE GIVEN TO THE HEROES OF LAGOON CITY, WHO PROTECTED US TODAY. AND BY HEROES, I MEAN EXO AND FURY.
WHO KNOWS? THE CITY IS SAFE. AND THAT'S ALL THAT MATTERS TO ME. WE SHOULD GET BACK TO THE LAB.
AGREED. YOUR HEART RATE IS OFF THE CHARTS.

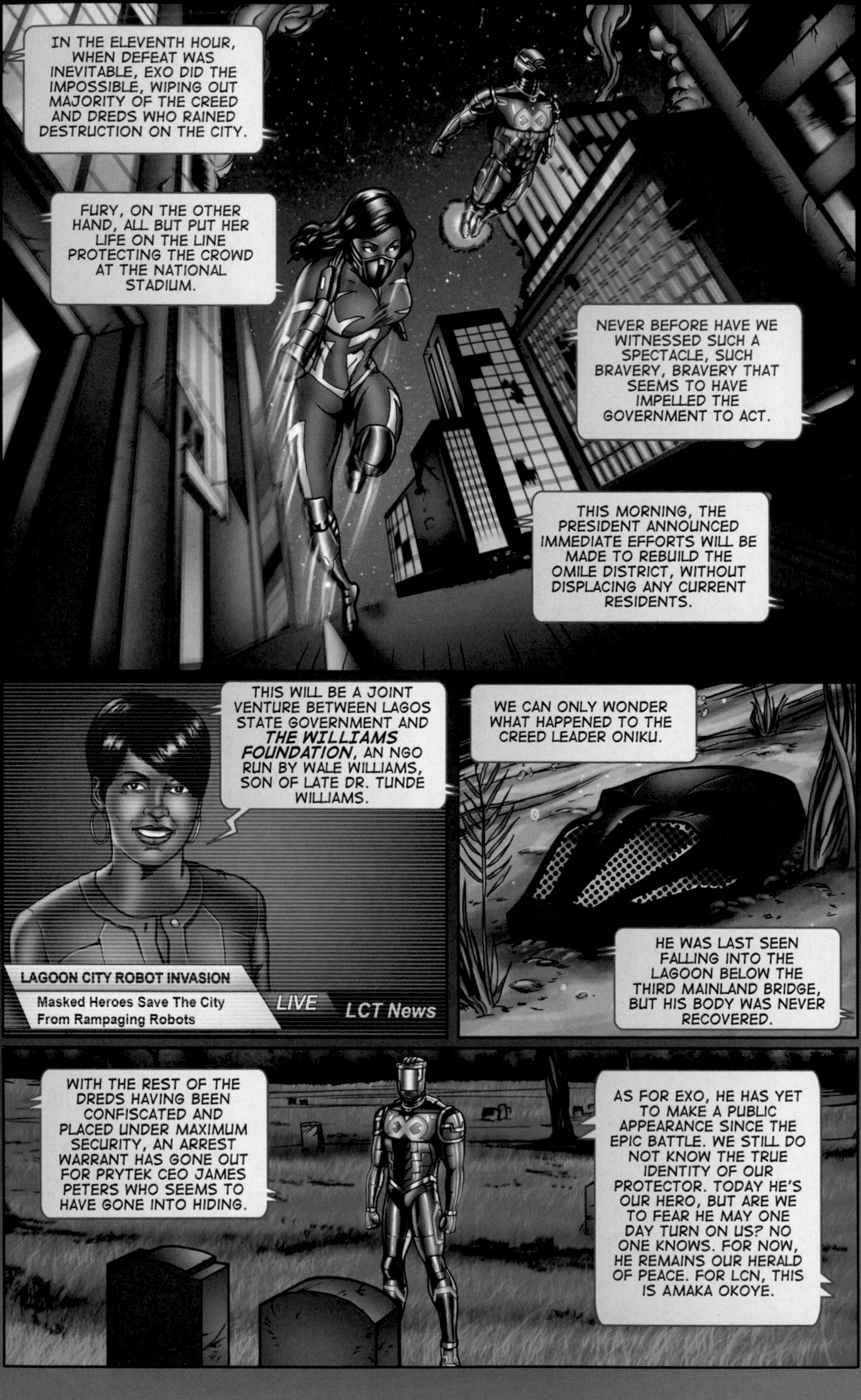
IN THE ELEVENTH HOUR, WHEN DEFEAT WAS INEVITABLE, EXO DID THE IMPOSSIBLE, WIPING OUT MAJORITY OF THE CREED AND DREDS WHO RAINED DESTRUCTION ON THE CITY.
FURY, ON THE OTHER HAND, ALL BUT PUT HER LIFE ON THE LINE PROTECTING THE CROWD AT THE NATIONAL STADIUM.
NEVER BEFORE HAVE WE WITNESSED SUCH A SPECTACLE, SUCH BRAVERY, BRAVERY THAT SEEMS TO HAVE IMPELLED THE GOVERNMENT TO ACT.
THIS MORNING, THE PRESIDENT ANNOUNCED IMMEDIATE EFFORTS WILL BE MADE TO REBUILD THE OMILE DISTRICT, WITHOUT DISPLACING ANY CURRENT RESIDENTS.
THIS WILL BE A JOINT VENTURE BETWEEN LAGOS STATE GOVERNMENT AND THE WILLIAMS FOUNDATION, AN NGO RUN BY WALE WILLIAMS, SON OF LATE DR. TUNDE WILLIAMS.
LAGOON CITY ROBOT INVASION
Masked Heroes Save The City From Rampaging Robots
LIVE
LCT News
WE CAN ONLY WONDER WHAT HAPPENED TO THE CREED LEADER ONIKU.
HE WAS LAST SEEN FALLING INTO THE LAGOON BELOW THE THIRD MAINLAND BRIDGE, BUT HIS BODY WAS NEVER RECOVERED.
WITH THE REST OF THE DREDS HAVING BEEN CONFISCATED AND PLACED UNDER MAXIMUM SECURITY, AN ARREST WARRANT HAS GONE OUT FOR PRYTEK CEO JAMES PETERS WHO SEEMS TO HAVE GONE INTO HIDING.
AS FOR EXO, HE HAS YET TO MAKE A PUBLIC APPEARANCE SINCE THE EPIC BATTLE. WE STILL DO NOT KNOW THE TRUE IDENTITY OF OUR PROTECTOR. TODAY HE'S OUR HERO, BUT ARE WE TO FEAR HE MAY ONE DAY TURN ON US? NO ONE KNOWS. FOR NOW, HE REMAINS OUR HERALD OF PEACE. FOR LCN, THIS IS AMAKA OKOYE.

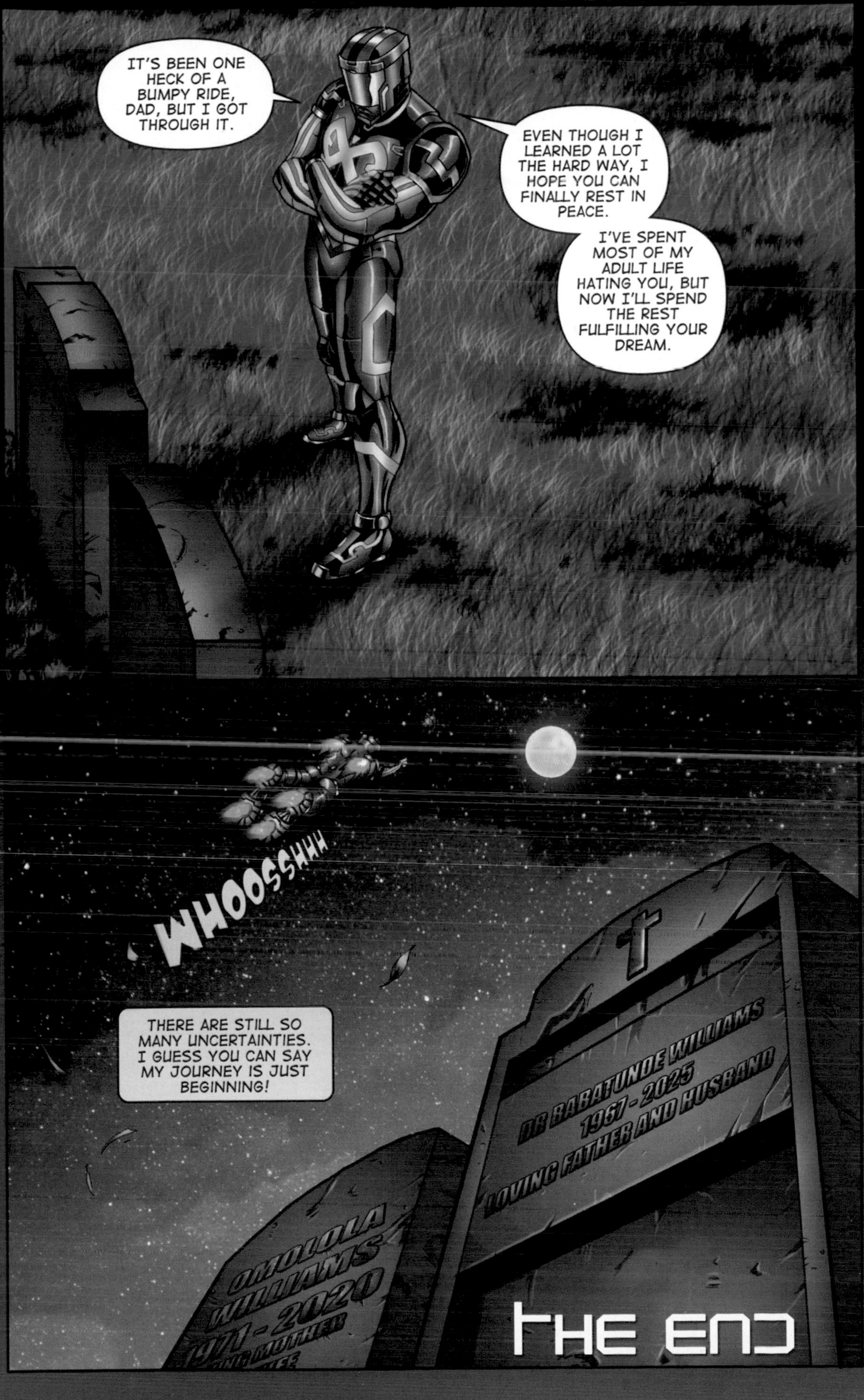
IT'S BEEN ONE HECK OF A BUMPY RIDE, DAD, BUT I GOT THROUGH IT.
EVEN THOUGH I LEARNED A LOT THE HARD WAY, I HOPE YOU CAN FINALLY REST IN PEACE.
I'VE SPENT MOST OF MY ADULT LIFE HATING YOU, BUT NOW I'LL SPEND THE REST FULFILLING YOUR DREAM.
WHOOSSHHH
THERE ARE STILL SO MANY UNCERTAINTIES. I GUESS YOU CAN SAY MY JOURNEY IS JUST BEGINNING!
DR BABATUNDE WILLIAMS
1967 - 2025
LOVING FATHER AND HUSBAND
OMOLOLA
WILLIAMS
1971 - 2020
THE END

MEANWHILE...

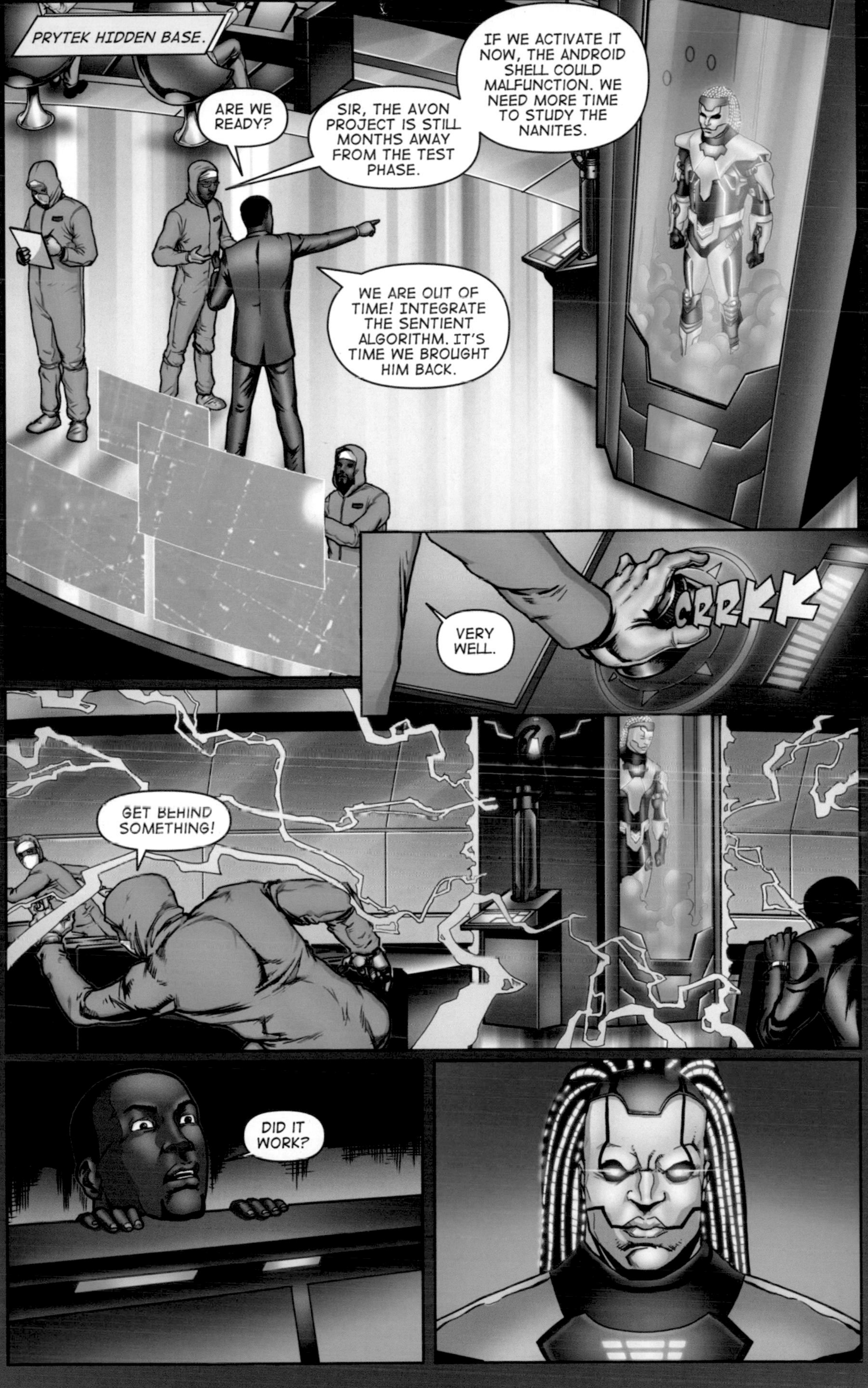
PRYTEK HIDDEN BASE.
ARE WE READY?
SIR, THE AVON PROJECT IS STILL MONTHS AWAY FROM THE TEST PHASE.
IF WE ACTIVATE IT NOW, THE ANDROID SHELL COULD MALFUNCTION. WE NEED MORE TIME TO STUDY THE NANITES.
WE ARE OUT OF TIME! INTEGRATE THE SENTIENT ALGORITHM. IT'S TIME WE BROUGHT HIM BACK.
VERY WELL.
CRRKK
GET BEHIND SOMETHING!
DID IT WORK?

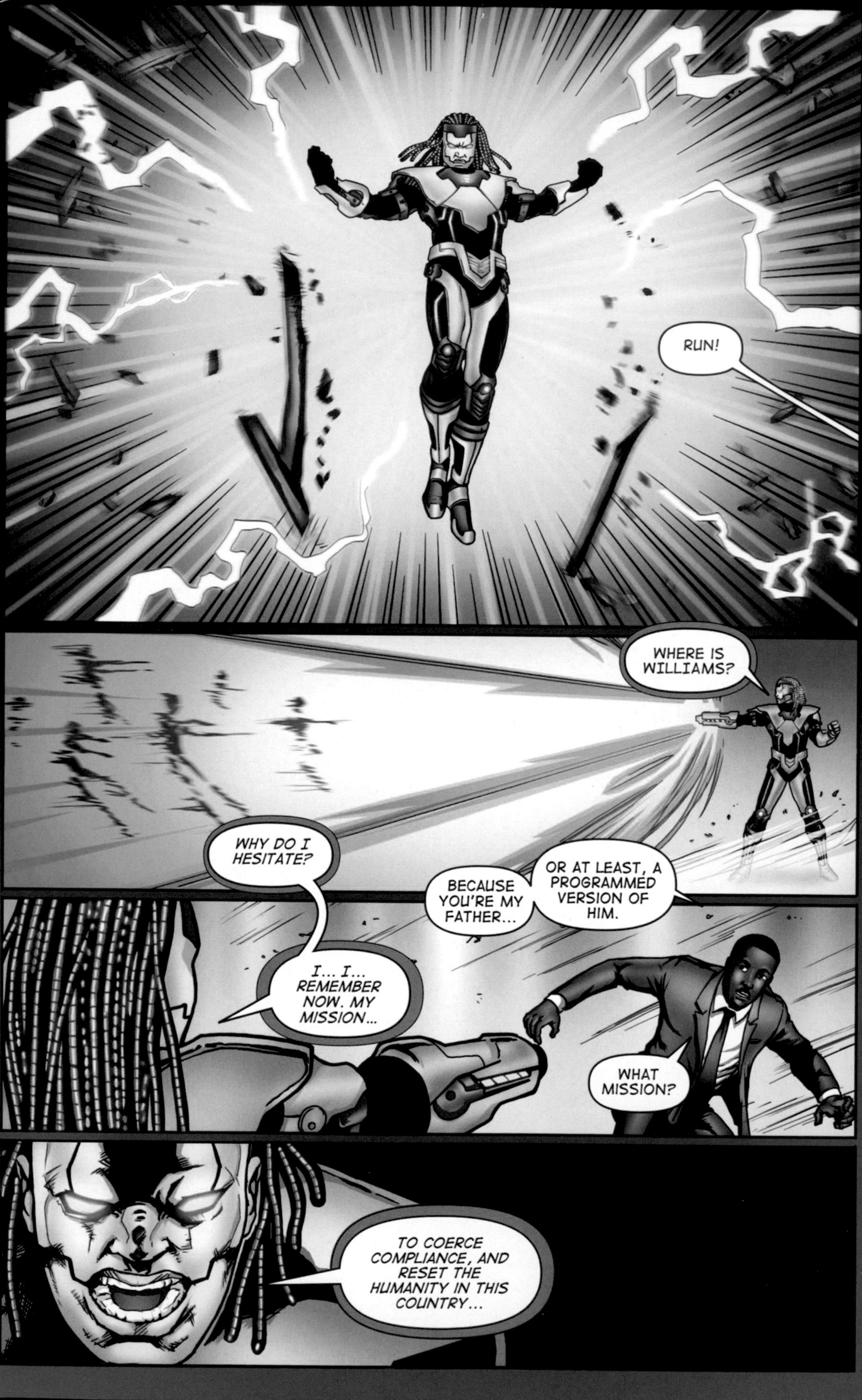
RUN!
WHERE IS WILLIAMS?
WHY DO I HESITATE?
BECAUSE YOU'RE MY FATHER...
OR AT LEAST, A PROGRAMMED VERSION OF HIM.
I... I... REMEMBER NOW. MY MISSION...
WHAT MISSION?
TO COERCE COMPLIANCE, AND RESET THE HUMANITY IN THIS COUNTRY...

Enjoying the E.X.O. story so far? Of curse you are!
Well, this is just the beginning! To experience more
"YouNeek" stories and download tons of free stuff
(animation, comics, creative "how to's" etc.)
sign up today on our website: youneekstudios.com/more

As one saga ends, another begins...

EXO will return in

The second saga in the E.X.O. series begins
Summer 2017.

But first, get ready for...

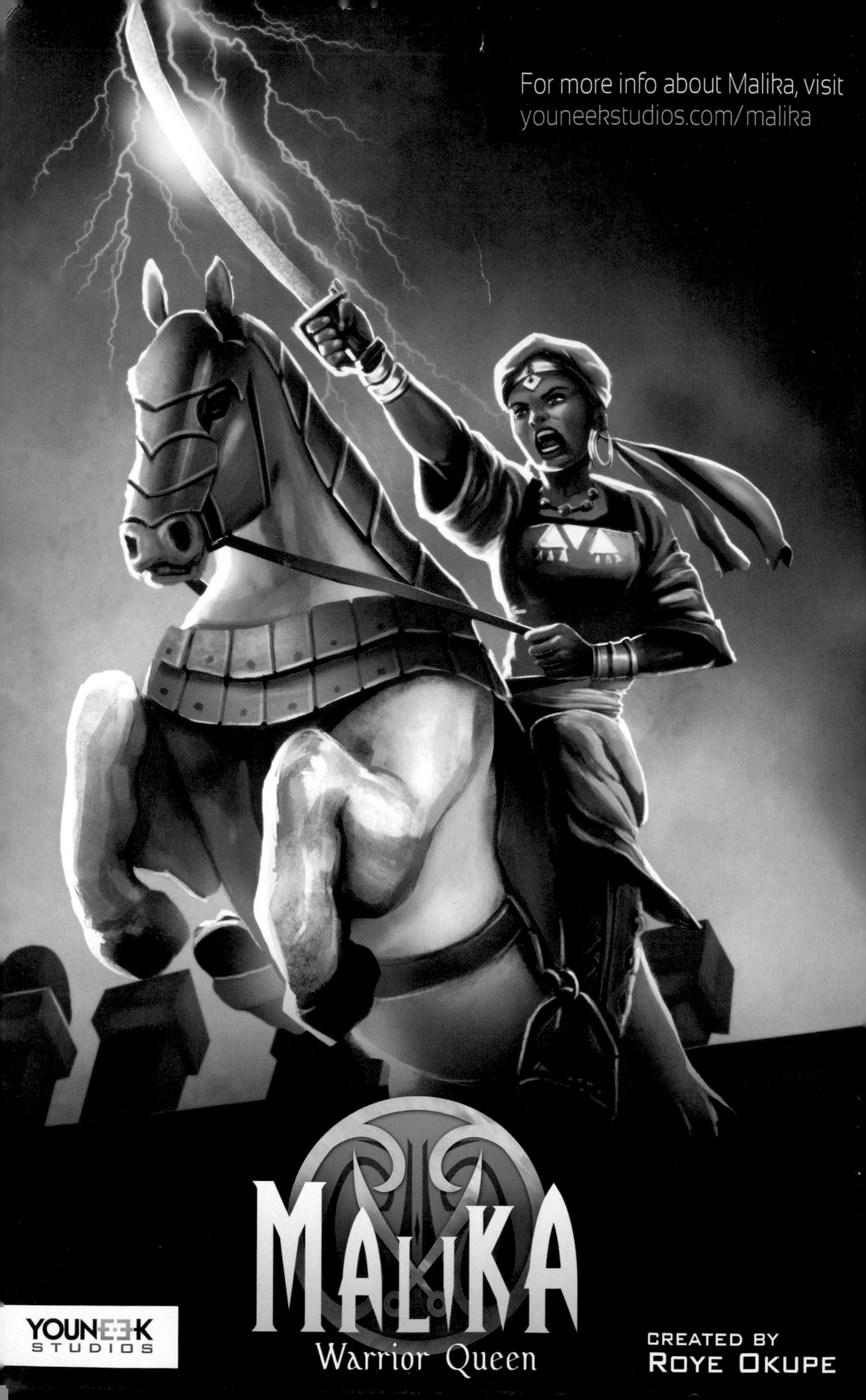
For more info about Malika, visit
youneekstudios.com/malika
MALIKA
Warrior Queen
YOUNEEK STUDIOS
CREATED BY
ROYE OKUPE

A SPECIAL THANK YOU TO OUR
KICKSTARTER BACKERS

Omotola Thomas

Vomoz Communications

Brian Loebig

Abimbola Adeniranye

Ayobami Oluokun

Adewale Odusanya

Meta Nabou Cisse

Pelumi Olatinpo

Naomi Nwaokoru

Ade O.

Tasha Turner Lennhoff

Wale Akingbade

Jose Pahissa

Paul Hance

Olukunle Malomo

Leke Adebayo

Shade Salisu

Artise Gill

Oluwatoyin Adewumi

Thomas Henn

Desiree Scudder

Sean Scott

Eric Outley

ANGELA BLACKMAN

Justin Payne-Brissette

Brian Cooper

Michael Hajdu

Feyisola Ogunfemi

James Ramirez,

Shamsiddin Muhammad Jr

Robert Early

Oladipo Oladapo

Chad Bowden

Richard Eddington

Brian Grefsrud

Kimmi Mackenzie

Ro Olufunwa

Alim Muhammad

Eze Wosu

malcolm payne

Andre Nedderman

Felisha Mason

Aramis Ofoma

Marc Presley

Heather Parra

Jene Radeke

Chad Sharpe

Jason Jackson

John F Hale III

Matt Fogel

Martine Thomas

Jerry D. Grayson

Eljee Javier

Dorphise Jean

Desayo Dellie

Kenyeda Adams

Chancellor Sims

Titi Okupe

Len Ahgeak

Olufemi Agunbiade

Tyrone Ross

Trevor Joy

Christopher Oladapo

Rick Johnson

Dwayne Simon

William A Anderson

Aderike Adalemo

Adeola omotayo

Dion Baccus

Mayowa Ogundiyun

Adedamola Adefemi

Paolo Butera

Jacob Roberts-mensah

Jimi Ogunduyile

Cheslan Simpson

Kunle Bello

Babatunde Ogundiyun

Tyrone Jackson

Cas Thomas

Curmeal Broadway

Solomon Gamra

Nikki Woolfolk

Nana Offei-Addo

Sandra Threadcraft

Sheilla Osayogie

Julian Herring

Joe Anugo

Ijeoma Lasebikan

Devon Camel

Josh Nowicki

Matt Kansy

kalina vanderlei silva

Remi Fayomi

Wumi Balogun

Elisabeth Panzenboeck

Ted Buter

Douglas Davis

Christopher M Demarest

Roosevelt Pitt

Gavin Kam-Young

Ore-Ofe Iluyomade

Ramel Hill

Jason Longden

Wade Meyer

Kanayo Adibe

Derrick D Johnson

Gary Simmons

Tim Adams

Jaimel Hemphill

Jamal Howard

Mugabi Byenkya

Kofi Jamal Simmons

Dallas Rico

Jonathan Fung

Cameron Moore

Joshua Adams

marcus williams

DON WALKER

Kayode Malomo

Marcus R Carson

Jeffrey D. Pegues

Greg Anderson-Elysee

Greg Burnham

Brandon Thomas

Ricardo hinds

Sasha Layne

Short Fuse Media Group, LLC.

Ronald Stevens

Aura-Lee Carr

Mychal Willis

Stanley A Nerestant

Olayinka Agunbiade

Charles Shropshire

Steve McGlone

Ayotunde Ayoola

T.C. Thomas

Steven Bishop

Gboyinde Onijala

Brian Dysart

Dawneeyale Amariel

Steve Beaulieu

Brandon Easton

Kevin Parent

Oladapo Adeniranye

A SPECIAL THANK YOU TO OUR
KICKSTARTER BACKERS

Ben Hinson
Stephanie Onanuga
Narjes Ruyan
Dembi Huya-Kouadio
Isaac Johnson
William Potts
Ronald T. Jones
Saji Ijiyemi
Tevin Hill
Kenneth Bell
Brendan McGarvey
Kwanza Johnson
Labi Azeez Salu
Alexander Lyle
Kariane Lemay
Rikisha Sigler
Derek Freeman
Lars Nelson
Dare Ademola
Brander Roullett
Erno Newman
Jeffrey Underwood
Paul DeBaldo
Brent Lambert
Brenton Poke
Matthew Hill
Melchizedek Todd
Marion Dupinet
Jeremy Melloul
Darnel Sonnier
Christopher Turner
Nedrick Mclaren
Adam Brady
Temi Olly
Mike Grossman
Briana Bellamy
Tolu
Edem Dzodzomenyo
Jesse Lowther
Oroboghene Adia
Rene Williams
Justin Sabelko
Milton Symister
wayne cash
Jeanne Mahaffey
Fatima Iqbal
Matt Turull
Bill Eastman

DeNae Culp
James Burton
Lynda Ademola
Ibijoke Oke
Donati Ivan
JD Hornbacher
Jim Otermat
Tomas Burgos
Nicolas Izambard
Ed Adams
Olashade Abidoye
Rasheen Beats
Robyn McGlotten
James Lucas
Thomas Joseph
Liam Murray
Bisong Taiwo
Tyrell White
Emeka Anyadiegwu
Ashley C Holmes
Daudi Frederick-Cato
Siju Salami
Karama
Ben Jones
Everard McBain
Shawn Pryor
Thomas Werner
Kirk Lindo
Sincere Ignorance
Alex
J IHero Wright
Peter Campbell
Andrew Wilson
Shawn Tolidano
Devon
John Hildebrand
Martin Reese
Erin Subramanian
Akoda Nwachukwu
Kenneth A. Brown
Caitlin Jane Hughes
Jay Nelson
Shining Otaku
Darkspi
Yann Kieffoloh
adedayo onibokun
Glenn Fayard
Josh Medin

Kenneth Strickland
David Chaucer La Forest
Jake Palermo
Nay Marie
Aaron Duncan
Hameed Catel
Jayson
Gary Francis
Yemi
Yewande Giwa
Anthony Mendez
Lamide Osunsina
Adebola Adesoye
A. Salisu
Lara Okanlawon
Bambi
Rafael Lima
Olamide Harrison
Adeola Ajibade